Practical Guide to PC and Microsoft Office 2010

– Word, Excel, and PowerPoint –

Sergey K. Aityan

ISBN-10: 1478371129
ISBN-13: 978-1478371120

Preface

For many years, I have been teaching students, doing business, and observing people of different professions and technical skills in the way they use office or home computers and office software.

Computer problems happen but their results don't need to be so devastating. If we take certain precautions by arranging our computers in such a way that hardware or software failures would lead to minimal loss, it would take less effort to restore the computer and information in it.

Word processing, spreadsheets, and presentations are the most popular office applications people use to develop documents. Modern office software offers quite sophisticated functionality that allows users to develop documents with high professional and publishing quality. Though some people are technically savvy and use full functionality of office applications, the majority of people continue to use word processors like typewriters, spreadsheets like calculators, and presentations like simple text and image placeholders. Such severe underutilization of office software functionality results either in low publishing quality of documents or in enormous amounts of time wasted to elevate the documents to the desired level of quality if it is even possible.

Most modern-day office applications are quite intuitive, so beginners can start working with them practically right away in a primitive way as described above. To use the applications in a more sophisticated way requires some knowledge which users can get from user manuals. User manuals normally are comprehensive sources that contain a lot of useful information. Experienced users can easily navigate through user manuals and find information to learn the needed functionality. However, beginners can easily get overwhelmed with comprehensive user manuals because it is not clear what functionality to look for. It is a common perception among beginners that user manuals are confusing because they contain too much information. Without preliminary knowledge it is not clear how much advanced functionality can help you, and it takes too much time to find what the user really needs to implement his/her vision of the document. Even more, sometimes beginners are not even aware about which functionality can help them.

This book is written for beginners who already know how to use their computers and office applications at a very entry level. It is not describing how to turn a computer on/off, how to select fonts in word processing and print documents, how to add or subtract two numbers in a spreadsheet, or how to put a text or an image in a presentation slide. The goal of this book is to help beginners move to the next level where they understand how to arrange their personal computers and use Microsoft Word, Excel, and PowerPoint functionality to develop professionally clean documents. By no means does this book aim to present complete functionality of office software. On the contrary, this book presents the bare minimum necessary to develop high-quality documents and self-learn more if needed. As an example, this book was written and formatted with Microsoft Office 2010 by using only the functionality described in this book.

Thus this is a methodological book rather than a comprehensive user manual. This book will help beginners reach a certain level of proficiency in managing their PC desktops and laptops, and learn very important functionality of Microsoft Word, Excel, and PowerPoint so they can better develop well-prepared documents and build a stronger foundation for further self-learning.

I would like to express my deep appreciation to Ms. Nicole Marsh for her valuable help in preparation of this book for publication.

Sergey K. Aityan

Table of Contents (Brief)

Table of Contents

1   Introduction

Business has always been associated with developing and managing a variety of written documents, calculations (including financial calculations), presentations, data and projects. In the 21st century, practically almost all this work is being done with the aid of computers and appropriate software applications.

Well-prepared documents improve communication of ideas, concepts, business strategy, collaboration, business operations, investment, and other business activities. A better organized process for document preparation and management dramatically improves the quality of documents, reduces preparation time, and helps with document and data management. Though people and businesses use different software for document preparation, it is a common mistake to ignore powerful features of the software that aim to help users prepare and manage documents. This results in document creation taking an unnecessarily long time and the final a low-quality final product.

All office applications have very powerful features that allow users to do professional work. However, though some additional knowledge of these advanced features would dramatically improve the quality of their work, most users still use the software at a beginner level.

One of the goals of this book is to show how learning a few powerful advanced features of office software can help make significantly better documents, calculations, presentations, and better manage data. This book is neither a complete user manual, nor a complete review of office software features. Its purpose is to bring users to the next level of better organization and management of personal computers. Learning the power of office applications with a few additional features and a little effort can make a major difference in results.

This book presents only the most practical and helpful features of the office software necessary to make well-formatted clean documents, present business ideas, and manage businesses in the most efficient way.

This book addresses Microsoft Office. However, since office software products offered by other vendors have similar features, readers will have no problem applying the tips and procedures they learn here with other office software.

The major office applications being widely used to develop documents are:
- word processing
- spreadsheets
- presentations

For this reason in this book, we will focus mostly on mastering the use of these applications.

Good tools always help improve the quality of a job and the efficiency. However, please remember that your document can only be as good as you are able to see it in your mind. Tools help you do the work better and faster, but cannot do the work for you.

1.1   Major Office Software and Vendors

Traditionally, office software is installed on the computer where it runs. Among the variety of office software vendors, the major players in today's market are shown in Table 1-1.

Table 1-1: Major computer-installed office software and vendors

Software Suite Name	Vendor's URL	Commercial / Free
Microsoft Office	http://office.microsoft.com/en-us/	Commercial
OpenOffice	http://www.openoffice.org/product/index.html	Free
WordPerfect Office	http://www.corel.com/corel/allProducts.jsp	Commercial

Microsoft Office and WordPerfect Office are commercially available office applications while OpenOffice is an open-source application available free of charge. There are also other vendors offering office software, however, they are not playing major roles on the market.

1.2   Office Software in a Cloud

Office application software has become so popular and demand on them has grown so dramatically in the recent years, thus many vendors began offering office application on-demand to run on the network cloud. These online products allow users to create, edit, and share the documents directly from the Web.

Table 1-2 presents some major on-demand online office applications and their components by vendor. These applications do not require any downloads or installation on the user's desktop computer and the user can work online directly from a web browser.

Table 1-2: Major on-demand online office software products and vendors

Company	On Demand Software			Vendor's URL
	Word processing	Spreadsheets	Presentations	
Microsoft	√	√	√	office.microsoft.com
Google	√	√	√	www.google.com
Zoho	√	√	√	www.zoho.com

Though working online is sometimes very convenient, the flip side of the coin is that online applications have relatively limited functionality with features that can only be used for quite simple documents.

2   Organizing Your Computer

Most users use PC or MAC computers at their offices and home. Modern computers normally have huge capacity hard drives that can store an incredible amount of information. The downside of the huge capacities of modern hard drives is that they may have difficulty locating information you need or even losing data due to software or hardware failures.

This chapter addresses the issue of data organization and information protection on your personal computer to reduce the hardship of finding information and reduce the risk of losing stored information.

Good data organization is important to ensure that information on your computer is safe, easy to find, and easy to track. If your data is poorly organized, there is a high chance of losing data or having problems finding it. Like in a library, it would be an unbearable task to find any book if books were just stacked in a big disorganized pile. In a warehouse, the inventory must be thoroughly organized to make the warehouse operational rather than a graveyard of goods. Even at you own home, and we all have such experience, poor organization of your household items typically results in a frustrating loss of time in attempts to find things. Your computer is no different.

2.1   Organizing Your Hard Drives

It's possible that a personal computer may have several physical hard drives, but most brand name personal computers come with a single high capacity hard drive. Every physical hard drive may be configured to have a number of partitions called logical drives, say, C:, D:, and so on.

It is common that a computer has one physical hard drive with a capacity of hundreds of gigabytes or even several terabytes and only one partition (logical hard drive) C:. Microsoft operating system by default offers users a directory (or folder) called *MyDocuments* for all user documents. At first glance it looks very convenient, but such organization has many hidden problems that may cause inconvenience or even severe problems.

The major inconvenience of this approach to document management is that all your documents and data are stored in the same directory (or folder). Even if this directory is segmented into many different subdirectories (or subfolders), you may end up with a long list of subdirectories which are difficult to manage or a very deep cascade of included subdirectories.

A much better way to organize your hard drive is to reformat it for a number of partitions depending on you practical needs. For example,

C:/System,
D:/Business,
E:/Personal,
F:/Photo,
and so on.

Figure 2-1 shows the relationship between a physical hard drive and its logical drives, or partitions. With such partitioning, you get much better organization of your information and data by classification that significantly improves your ability to find and work with appropriate documents, and at the same time provides better computer performance and protection from information loss.

Logical drives (partitions) C:. D:, E:, F: …

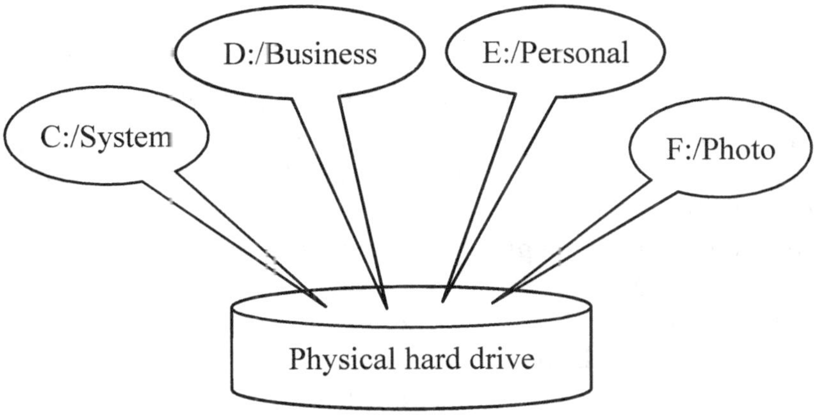

Figure 2-1: Physical hard drive and its logical partitions

However there are even more compelling reasons for your data, documents, or other information to be stored in separate partitions (logical drives) or away from the partition used for the operating system and software applications. We will discuss these reasons below. Note that *MyDocuments* folder is located in the same partition (logical drive) as the operating system.

2.1.1   Organizing the System Drive

The main partition or logical drive on your computer is C:, which is typically called the system drive. Unfortunately most computer vendors deliver their computers with the single physical and logical hard drive C: only.

If your computer is supplied with a single physical and logical hard drive C: only it is strongly recommended that you repartition the physical hard drive by creating several partitions (logical drives)—D:, E: and so on—for your documents, data and other information, following common sense and logic of organizing information and leaving logical drive C: only for the operating system and standardly installed applications. If your data, documents, and other information do not have complex logical structure, make at least one additional partition D: for them and never store your data, documents and other information in the same partition (logical drive) C: where you have the operating system and standard software applications.

You can repartition the hard drive without reinstalling the operating system and application software. The computer management tools supplied together with the operating system allow you to do so practically effortlessly. When selecting the size of partitions (logical drives), please keep in mind that logical hard drives show good performance if they have at least 20% free space; a bare minimum of 15%.

- Create a number of partitions (or logical) hard drives on the hard drive(s) of your computer. Choose the number of additional partitions following common sense and the complexity of your data organization.
- Install operating system on the system hard drive (C:) only. (See *** Note below)
- Install standard software applications, which you can easily reinstall if needed, on the system drive (C:). (See *** Note below)
- Configure all software applications installed on the system drive (C:) in such a way that the documents and data they generate are stored on other logical drives.
- Do not use the system drive for any documents or data other than standard documents and data supplied with the software applications which could be easily reinstalled with the software.
- *** Note: If the operating system and software applications have already been installed on your computer, you can shrink partition (logical drive) C: and set new partitions on the freed space on the physical hard drive using computer management tools supplied together with the operating system.

For example, if Microsoft Outlook is being used as your email tool and it is installed on the system drive along with the Windows operating system, in the case that you need to reformat drive C:, your emails are going to be lost. To avoid this inconvenience, there is an option to configure Outlook in such a way that all emails will be stored in some other partition (logical drive). Another example: if you have Microsoft Word installed on the system drive but all documents you have created with Microsoft Word are stored on other logical drives, no documents will be lost if system troubles happen on drive C:.

Why is it practical and helpful to follow such disk organization? There are many reasons. The main ones are data loss protection, improved computer performance, and convenience.

Data Loss Protection

The system drive is the most vulnerable logical hard drive on your computer. All of us, who have been using personal computers for a while, have had unpleasant experiences when the operating system on your computer gets corrupted. Unfortunately this periodically happens because of internal failures in the operating system, conflicts with installed software applications with the operating system or between themselves, or computer viruses. We are talking about software or system failures rather than physical hard drive failures.

Most of the time, the only remedy is to reformat the system hard drive and reinstall the operating system, and all applications. Such action results in the loss of all data on the system hard drive including your documents, emails, and other information stored on that hard drive. Most likely you may have the CDs, DVDs or other media with the operating system and software applications, so reinstalling them is just a matter of a couple of hours, but how about your data and documents? You lose the data and documents too. If your data and documents are stored on other drives, you do not lose them in the process of fixing the system hard drive.

To Improve Computer Performance

The system drive is hardest working hard drive in your computer. Intensive file operations cause significant file fragmentation on the drive. Significant file fragmentation causes a significant reduction in computer performance and, sometimes, can even lead to a system lock and loss of data. Therefore it is strongly advisable to defragment the most intensively used hard drives at least bimonthly if the computer is being used intensively. The hard drive that works harder experiences more fragmentation and should be defragmented more frequently. By separating the system drive from other drives, one can reduce the degree of fragmentation and time needed for defragmentation, and improve computer performance.

Convenience

If your computer has several logical drives (or partitions), then organizing data on them is more convenient than on a single partition. The analogy can be made by comparing a single-room studio apartment, even a big one, with a four-bedroom apartment where each room has its own purpose. Another good analogy is one large cabinet where you store food, clothes, shoes, and sporting equipment versus a number of different cabinets where things are stored by category of use.

2.2   Version Tracking

Though some advanced software applications offer automated version tracking, most users track different versions of their documents manually by adding modifiers to the document filename like version numbers or dates of modification. It is strongly recommended to add the version modifiers to the end of the file name rather than to the beginning or the middle. The reason is very simple. If the modifier is added to the end of the filename then all versions of this file will be shown together in the file managing system ordered alphabetically by name. Otherwise the versions of the file will be spread around in the folder, and that makes it very difficult to find them. For example, suppose you want to make several versions of your resume stored with the file name "resume.docx" and you've added appropriate file name modifiers to track different versions of the document.

accounting_files.xlsx	accounting_files.xlsx
books.docx	books.docx
editorials.docx	edited_resume.docx
kitchen_recipies.pptx	editorials.docx
global_economy.docx	final_resume.docx
resume_1.docx	global_economy.docx
resume_final.docx	good_resume.docx
resume_edited.docx	kitchen_recipies.pptx
resume_good.docx	neuroscience.docx
resume_perfect.docx	perfect_resume.docx
neuroscience.docx	resume_1.docx
sport_magazines.docx	sport_magazines.docx
(a)	(b)

Figure 2-2:   Filenames with modifiers (a) at the end of the filename and (b) in the beginning of the filename. Filenames of "resume" files are highlighted just to make them easy to see

Figure 2-2 shows how the versions of the document would look in the file management system if the modifiers are added (a) to the end of the filename (b) and in the front of the filename. It is clearly seen from Figure 2-2 (a) that in the case of modifiers at the end of the filename all versions of the resume file are shown compactly together, while in the case of adding modifiers in the front of the filename all versions of the file are confusingly mixed with other files as demonstrated in Figure 2-2 (b).

If the filename modifier is supposed to track version number, the recommended format for the version number should include enough leading zeros to account for the length of the highest version number. For example, if the number of versions will not exceed 9, then the versions could be shown as 1, 2, 3, ... On the other hand, if the number of versions exceeds 9, then the versions should be shown with two digits as 01, 02, 03, ..., 10, 11, ..., or more depending on how many total versions you anticipate.

If the modifier shows the date of the new version of the file, then the recommended format for the date is YYMMDD where YY stands for year, MM stands for month and DD stands for day. Though such a format for date with the leading year is not typically used in common life and looks quite unusual and weird, it is very convenient for computers. This is based on the general ordering concept—first comes the "heaviest" part (year), then the "less heavy" part (month) with the "least heavy" part (day) at the end.

my_resume_01.doc	my_thesis_121204.doc
my_resume_02.doc	my_thesis_121212.doc
my_resume_03.doc	my_thesis_121223.doc
my_resume_04.doc	my_thesis_121228.doc
my_resume_05.doc	my_thesis_130105.doc
my_resume_06.doc	my_thesis_130107.doc
my_resume_07.doc	my_thesis_130111.doc
my_resume_08.doc	my_thesis_130115.doc
my_resume_09.doc	my_thesis_130119.doc
my_resume_10.doc	my_thesis_130121.doc
my_resume_11.doc	my_thesis_130124.doc
my_resume_12.doc	my_thesis_130125.doc

Figure 2-3:   Document order with recommended formats for version numbers and dates

Such formats ensure correct ordering by version number or by date on the file list in the file management system. Figure 2-3 shows the files with the recommended version date formats as they are displayed in the file system on the computer monitor.

If the user does not use a full-digit format for version numbers or a different format for dates, like DDMMYY or MMDDYY, then the ordering on the file list would be quite disorganized. For example, Figure 2-4 shows the file ordering for the same files in Figure 2-3 with least-digit version number and *DDMMYY* date format.

my_resume_1.doc	my_thesis_041212.doc
my_resume_10.doc	my_thesis_050113.doc
my_resume_11.doc	my_thesis_070113.doc
my_resume_12.doc	my_thesis_110113.doc
my_resume_2.doc	my_thesis_121212.doc
my_resume_3.doc	my_thesis_150113.doc
my_resume_4.doc	my_thesis_190113.doc
my_resume_5.doc	my_thesis_210113.doc
my_resume_6.doc	my_thesis_231212.doc
my_resume_7.doc	my_thesis_240113.doc
my_resume_8.doc	my_thesis_250113.doc
my_resume_9.doc	my_thesis_281212.doc

Figure 2-4: Document versions with inconvenient version numbers and dates

If you don't use the recommended formats then the file order goes neither by versions nor by dates, as clearly seen from Figure 2-4.

Questions and Exercises

Questions

1. What disk partitioning provides better protection from hardware and software failures?
2. What is the most secure way of organizing your hard drive?
3. Is it possible to set up multiple logical hard drives if your computer has only one physical hard drive?

4. Which hard drives are most optimal to install operating system, applications, and to store working data and information?

5. Is it possible to have an application installed on one hard drive but the data associated with this application on another hard drive?

6. What may cause problems with your computer performance?

7. Why is disk defragmentation needed?

8. How do you track versions of documents stored on your computer?

9. What is the most convenient file version numbering to provide better file ordering?

Exercises

1. Review your computer hard drive organization and decide if there are any improvements possible to provide better protection from hardware or software failures.

2. Review your computer performance and run disk defragmentation if needed.

3. Review how you track versions of files stored on your computer and change the format of filename numbering or date tags in the filenames if needed.

3   Information Security

Information security is one of the most important issues to address in order to prevent computer system failure, which may have a devastating impact on your business or personal life. Information security is a broad term that embraces a wide spectrum of threats ranging from disturbing you with unsolicited commercial offers to information loss to information theft and its usage for hostile purposes.

In this chapter, we address the major aspects of information security related to your personal computer and offer ways to improve your information protection.

3.1   In-Office Information Security

3.1.1   Backups

If not from personal experience, everyone has at least heard scary stories about information loss caused by a hard drive malfunction or an operating system failure. Such failures and malfunctions may happen to any electronic and mechanical equipment at any time, and not only it is very difficult to prevent, information recovery from a corrupted hard drive is very complex and expensive. It's much better not to get to that point.

There are ways to significantly minimize the chance of losing valuable information. Information backup is the most common one, and is very effective. It is simply copying the information to another carrier so that there is a duplicate in case of equipment failure. Though all this sounds very easy at first glance, an effective backup is not a simple one-time copying action, but rather a serious strategic and repeating procedure that has to be carefully planned and systematically executed.

If you keep manually making a backup every time a new modification of the information on your computer occurs, you would probably not be very productive. Therefore all backups must be performed in a consistent and planned manner. For information on your computer that is not being frequently changed, you do not need frequent backups. On the other hand, information on your computer that is being modified very frequently requires frequent backups.

A simple backup

If you only have a small amount of valuable information stored on your computer, you do not need to buy any sophisticated external backup devices. In this case, just use a flash memory stick to copy this information that you can't afford to lose with a frequency that you feel comfortably secures protection from possible information loss.

An external hard drive

If there is a high volume of information on your computer you want to back up, you can use an external hard drive. Most external backup hard drives come with specialized software that ensures scheduled or even incremental backup. Incremental backup automatically updates the backup files incrementally as modification occurs. This process goes on in a background mode, i.e. while your computer is on idle, thus it does not disturb your routine work.

Online internet backup

There are many service companies that offer online backup. If your computer is connected to the Internet, you can sign up for these backup services and incremental backup will be performed online by the service company. In the case of information loss, you will be able to restore the information from the backup copies on the service provider server. However, though such backup is very convenient, it may leave some concerns about unauthorized access to your proprietary information.

3.1.2   Password Protected Access

Personal computers and laptops may be used by a single user or by a number of users. To protect the information on your computer from unauthorized access, use, copying, or destruction, it is wise to set up password-protected access to your computer or to your account on the computer you use.

However, if you are a single user and there is no sensitive information on your computer that you don't want other people to access, you do not need password-protected access to your computer.

3.2   Internet Security

The Internet has changed the entire landscape of business and personal life. Nowadays, it is very difficult to imagine any business without it or any person who does not use the Internet at least occasionally. However a coin always has two sides and the opposite side of the Internet is a variety of security threats.

3.2.1   Firewalls

Firewall is a software program or an electronic hardware device that protects your computer or a group of computers from unauthorized access from the outside network. A firewall can be provided by the hardware router that connects your computer or a group of computers to the network. A firewall could be provided by the software included in the operating system on your computer, or it could be part of the specialized internet security software you that purchase separately and install on your computer. Despite of a variety of forms, the firewall is an important barrier that protects your computer from the hostile environment on the outside network. You have to have an active firewall on your computer to protect it from unauthorized access.

3.2.2   Viruses

A computer virus is a computer program that can copy and incorporate itself into other programs and infect a computer without the user's permission or knowledge. These programs are called viruses because they act exactly the same as real viruses in nature, which incorporate themselves into live cells of other organisms, using the host cells for their (viruses) support and reproduction, and in result. most likely, destroy the cells. Computer viruses show the same pattern. Computer viruses are software programs which can incorporate themselves into legitimate programs—host programs—running on the computer. Then the host program becomes infected. Computer viruses spread by transmitting from an infected program to uninfected ones. Viruses modify functionality of infected programs and the modified functionality can be quite harmful. Every virus has a main function, and in this way too, computer viruses are very similar to the natural viruses.

Some computer viruses are practically harmless. They just lead to some strange computer behavior and make your computer contagious to other computers. A classic example of a harmless virus is a very old virus called Yankee Doodle. If a computer gets infected with Yankee Doodle, the only impact from the virus is that every day at five o'clock the computer plays the Yankee Doodle tune. Though such virus behavior is quite harmless, it is still very unwelcome.

Most computer viruses, however, are quite dangerous and may pose a devastating effect on your computer and the information on it by their malicious impact. Viruses can steal proprietary data from your computer including your financial information, bank passwords and other very sensitive information. They can also track your actions, destroy your data, make software inoperable, and even destroy hardware by forcing it to act in such a way that it leads to self-destruction. For example, some computer viruses may interfere or take over the hard drive control and force the hard drive to perform head motion which conflicts with the spinning part of the hard drive destroying it in the process. This is just one example of many malicious virus activities that can destroy computer hardware.

There is a broad variety of types of computer viruses and they differ by their functional behavior, reproductive features, and malicious impacts.

3.2.3   Spying Software

Some malicious programs, called spyware, are able to infiltrate your computer, remain stealthy without any visible track of their existence, collect proprietary and sensitive information on your computer, and send it over the internet to some other location mostly for the purpose of hostile actions. Spyware is difficult to identify without special software due to their stealth and technically harmless behavior. However, letting spyware reside on your computer may cause you enormous damage.

There is antispyware software available from various vendors, and typically protection from spyware is a standard function of most internet security and virus protection packages.

3.2.4   Cookies

Cookies are passive data files that collect your workflow information for the sake of the user's convenience. For example, cookies can store your username and password to provide automatic login to some programs or web accounts. Some software applications insert cookies into your computer to store system settings and configuration for the user's convenience. The downside of this convenience is that cookies may be used to collect your proprietary information for unauthorized use.

Most websites use cookies for the user's convenience, however, be vigilant as some cookies can be quite harmful because they may store your proprietary information and allow outside programs to access your proprietary and sensitive information. Try not to allow cookies if it is not necessary. At least, agree to use cookies only if there is no other way and their use is safe.

3.2.5   Vulnerability

Internet vulnerability is one of the most important issues for all software including operating systems. Modern software is so complex that it inevitably has some weak points where internet security can be compromised or broken by providing back door access to your computer and the information on it. Hackers typically use such vulnerabilities to break into a computer system. Software vendors do their best to fix vulnerabilities in their software products and offer software patches to fix any identified problems. The only advice regarding software vulnerabilities is to keep your software up-to-date and install the updates and patches offered by the vendors.

3.3   Internet Fraud

Internet fraud typically refers to fraudulent activities over the internet by using email, websites, chat rooms, social networks, and other internet programs and services. There are a variety of internet fraud schemes and approaches, so be internet-smart watch what you do, and do not become a victim of internet fraud.

3.3.1   Spam

The term "Spam" refers to unsolicited and undesirable bulk emails that typically carry commercial or other offers. At first glance, Spam looks quite innocent but just annoying. However, you should be careful. The goods offered by spammers may be of poor quality or spam may be associated with malicious viruses and other forms of internet fraud including identity theft.

Suppose you are offered something you really like at an affordable price, so you pay for the goods with your credit card and provide some personal information for verification. This could be a catch. Spammers may use the offered products or services as bait. The spammer may even send you the purchased goods to avert any suspicions. but at the same time the spammer gets possession of your credit card and other personal information for identity theft or other fraudulent activities. Use your common sense and be internet-smart to avoid such situations, but at the same time, don't become extreme and overly cautious by refusing any internet sales. Good eCommerce companies are very reliable and take very good care of their customers and their personal information.

3.3.2   Phishing

Phishing refers to fraudulent activities on the internet that aim to acquire a user's personal and sensitive information by mimicking legitimate websites. Modern internet technology provides the technical ability to send emails that pretend to be from any sender and mimic well-established eCommerce or other websites. The term "Phishing" is an analogy to real fishing and is used to emphasize the kind of internet fraud where a fisherman, i.e. "hacker", puts bait on a hook and waits for the fish to bite.

You may have received emails pretending to be from your bank, eBay, the government and so on, with a request for you to login by clicking the provided link and update your personal information including your name, address, password, bank account details, social security number and so on. If you do this, you're like the fish getting on the hook. First of all, you are providing personal and sensitive information that could be used for illegal activities including identity theft, bank account access, etc. In addition to this, by clicking on the link provided, you may infest your computer with malicious viruses or spyware that take control over the information on your computer.

To protect yourself from Phishing you have to be internet-smart, cautious in your actions, and knowledgeable of major rules that legitimate banks, eCommerce vendors and other organizations have used to protect their customers from fraudulent activities on the internet. Several simple rules may help you avoid potential problems:

- Remember, legitimate eCommerce vendors never ask for your personal information over email.
- If you receive an email from an unknown source with a request to click on the provided link, just ignore it.
- If you receive an email that looks legitimate and there is a request to click on the provided link, still do not do it. Instead, open a new browser and go the appropriate website of the service provider. If there is anything you need to know or there is any information you need to provide or update with that service provider, you will always find it on the website.
- If you still want to use a link received over email, bring the cursor to that link and click the right button of your mouse to see properties. You will see a real link in properties that helps you identify if it is a fraudulent or legitimate link.

Protecting yourself and your computer from Phishing

- Legitimate banks, eCommerce vendors and other organizations never ask for your password or any personal and sensitive information in unsolicited emails.
- If you receive an email that you suspect to be a Phishing one, delete it at once. Never click on any links provided in emails if you have any suspicion of Phishing. Instead, go to the legitimate website by opening a new browser and typing the appropriate URL, logging in, and checking if there are any problems you have to fix or any information you need to update in your account.
- If you open a legitimate website but have a suspicion that you were redirected to a Phishing website by fraudulent activities on the internet name server, close the web page and call customer service.
- Some advanced eCommerce websites have already introduced a vendor identification step in the login process. Traditionally, only customers identify themselves with the username and password. However, with the threat of Phishing, some internet services like Bank of America have introduced vendor checking by providing a specific identification selected by the customer to make sure that the customer gets on the legitimate website rather than on the Phishing replica of it.

3.3.3   Identity Theft

Identity theft is the term used for illegal activities involving the usage of another individual's identity. The main purpose of identity theft is to collect a sufficient amount of personal information on another person to use for criminal activities like establishing credit in the victim's name, using his or her bank account, or establishing bank credit and leaving the victim responsible for it. There are also many other illegal uses of a stolen identity. The consequences of identity theft are typically devastating for the victim and difficult to recover from.

To prevent identity theft one has to be vigilant in not providing personal information to any suspicious or unknown business entities or people. For example, if you are paying for any goods or services over the internet and can do it through PayPal or other known and verified providers, you should do that.

3.3.4   Farming

Internet link farming is a fraudulent activity based on the automated redirection of a website to a cascade of other websites for the purpose of Spam or other illegal activities. The user opens one website and a cascade of other websites uncontrollably pop up on the computer monitor. Though it just looks extremely annoying, sometimes it can be harmful as it may be associated with spyware, phishing and other internet fraud activities. No legitimate internet companies use farming and it is considered part of internet fraud.

3.4   How to Protect Your Computer and Yourself

To protect your computer and yourself from the devastating impact of viruses, spyware, and internet fraud of all kinds, you should install powerful internet security software and keep your protective software up-to-date. Keep in mind that installing two different internet security systems on one computer may lead to conflict between these two systems that eliminate any protection, so keep only one internet security system on your computer at any time.

Never send personal and sensitive information over an unsecure internet connection. A hint: secure websites typically have a URL that begins with "https://" rather than "http://". However, be aware that a secure connection can still be mimicked by malicious programs.

Technical Measures

- Install firewall and internet security software including virus protection, spyware protection and others.
- Keep internet security software up-to-date.
- Keep updating the computer operating system and installed software applications by downloading the security patches from the software vendors.
- Do not use two or more different internet security systems on your computer at a time because they may conflict with each other resulting in no protection at all.

Also be aware that technology does not solve this problem itself. You must be vigilant, internet smart, and behave in such a manner that you reduce the chance of viruses getting in your computer and your personal information becoming known to suspicious businesses and individuals. Using the human analogy, one can say that virus protection software plays the role of medication or a flu shoot, while a human's protective behavior helps avoid undesirable and potentially harmful contact and personal hygiene may significantly reduce chances of catching the flu. To protect your computer from viruses and prevent your personal information from being stolen, you have to take both technical and personal discipline measures.

Discipline Measures

- Never install any non-proven or suspicious software on your computer.
- Never open any suspicious web pages or emails.
- Ask your friends and colleagues to be very specific in the email subject line to identify that the email really comes from them.
- Never provide your proprietary or sensitive information on the web unless the recipient is well-known and the connection is secure. Just having a secure connection does not save you from identity theft.
- Be internet-smart by analogy of street-smart. This means keep your eyes and mind open to possible dangers in the environment.
- Apply common sense and be aware of commonly used protective rules.

Questions and Exercises

Questions

1. Why is backup needed?
2. How often do you have to make a backup?
3. What does it mean to backup online?
4. What is needed for online backup?
5. Why is password protection needed for your computer?
6. In what case does your computer not need password protection?

7. What major issues are involved in internet security?

8. What is a firewall and why is it needed?

9. What are computer viruses?

10. Why are computer viruses dangerous?

11. What does spying software, or spyware, mean?

12. What are cookies and what do they do?

13. Why are cookies sometimes harmful to your computer?

14. What does system vulnerability mean?

15. What does internet fraud mean?

16. What types of internet fraud do you know?

17. What kinds of activities are associated with internet fraud?

18. What damage could internet fraud do to your computer and to you?

19. How do you protect your computer and yourself from internet fraud?

20. What does the term Spam mean?

21. What kinds of activities are associated with Spam?

22. What damage could Spam make to your computer and to you?

23. How do you protect your computer and yourself from Spam?

24. What does the term Phishing mean?

25. What kinds of activities are associated with Phishing?

26. What damage could Phishing do to your computer and to you?

27. How do you protect your computer and yourself from Phishing?

28. What does the term Identity Theft mean?

29. What kinds of activities are associated with Identity Theft?

30. What damage could Identity Theft do to your computer and to you?

Exercises

1. Review your computer security system and plan improvements to provide better protection if needed.

2. Review your computer virus and spyware protection and plan improvements if needed.

3. Review your work habits and make the appropriate changes to provide better protection from internet fraud.

4. Review your work habits and decide what you can do to protect yourself from identity theft.

4   Writing with Styles

This chapter introduces the reader to some advanced features of modern word processing and technology, and provides a writing methodology that creates clean and impressive documents while saving time and effort in the document preparation process. By no means is this book a comprehensive user manual. Rather, it presents a minimum set of the most important advanced word processing features and document preparation methodology for those already familiar with the basics to bring readers up to a level where they can effortlessly create professionally looking documents which are easy to format and modify.

There are a variety of good and advanced word processing applications currently available on the market. The most popular are Microsoft Word, Corel WordPerfect, and the relatively new OpenOffice Writer.

Microsoft Word and Corel WordPerfect are well-established commercially available applications that offer the most features for document writing and publishing. OpenOffice Writer, on the other hand, is a relatively new open source application available free of charge with the same major advanced features as Microsoft Word and Corel WordPerfect. OpenOffice is maturing at an incredibly high rate and has huge potential to become the most powerful word processing application in the near future. Its market share keeps growing.

Since each of these office applications are so similar—primary differences being user interface and specific menus and buttons—this book is equally applicable to all of them. For simplicity's sake, however, we will focus our attention primarily on Microsoft Office 2010, the most recent version of Microsoft Office and the most popular and widely used of the office application suites. To prove the power of this application, this book itself was written and formatted with Microsoft Word 2010.

4.1   Introduction to Microsoft Word

Microsoft Word is the word processing application of the Microsoft Office application suite. Document files written with Microsoft Word have extension ".docx" for versions 2007 and 2010 and ".doc" for 2003 and preceding versions. These two extensions imply differences in the internal structure of the documents for versions before and after 2007, however, files can be converted from one format to another if needed with some possible minor loss of formatting functionality.

This book addresses Word processing with Microsoft Word 2010 functionality. The user interface of Microsoft Word, as well as other Microsoft Office applications, has the following structure:

The main menu addresses major divisions of functionality. Main menu items are called tabs. For example, **Home** tab, **Insert** tab and so on as shown in Figure 4-1. Each tab (main menu item) leads to a collection of related functions. Each of these functions is displayed in the form of an icon on a panel below the main menu. This panel is referred to as a **Ribbon**. The functions displayed in each **Ribbon** are specific to a particular tab, which means that switching a tab results in changes in the **Ribbon**.

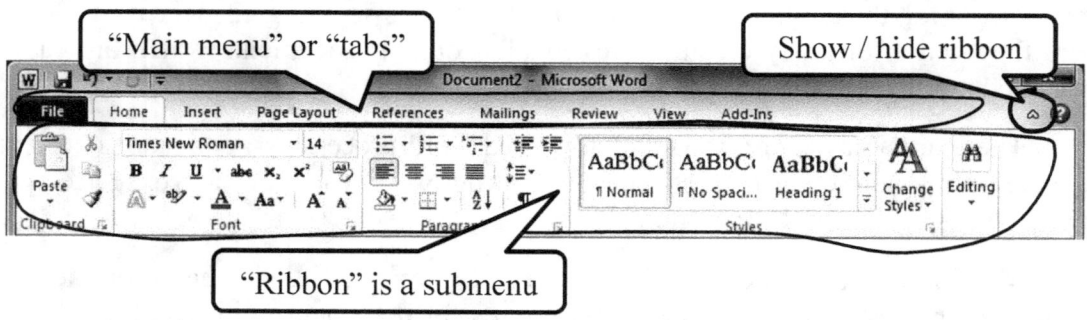

Figure 4-1: Tabs and ribbons

As soon as ribbon takes a certain portion of the screen, sometimes it is convenient not to show the ribbon all the time. Users can show or hide the ribbon by pressing an icon indicated in Figure 4-1. Placing cursor to a ribbon and rolling the mouse wheel causes sequential switching the main menu tabs along with their ribbons.

4.2   About Styles

4.2.1   Why Styles?

It is presumed that the reader has some elementary knowledge of Microsoft Word, i.e. knows how to open a new or an existing document, type in the text, modify the fonts, cut/copy and paste portions of text, control the layout of the document, and save the document in the specified directory (or folder). If for some reason, you do not know how to do it, don't worry, just open Microsoft Word and learn it in a practical manner; it is very easy and intuitive, so we would not spend time on such basics in this book.

Most people use just the basic features to develop documents with Microsoft Word, i.e. open a new or an existing document, type/cut/copy/paste text, modify fonts, control the layout of the document, and save the document in a specified directory (or folder). At first glance, it seems that is enough to write good and clean documents. I am afraid that it is not exactly the case. If you have any experience writing documents, you should remember how many times you have struggled with stubborn fonts, line spacing, line indents, bullets, document layout, and have been engaged in other losing "formatting battles".

Matching numeration of document sections and subsections, figures, and tables, cross references, and table of contents are especially unnerving and frustrating procedures, particularly when some of the portions of the document have been changed, added or removed during the document preparation. It would be practically impossible to find a somewhat complex and long document prepared with successfully matching numeration of sections, figures, tables, equations, cross-references, and tables of contents if all this was done manually and if the document had been significantly changed several times in the process of its development. In the end, you will surely find a lot of flaws in the document.

Imagine for a second that after you completely format your paper, you find out that all formats have to be changed because of special formatting requirements or because you have to add or remove some sections, figures, tables or equations. I have seen horror in the eyes of people who faced this problem and tried to keep their documents clean. People spend enormous amount of time and effort in cleaning up documents, matching up the numeration of sections, figures, and tables, verifying cross-references and fixing the table of contents, and still the result is a document with many flaws.

Is this problem solvable? Is there any way of writing a clean and nice document without wasting so much time on technical cleanup? The answer is yes. Write documents with Styles!

4.2.2   What is a Style?

Styles are a simple solution to formatting your document so that making changes is much easier and more consistent.

Imagine that you have a 100-page document with 20 section headings. Now, say you wanted to change the font size and bold of all the heading titles. It would take a lot of time, and an accurate eye, to change every single heading individually. And, then, what if after changing them all, you don't like the look – you could be repeating this action again and again.

Similarly, if you assign properties like font face and size, line spacing, indents, numeration, cross-referencing and other formatting features directly to selected parts of the document, then changing any of them is a big problem because you must go through the entire document and make the appropriate changes to each and every part that should be consistent. This is practically an unbearable task to accomplish for large documents, or at least it is very difficult, time consuming, and unnerving to complete this task with success.

Styles:

- Styles are standard or user-defined types of text or other document components that can be assigned to different parts of the document.
- Each style is given a unique name.
- Each style contains text properties that are automatically applied to the portions of the document that have been assigned that style.

The solution is to apply "styles" to different parts of your document. Styles are standard or user-defined types of text or other document components that you assign to the appropriate parts of the document. Then, when you need to make adjustments to those sections, you just change the properties of the style type and the appropriate changes will automatically propagate to the entire document. Nice and easy, fast and clean! For this reason, I advise to spend time to learn styles – you will appreciate it very much. In the end, it will save you a lot of time and ensure a clean and consistent document.

The concept of styles is illustrated in Figure 4-2. Style "Heading 1" is associated with all first-level headings in the document, style "Heading 2" with all second-level headings, and style "Body Text" with all paragraphs of the document.

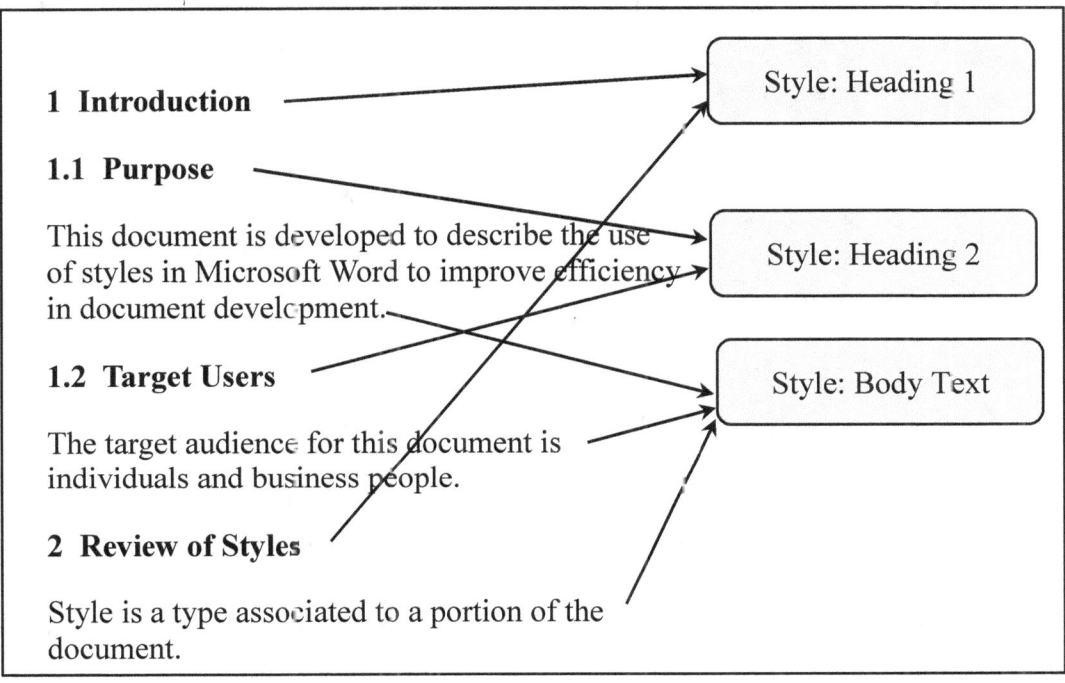

Figure 4-2: Portions of a document with the associated styles.

"Body Text" style is used for the document text in Figure 4-2 as an example. If you want to change the font size and indent the first line in all paragraphs of the document, all you need to do is modify the style "Body Text" and all paragraphs in the entire document associated with that style will automatically change accordingly.

4.3   Basic Style Properties

Let's start with some basic style properties that control text, paragraphs, line spacing, and indents. Even with these basic style properties, you will definitely get a lot of relief in writing documents.

4.3.1   Text, Paragraphs, Line Spacing, and Indent

Assume, you are writing a diary and your initial text looks like shown in Figure 4-3. So, you did everything manually:

- Typed everything in Times New Roman font size 12.
- Manually made the headings "bold."
- Manually made the first line indent by using "*Tab*" key on the keyboard.

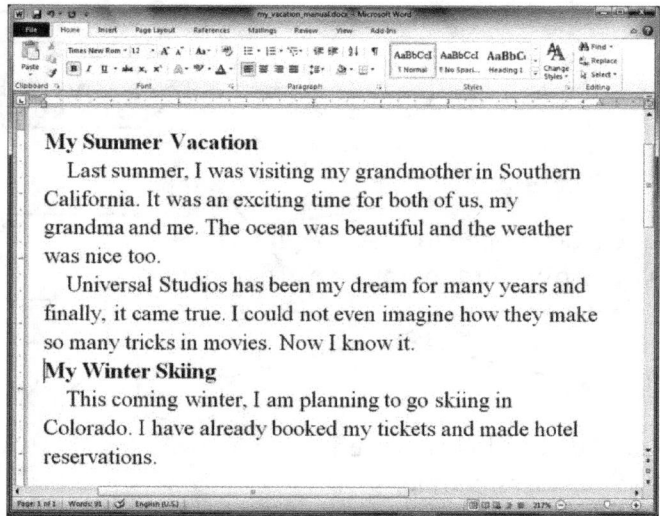

Figure 4-3: Manually formatted sample document

Everything looks just fine, however, what if you decided to make the following changes:

- change font face from "Times New Roman" to "Arial" through the entire document,
- change font size to 14 for the headings,
- make headings centered,
- increase space between paragraphs in the text but make it less than an entire empty line,
- increase space between headings and text more than between paragraphs,
- make the first line indent longer in each paragraph,
- change text alignment from left to justified.

So, you begin making all these formatting changes manually again by

- directly changing font face and size by selecting the appropriate text or heading and setting up font face and size,
- adding another tab for the longer indent,
- making alignment justified,
- changing heading alignment to centered,
- adding empty lines between paragraphs and between headings and paragraphs.

Did you notice? You've already got your first problem. You have no control over the space between paragraphs and between headings and paragraphs. The only thing you can do is add an empty line between paragraphs as well as between headings and paragraphs, but in this case you get a larger space than you wanted. You wanted just a tiny space between the paragraphs rather than an entire line. If you try to control the space between paragraphs by changing the font size in the empty lines, you are looking for even more trouble in the future, bringing your document formatting out of control.

Then let's remember that all of us are humans and humans can miss or overlook something. You may believe that you changed everything you meant to change, but inevitably in a large document you will miss some. For example, you may overlook modifying the second paragraph and heading. In that case, after you complete all your format modifications, the document may look something like that shown in Figure 4-4. This is not what you wanted; it is neither nicely formatted nor clean at all. While this example is small enough to be manageable, it demonstrates the kinds of issues that occur with large documents when formatted manually.

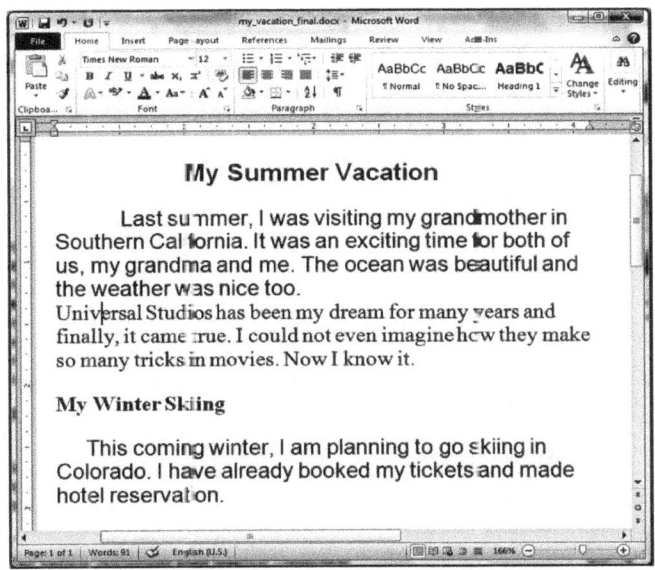

Figure 4-4: Sample document after manual correction

Assigning a Style

Now, let's do the work right. First of all, let's start everything over. We will not do any formatting directly in the text including "bold" font, extra lines, and manual indents.

Let's assign "styles" to each part of the document. In this particular document, we have two parts which need different formatting: text and heading. One of the ways to assign existing styles is to use ***Quick Style Selector*** in the "Home" tab as shown in Figure 4-5:

- Select the portion of the text in the document you want to assign a style.
- In tab ***Home*** chose a style from the ***Quick Style Selector*** section in the ribbon as shown in Figure 4-5.

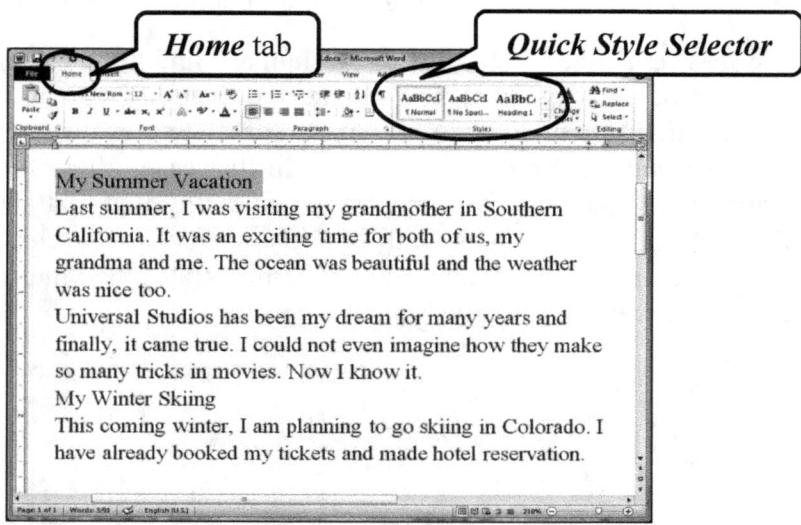

Figure 4-5: Assigning styles to parts of the document

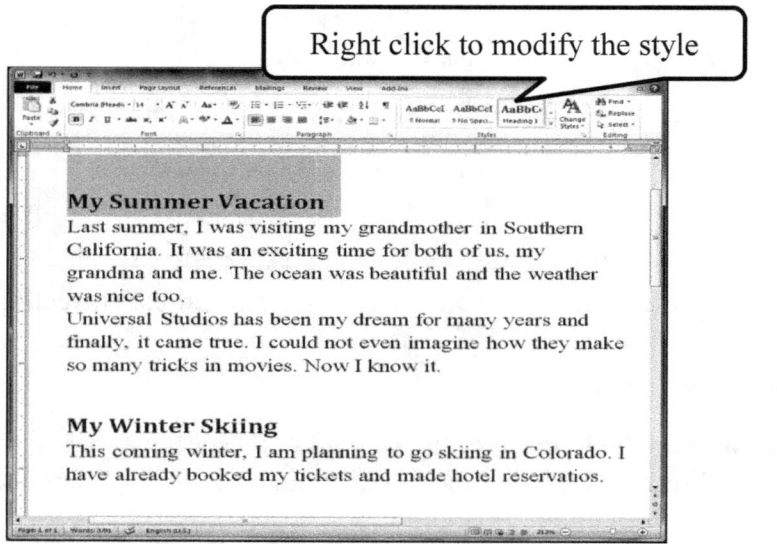

Figure 4-6: Document after initial style assignment

Style Modification

As you see in Figure 4-5, ***Quick Style Selector*** contains certain preset styles. First let's select first heading "My Summer Vacation" as shown in Figure 4-5 and assign style "Heading 1" to it by clicking on ***Heading 1*** icon in the ***Quick Style Selector***. Assign the same style to the second heading "My Winter Skiing" in your document. Keep style "Normal" for the text of this document. You can check an assigned style by clicking on that part of the document: the assigned style becomes highlighted in the ***Quick Style Selector***. In result, your document will look like Figure 4-6.

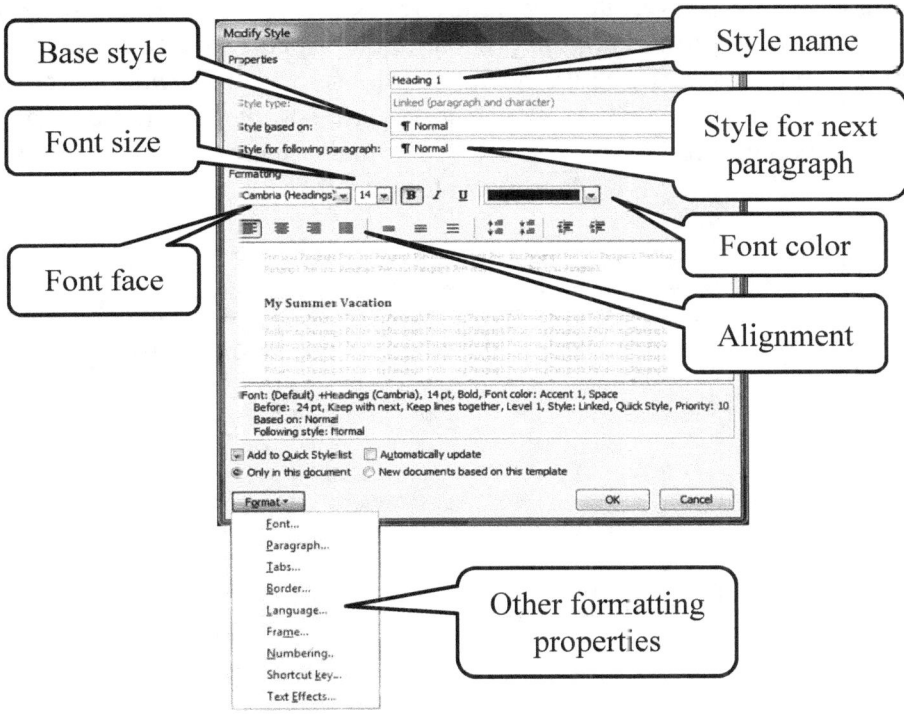

Figure 4-7: ***Modify Style*** window for style properties setting

As you see from Figure 4-6, the font color of all headings in the document turned blue, font face changed to "Cambria", and the space between paragraphs and headings became larger than you wanted it to be. It is not exactly what you want. It happened because style "Heading 1" was preset to those specific parameters. Let's now modify style "Heading 1" to set it exactly how we want it to be. By clicking the right button on the style icon in the ***Quick Style Selector*** section as shown in Figure 4-6, we open the ***Modify Style*** popup window where we can change the style settings as shown in Figure 4-7.

Using the ***Modify Style*** window (Figure 4-7) we can set the desired style properties. In our example, we set for style "Heading 1": font face "Arial", size "14", "centered", and color "Black". Then pressing ***Format*** button in that window we bring a list of other formatting options and select option ***Paragraph*** we open a control where we set the desired space before and after the paragraph in style "Heading 1". You must have noticed that as soon as you clicked on the "OK" button in the ***Modify Style*** window (Figure 4-7), all portions of the text assigned to style "Heading 1" changed their appearance to follow the new format settings.

Then let's select any paragraph of the regular text in our document (Figure 4-5) which is assigned to style "Normal" by right clicking on style "Normal" in ***Quick Style Selector*** (Figure 4-5) and following the procedure described above to set the formats for style "Normal". To make the first line indent we choose option ***Format → Paragraph*** to set up "First Line" indent to 0.5" as shown in Figure 4-8. Do you notice that as in the previous case all paragraphs assigned to style "Normal" changed their format as soon as you clicked the "OK" button in the ***Modify Style*** window.

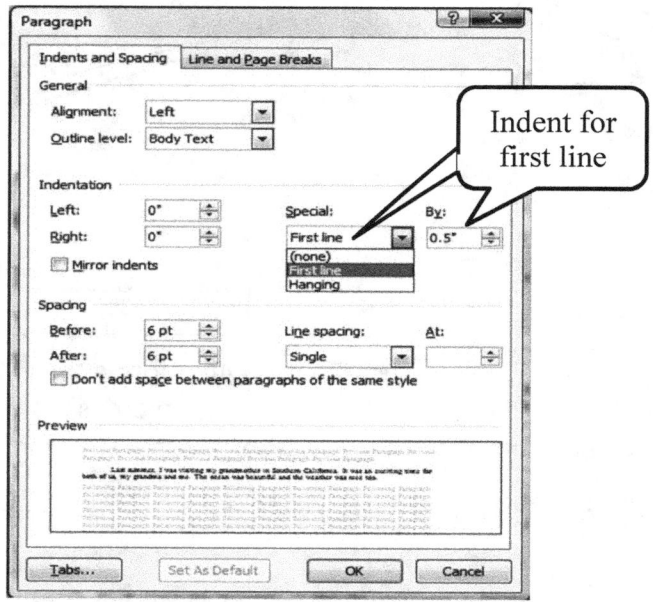

Figure 4-8: Formatting paragraph properties

All these procedures are quite intuitive, so you can easily learn them and become very comfortable with them after a couple of routine practice exercises.

In result, your text now looks as shown in Figure 4-9 which is exactly what you wanted.

Figure 4-9: Final version of the formatted document

The formatting of the final document shown in Figure 4-9 is now under control. If you decide to make any additional changes to the document, you just need to modify the properties of the assigned styles and the entire document will adjust to the new properties of the assigned styles.

Writing with Style: Basics

- Assign the appropriate styles to every portion of the document.
- Control the document formatting by adjusting properties of the appropriate styles rather than directly changing properties of the text. For example, if you need to change the font size, do it through changing the font size in the appropriate style properties rather than directly in the text.

4.3.2   Finding Styles

To find out what style is assigned to any particular portion of the document, place the cursor on that portion of the document and click on the left button; the assigned style gets highlighted in the **Quick Style Selector** as illustrated in Figure 4-5. However the style selector does not have room for many styles. There is a scroll bar on the right-hand side of the **Quick Style Selector**. You can use that scroll bar to see more styles. Clicking on the bottom of the scroll bar expands the **Quick Style Selector** (Figure 4-10).

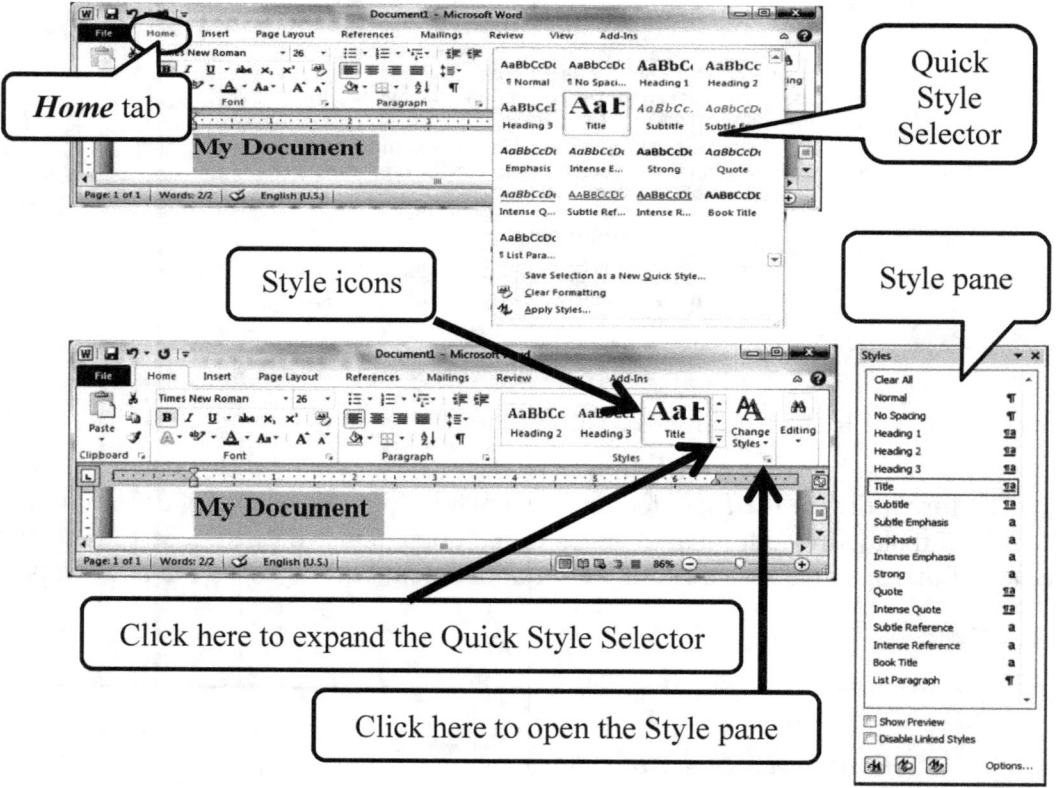

Figure 4-10: Style selection methods

The expanded **Quick Style Selector** contains the most recently used styles but its capacity is also quite limited. To see more styles click on the right side of the "style bar" in the ribbon below the **Quick Style Selector** as shown in Figure 4-10 to open the **Style Pane**. The style highlighted by a frame in the **Style Pane** shows the style associated with the appropriate portion of the document. Right clicking on a style in the **Style Pane** allows you to modify the style properties exactly the same way as described in section 4.3.1 above and illustrated in Figure 4-7.

The **Style Pane** (Figure 4-10) may show all defined styles or only styles used in this particular document depending on the viewing options setting. To control the viewing options on the style pane click on **Options** in the bottom-right corner of the **Style Pane** (Figure 4-11).

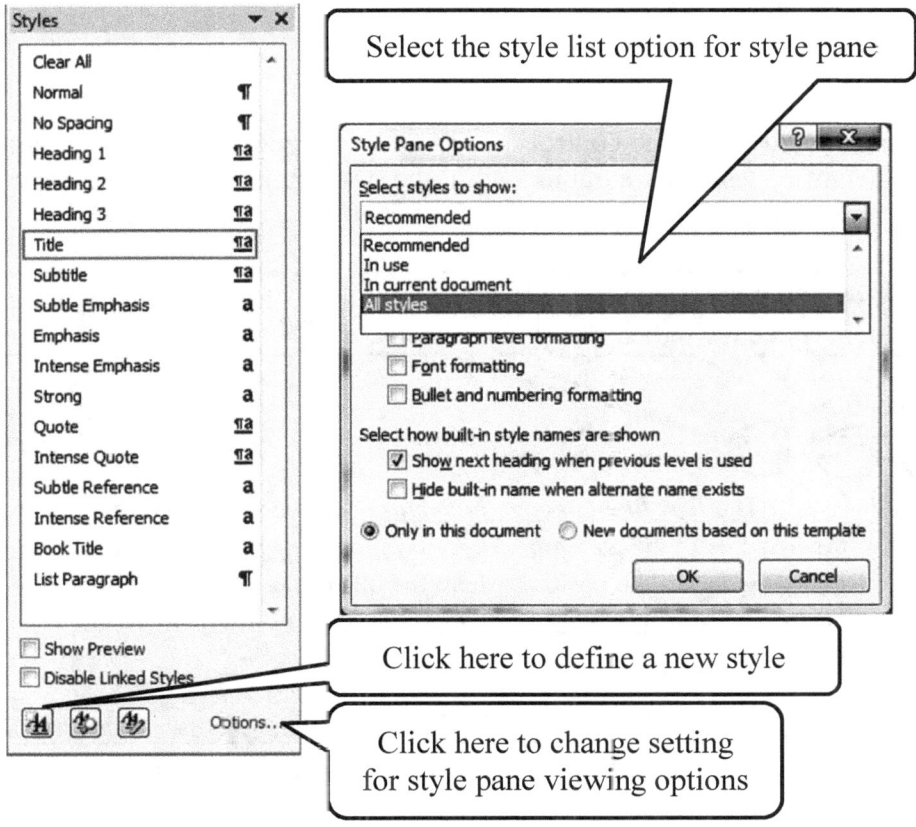

Figure 4-11: Controlling style pane options

4.3.3 Modifying an Existing Style and Defining a New Style

To modify properties of an existing style you have to select the style from the **Quick Style Selector** or from the **Style Pane**, right click on the style to open a list of options, then choose "Modify". This opens the **Modify Style** popup window (Figure 4-7). Use the **Modify Style** popup window to change the style properties to those you want. Immediately as you press the **OK** button the modified properties apply to all portions of the document to which this style has been assigned. We will discuss the most important style properties later in this book.

You may want to define a new style. In this case click on the **New Styles** icon in the bottom-right corner of the **Style Pane** as shown in Figure 4-11. A **Create New Style** popup window identical to the familiar **Modify Style** window opens which you can then use to define your own new style.

4.3.4   Tabs and Edge Indicators

Edge Indicators

Users should be able to control the left and right edges of the document as well as the left and right edges of paragraphs within the document by using the edge indicators shown in Figure 4-12.

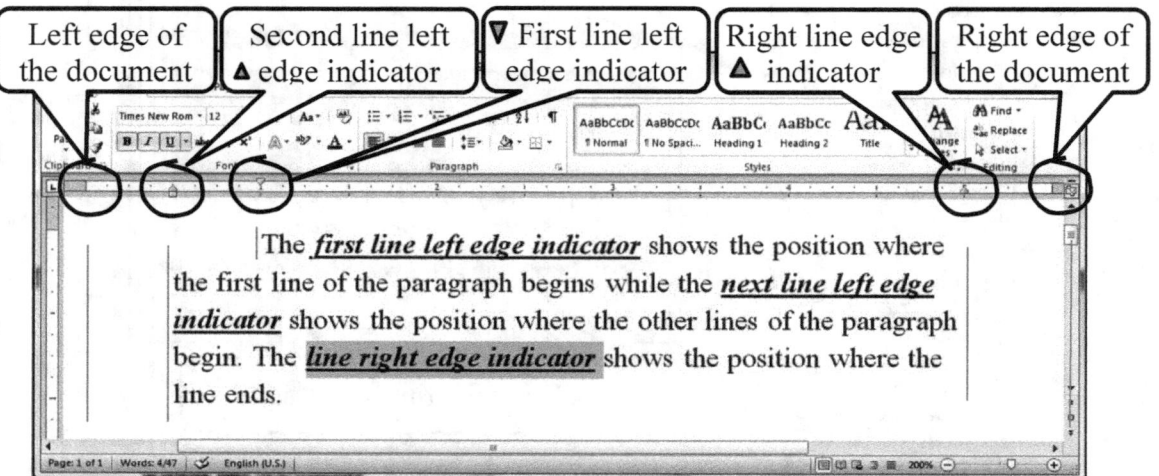

Figure 4-12: Document and paragraph line edge indicators

The left and right document edge indicators control the text area of the document and are shown on the document ruler as vertical separators between the shaded (margin) and clear (document) areas. Everything outside the working area is the document margin. The line edge indicators control the edges of the paragraph. The first line left edge indicator (a tip-down triangle in the upper part of the ruler area) controls the position where the first line of the paragraph begins while the second line left indicator (a tip-up triangle in the lower part of the ruler area) controls the position where the other lines of the paragraph begin. The right line edge indicator (a tip-up triangle in the lower part of the ruler area) controls the position where all lines of the paragraph end. By moving and setting the indicators one can accurately control the document and the paragraph edges.

Tabs

Using tabs allows users to shift text by a certain amount of space along a line to accurately control the text layout. Any attempt to do so by using the space key will not result in a nicely aligned shift due to different width of characters. On the other hand, tabs do the job. Tabs are the marks on the page ruler that show and control the exact position and alignment properties of the text when the user presses the **Tab** key while typing the text.

There are different types of tabs:
- left
- middle
- right
- decimal
- bar

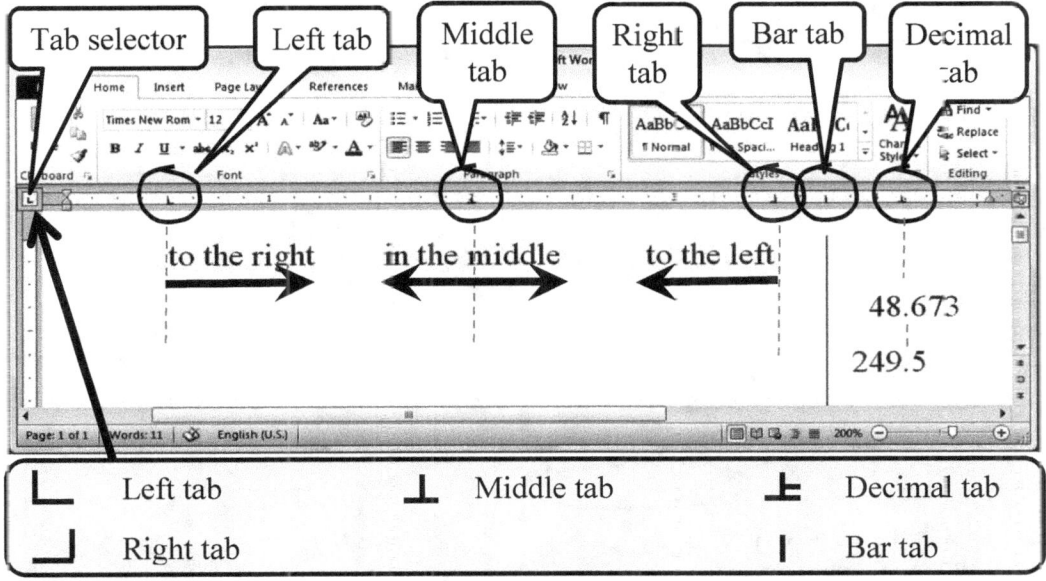

Figure 4-13: Tabs and their properties

Figure 4-13 shows the properties of these types of tabs. If a left tab is set in a certain position of the document, pressing the **Tab** key will cause the next portion of the text to be aligned to the right from the "left tab" position (Figure 4-13). The "middle tab" causes the appropriate portion of the text to align at the position of the "middle tab" mark always keeping the tab mark in the middle of that portion. The "right tab" aligns the text to the left from the tab mark. The "Decimal tab" causes the decimal point of a number to align at the position of the tab mark. The "Bar tab" draws a vertical line in the document in the position of the tab mark.

Users can select a tab type from the tab selector in the upper-left corner of the document window as shown in Figure 4-13. Every click on the tab selector changes the tab type. When a desired tab type shows up, click to the appropriate part of the horizontal document ruler to set the tab for the current or selected lines of the document.

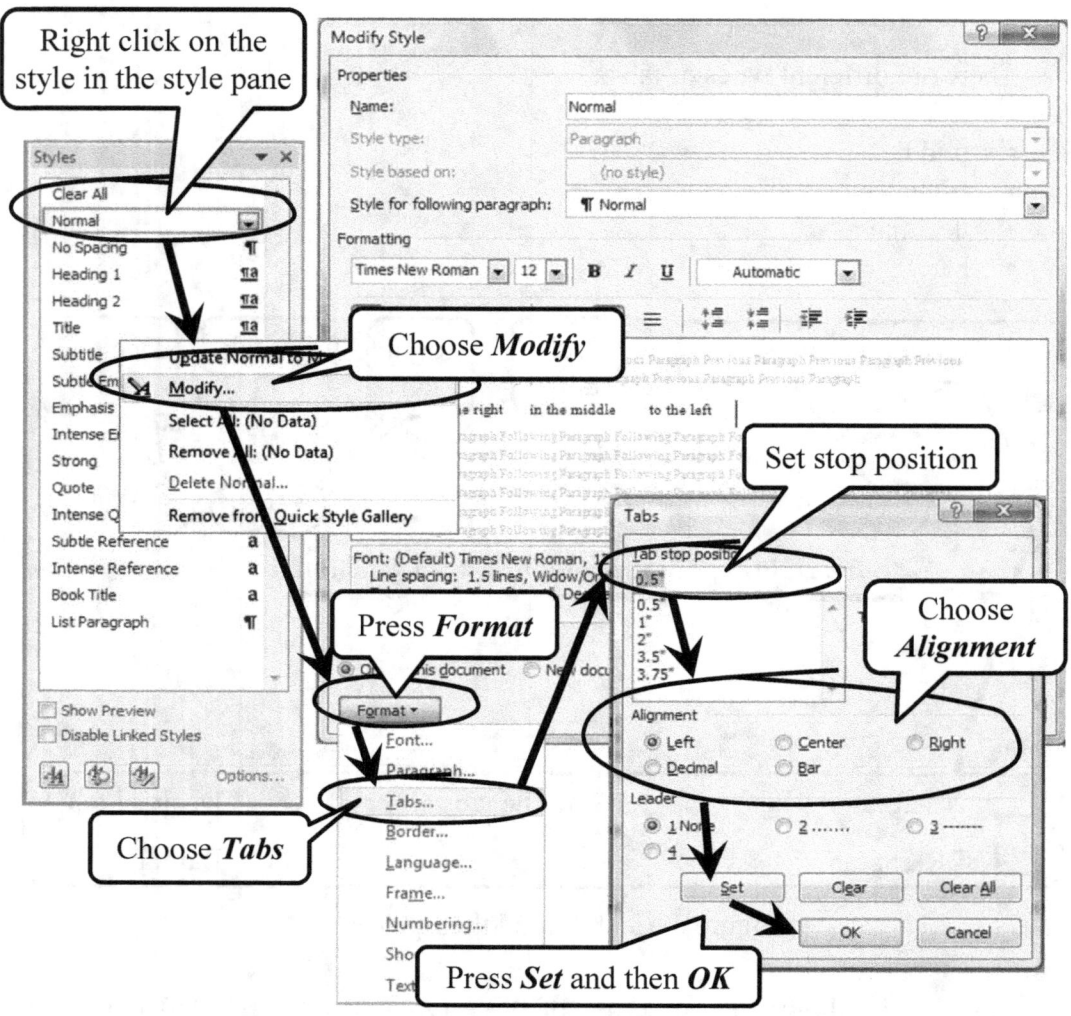

Figure 4-14: Setting tabs to a style

Setting tabs manually may cause confusing combinations of tabs for different portions of the document. It is strongly recommended that you set up tabs in appropriate styles as you would with any other formatting properties. This technique results in the consistent application of tabs for all portions of the document assigned to that particular style. To set tabs to a style, follow the procedure illustrated in Figure 4-14. First find the appropriate style in the style pane, then right click on that style and choose "Modify", press the *Format* button in the *Modify Style* popup window, and choose *Tabs*. The *Tabs* setting popup window appears. In that window set up the desired position of the tab, choose the tab alignment and press *Set* and then *OK*. After that, press *OK* in the *Modify*

Style popup window.

To remove a tab, perform the same procedure but when you come to the *Tabs* window, select the appropriate tab and press the *Clear* button.

4.3.5   First Line Indent and Hanging

In many documents, the first line of a paragraph may require a different indentation than other lines. The technique to set the indent for the first line of a paragraph was described in Section 4.3.1 and illustrated in Figure 4-8. However sometimes it is necessary to control the indent for the other lines of a paragraph, for example, if you need to write a bibliography as shown in Figure 4-15. In the sample bibliography each source is written as a separate paragraph. The second and all following lines of every paragraph should be indented relative to the first line, which has no indent.

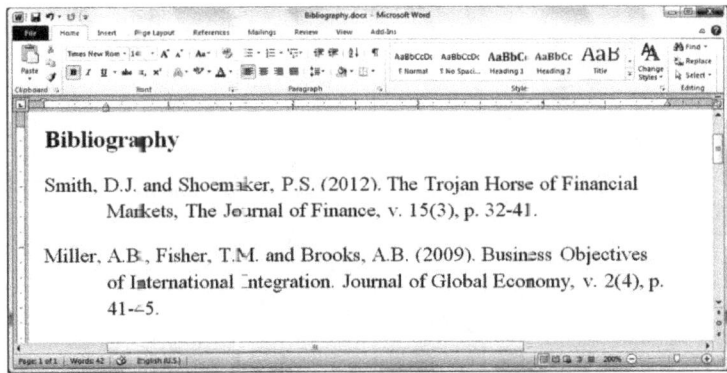

Figure 4-15: Sample bibliography

To format the text as shown in Figure 4-15 you have to set up a "Hanging" property at the top of the paragraph. To set up a "Hanging" property, select the appropriate portion of the text and assign a style to that text from the *Style Pane*. This procedure is shown in Figure 4-16. Right clicking on the style in the *Style Pane* opens the *Modify Style* popup window. In the *Modify Style* window press the *Format* button and choose *Paragraph*. This action opens the *Paragraph* popup window. In the section *Special* of the *Paragraph* window click on the drop down box, select option "Hanging" and enter the value of the indent you wish to set for all lines of the paragraph except the first line. Then click *OK* in both the *Paragraph* and *Modify Style* windows. The hanging style is set and your bibliography looks as desired.

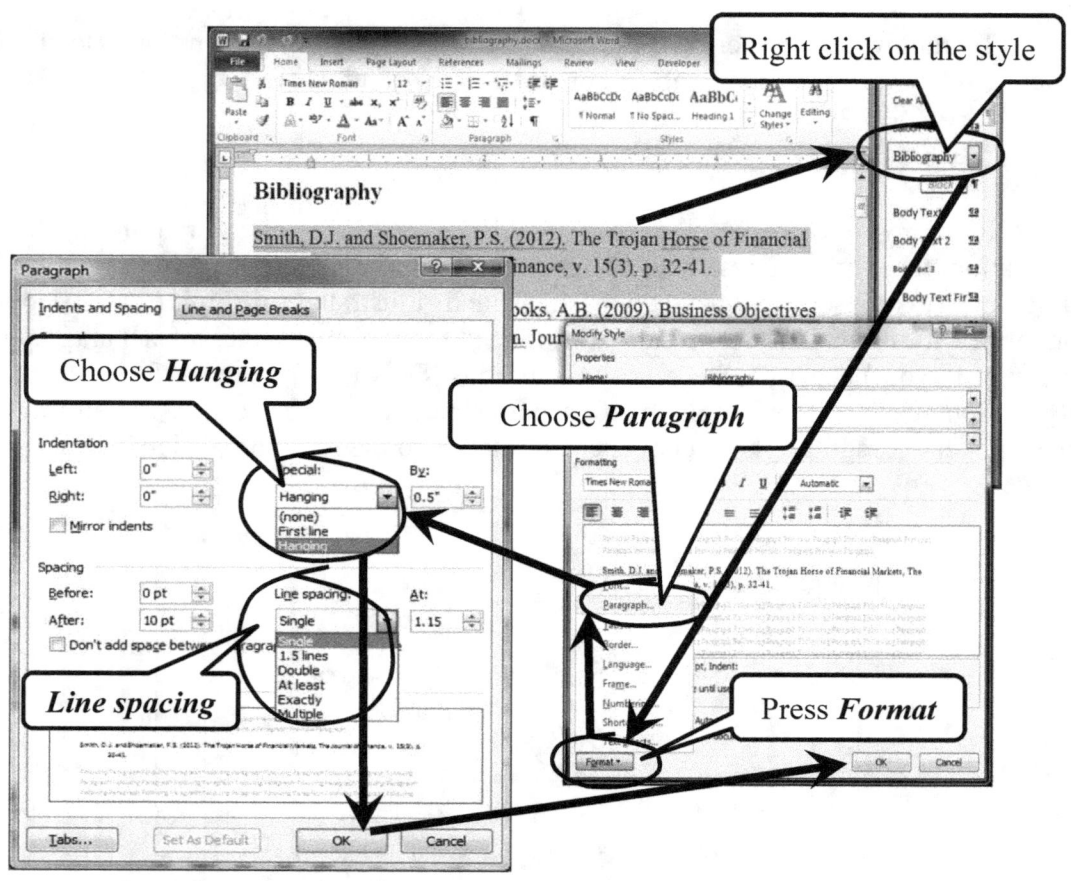

Figure 4-16: Setting hanging and other paragraph properties

4.3.6   Line Spacing and Text Alignment

The amount of space between the lines of text within a paragraph and between each paragraph, as well as the text alignment, are important formatting properties illustrated in Figure 4-17.

Paragraph alignment could be "left", "right", "centered", or "justified". With the "left" alignment the paragraph is aligned to the left edge of the pages' text area, with the "right" alignment to the right, with the "centered" to the center, and with "justified" to both left and right edges.

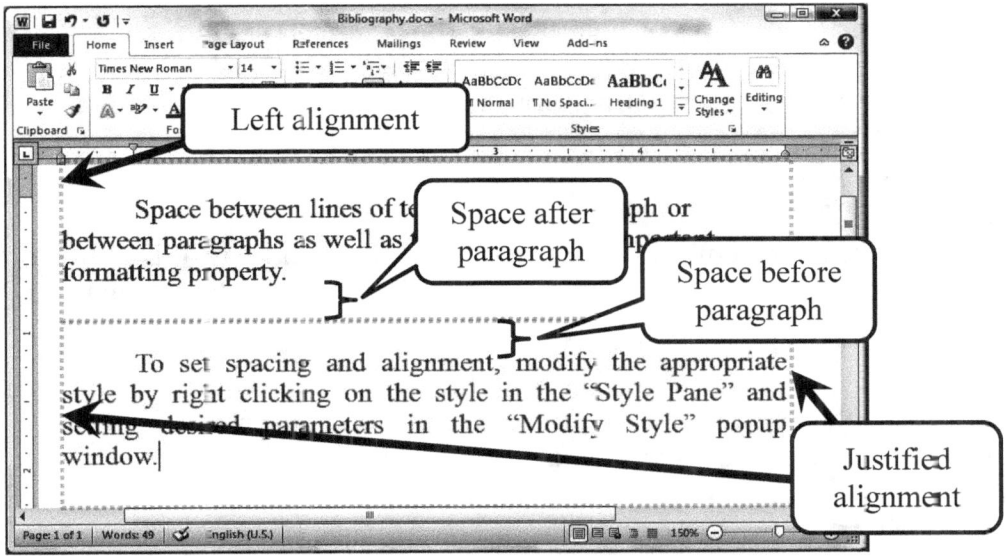

Figure 4-17: Spacing and text alignment

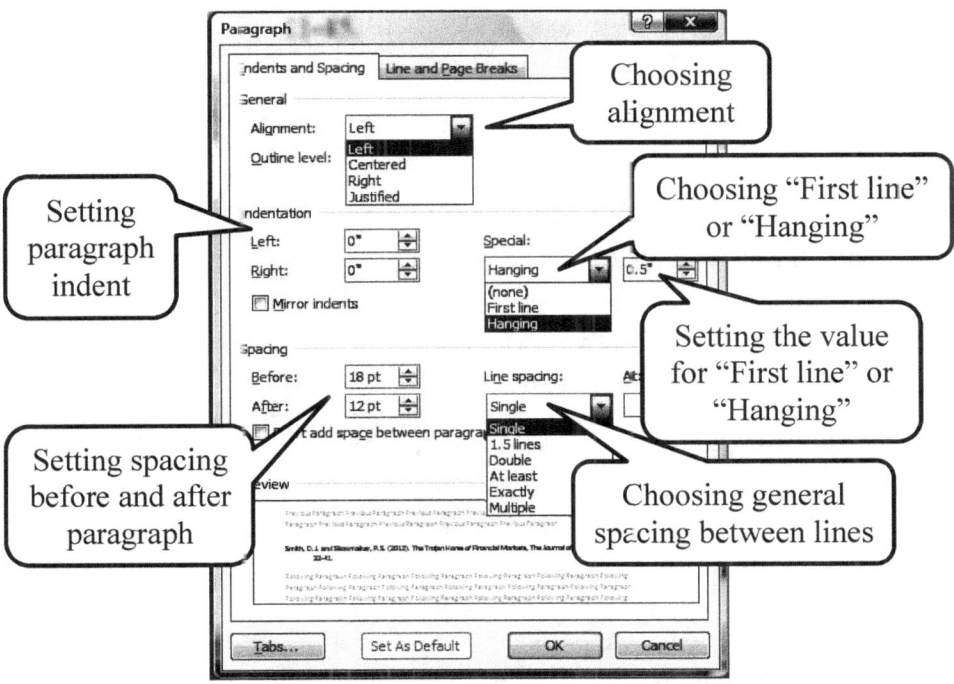

Figure 4-18: Paragraph setting

To set paragraph properties to a style, select a style in a *Style Pane* or in a *Quick*

Style Selector (Figure 4-10), right click on the selected style, choose "Modify", press *Format* in the *Modify Style* popup window, choose "Paragraph", and set the required properties to the style in the *Paragraph* popup window as shown in Figure 4-18

4.3.7 List Bullets

Bullets are part of style properties. Suppose you have text like in Figure 4-19 and want to format a portion of it containing a list of items (my-item 1, my-item 2, my-item 3) with bullets.

It seems natural to select the portion of the text containing my-items and set bullets using the bullet icon as shown in Figure 4-19. You can easily do this, but it's not a good idea from the point of view of maintaining formatting consistency in the document.

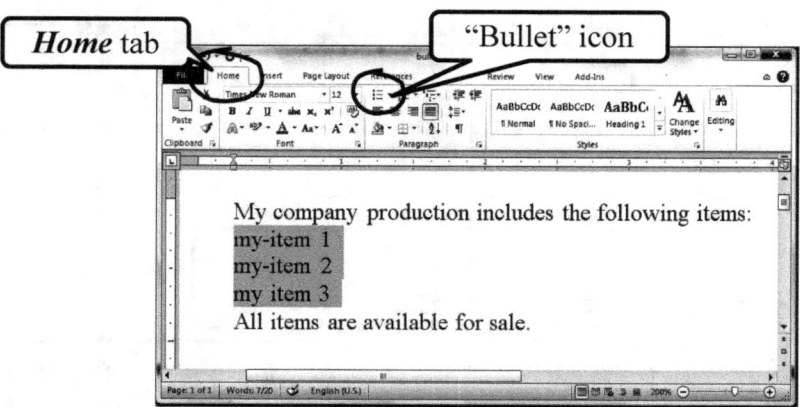

Figure 4-19: Initial text written with "Normal" style before setting the bullets

If you apply "bullets" directly to the required part of the text, you may lose some control over the document for the following reasons:

- The portion of the text to which you applied bullets was initially associated with style "Normal" which is most likely assigned to many other parts of the document and just supposed to be plain text. Thus, you start creating style conflict.
- The style conflict may propagate to parts of the document you could not even predict and corrupt the document look and feel.
- The style conflict may unexpectedly appear if you modify style "Normal" later, and you may be surprised to find that the bullets you set directly disappear altogether.
- Style conflict results in out of control documents and may lead to unpredictable results in document formatting.

Avoid setting up the bullets (as well as any other formatting properties) directly to the text because later you may occasionally modify the style assigned to the initial text and mess up either these bullets or other parts of the document. Instead, assign a preset bullet style to this portion of the text. You can also create a new bulleted style and assign it to that text.

Assigning List Bullet Style

Suppose the initial text is written with "Normal" style which looks like Figure 4-21. Select the text you want to format as bulleted, open the style pane as shown in Figure 4-10, find a "List Bullet" style in the style pane (Figure 4-20) and click on it to assign "List Bullet" style to the selected text.

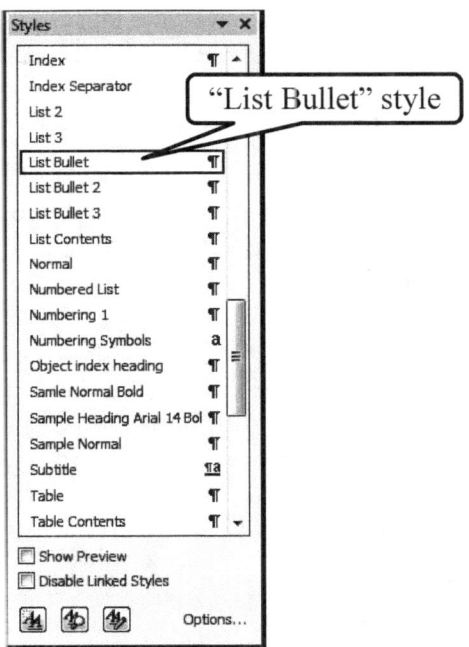

Figure 4-20: Assigning "List Bullet" style to the selected text

The selected text switches to "List Bullet" style and formats it in bullets as shown in Figure 4-21. With this operation you ensure that later formatting of your document will not mess up the current formats because the appropriate portions of the text have been assigned to specific styles.

You may assign the same "List Bullet" style to other portions of the document and all the bulleted portions of the document will be formatted consistently with the same type of bullets, indents and other properties. If for any reason you would like to change the bullet type, indent or other properties of the bulleted text in the document, you can do this by modifying style "List Bullet" and all portions of the document assigned to that style get automatically updated to the new properties set for this style.

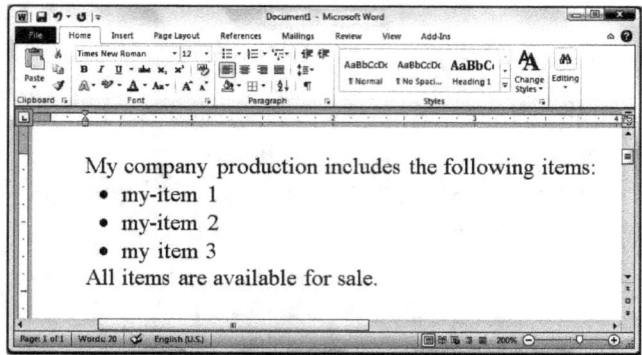

Figure 4-21: Bullets in the document text

There are several list bullet styles preset in the style pane, i.e. "List Bullet", "List Bullet 2" and so on. These styles differ in the length of line indentation. You may modify these styles and use them to format different types of bullets in the document.

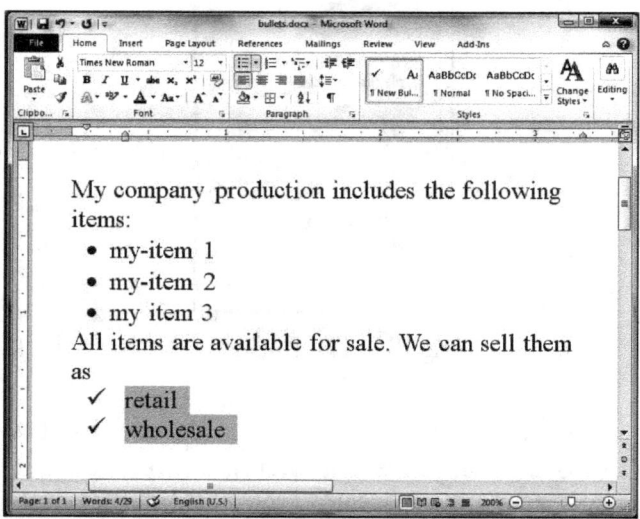

Figure 4-22: Bullets in the document text

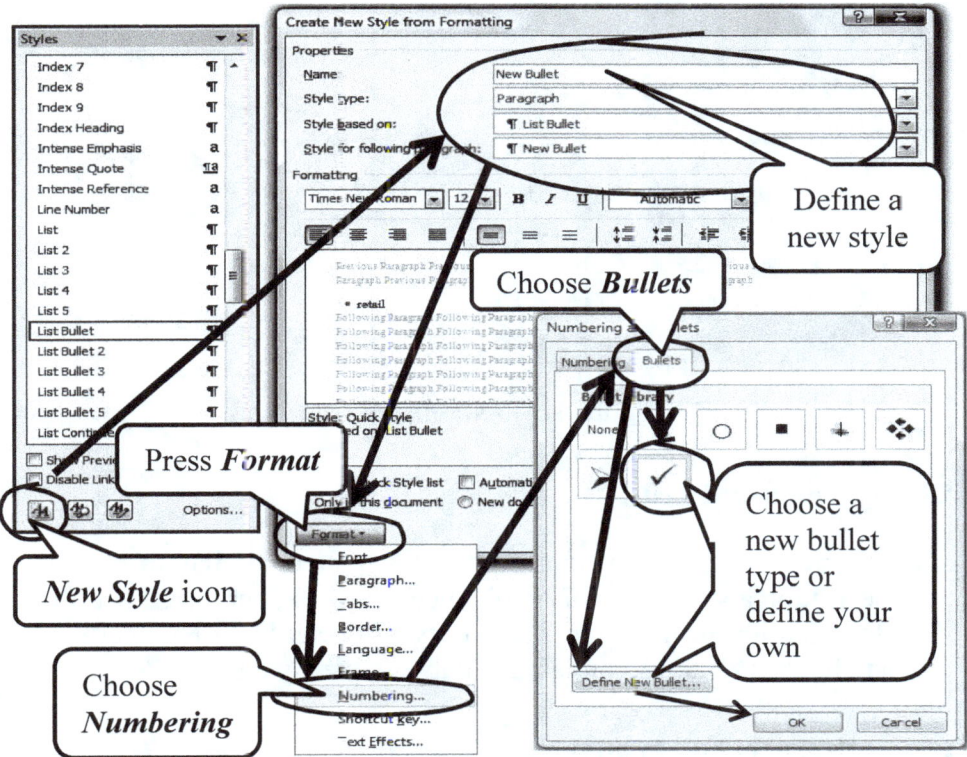

Figure 4-23: Bullets in the document text

To set up a different look for bullets, perform the following:

- select that particular portion of the text in the document for which you want to set a different bullet shape as shown in Figure 4-22,
- open the **Style Pane** as shown in Figure 4-10,
- click on the **New Style** icon as shown in Figure 4-23,
- in the bottom-left corner of the **Create New Style** pop-up window click on **Format,**
- select option **Numbering,**
- in the **Numbering and Bullets** popup window select the **Bullets** tab,
- choose the bullet shape you like from the displayed variety of bullet shapes,
- if you want some other shape of the bullet, click on the **Define New Bullet** button in the bottom-left corner of the **Numbering and Bullets** window and define you own bullet shape.

By following the procedure described above and illustrated in Figure 4-23, you get the bullets exactly as you wanted (Figure 4-22).

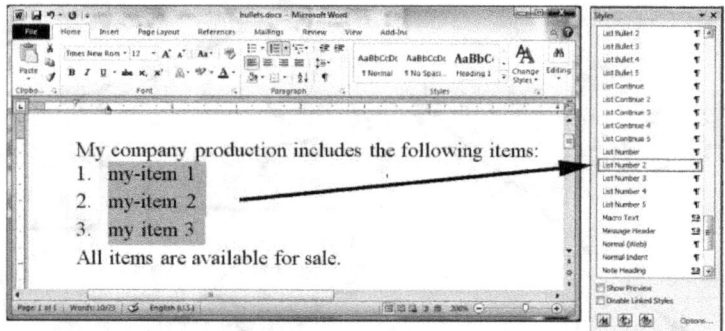

Figure 4-24: Numbered list

4.3.8   Numbered Lists

You may need to create a numbered list which is similar to the bulleted list described in the section above. The only difference is that the numbered list uses numbers instead of bullets. Similar to list bullets, a variety of preset "List Number" styles ("List Number", "List Number 2" and so on) are available in the style pane.

4.3.9   Headers and Footers

Headers and footers are important parts of a document. Documents with headers and footers look much nicer than those without, and the information in headers and footers helps the reader navigate through the document. Headers are located on the top of the page and footers at the bottom of the page.

Writing with Style: Bullets and Lists

- Do not set bullets directly to the document text.
- Set bullets and numbering to the portions of the document by assigning the appropriate style only.

Setting up a Header or Footer

A header or footer may consistently repeat content on all pages throughout the document or they may provide different content for different sections, such as odd and even pages as normally used in books, or for other reasons. The user can choose header and footer properties for the document by making the appropriate selection from *Header* or *Footer* in the *Insert* tab as shown in Figure 4-25.

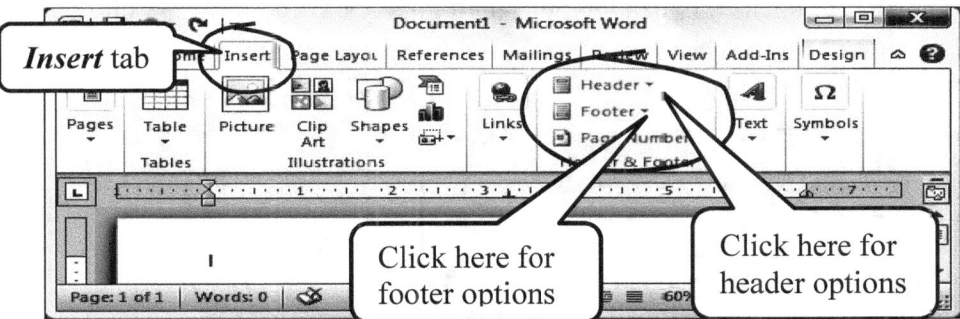

Figure 4-25: Setting headers, footers, and page numbers

By clicking on *Header* or *Footer* options the user can view and choose the preset properties (look and feel) of the appropriate features as shown in Figure 4-26 and Figure 4-27.

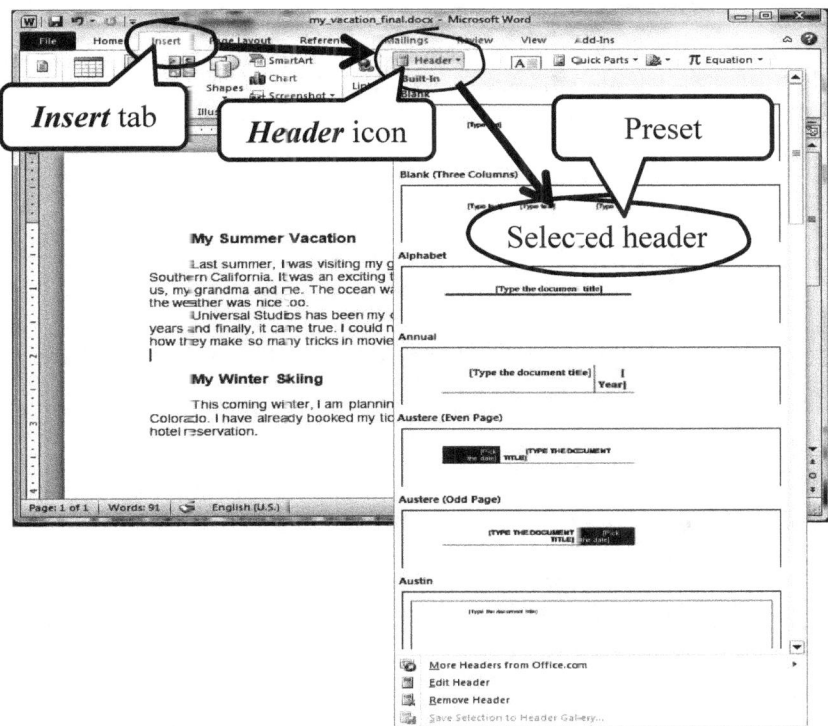

Figure 4-26: Preset header formats

Let's suppose you selected the second header option "Blank (Three Columns)" as in Figure 4-26. A blank header would appear in your document containing three text fields as shown in Figure 4-32. To place desired text in those text fields select a text field and type the phrase you want to be placed there. You may fill up all three fields in this way. The text you enter in this header field then appears at the top of each page of your document. A similar methodology applies for footers.

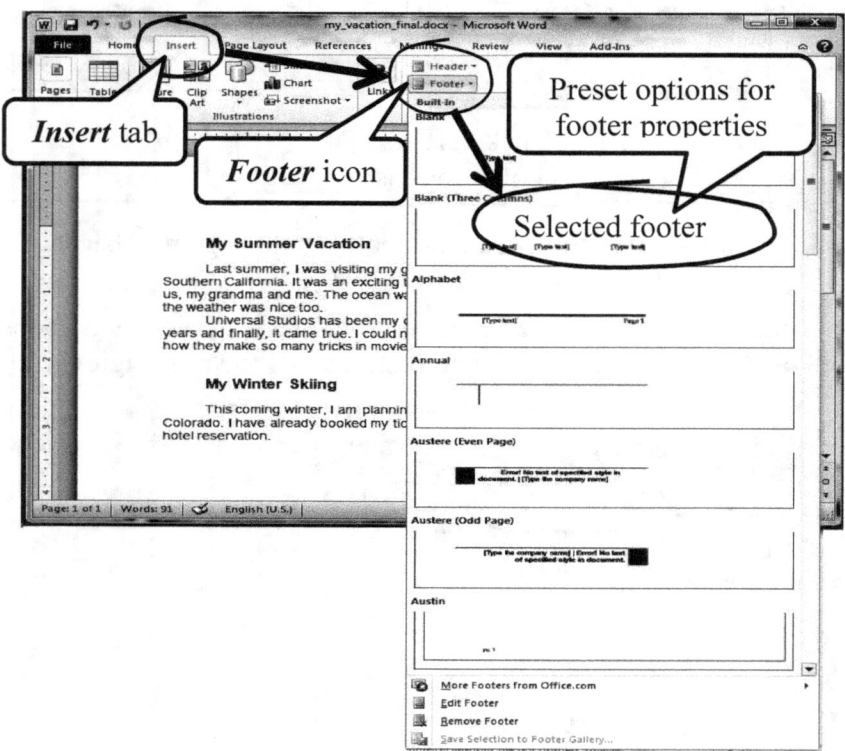

Figure 4-27: Preset footer formats

Header and Footer Styles

If you want to change formatting properties of a header or footer, select the header or footer in the document and open a style pane as described in section 4.3.2 and illustrated in Figure 4-10. Scroll through the style pane until you find the appropriate header or footer. Once the appropriate style is selected (in a frame) as shown in Figure 4-21 and Figure 4-30, right click on the "Header" or "Footer" style and modify it accordingly to you desires.

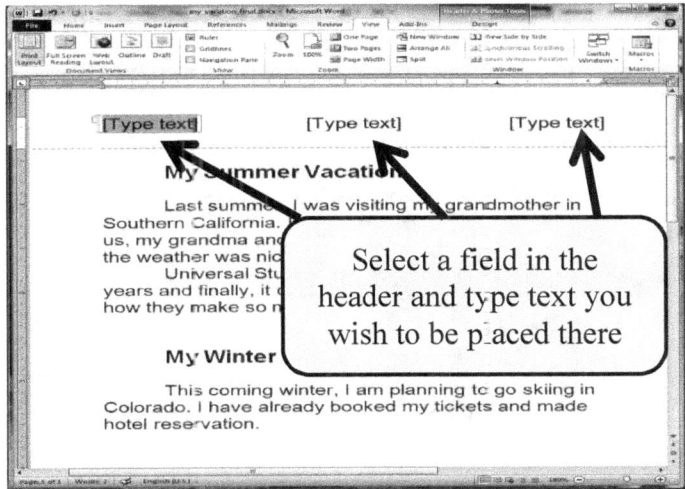

Figure 4-28: Preset header formats

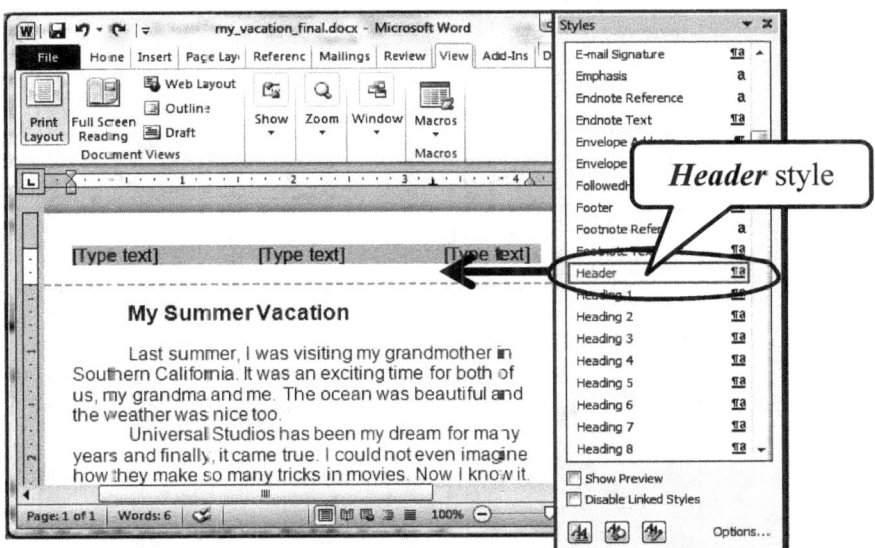

Figure 4-29: The header style

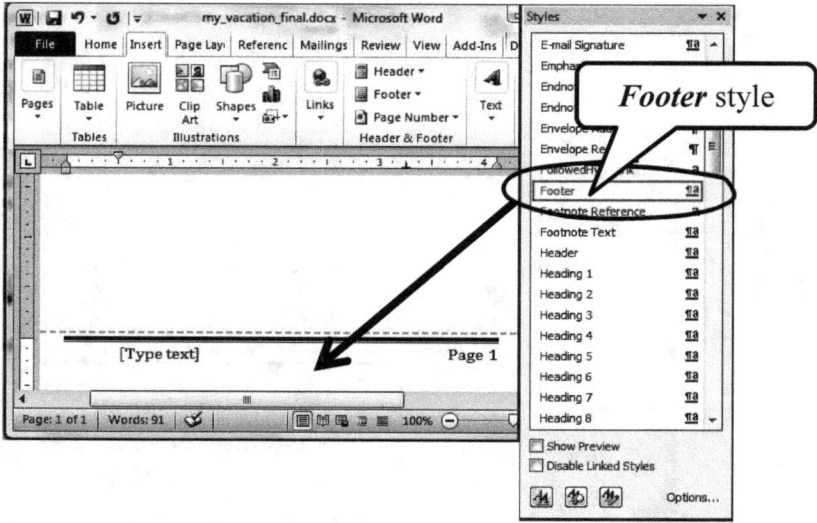

Figure 4-30: The footer style

Managing Header or Footer by Pages

Different documents utilize headers and footers differently. For example, some may have the same header appear on every page, while others may have a different header or footer on odd and even pages, or a unique header and footer on the first page. To control the appearance of the header or footer, select it by clicking on it. You will immediately notice tab *Design* appear in the main tabs line as shown in Figure 4-31.

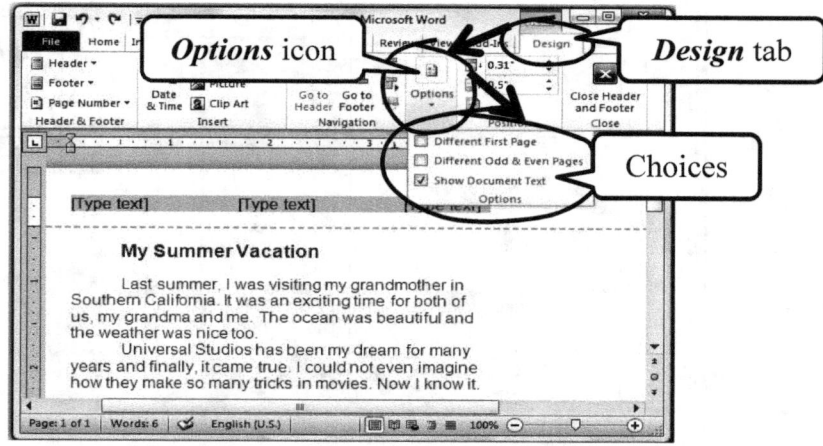

Figure 4-31: Header and footer properties

Using the options in this tab allows you to control many properties of headers and footers, such as their size, position, etc.. Take time to experiment with the functions in this tab to find out how they work. To control where the headers and footers will appear by page, go to tab *Design*, click on Options and then check an appropriate check box as shown in Figure 4-31.

Page Numbering

Most documents require page numbering. It is easy to set this feature and there are different ways to apply page numbers in Microsoft Word 2010.

In the *Insert* tab click on *Page Number* and select your preferred format for displaying page numbers in your document as shown in Figure 4-32. Then, similar to headers and footers, you can control the style and appearance of page numbering in the document.

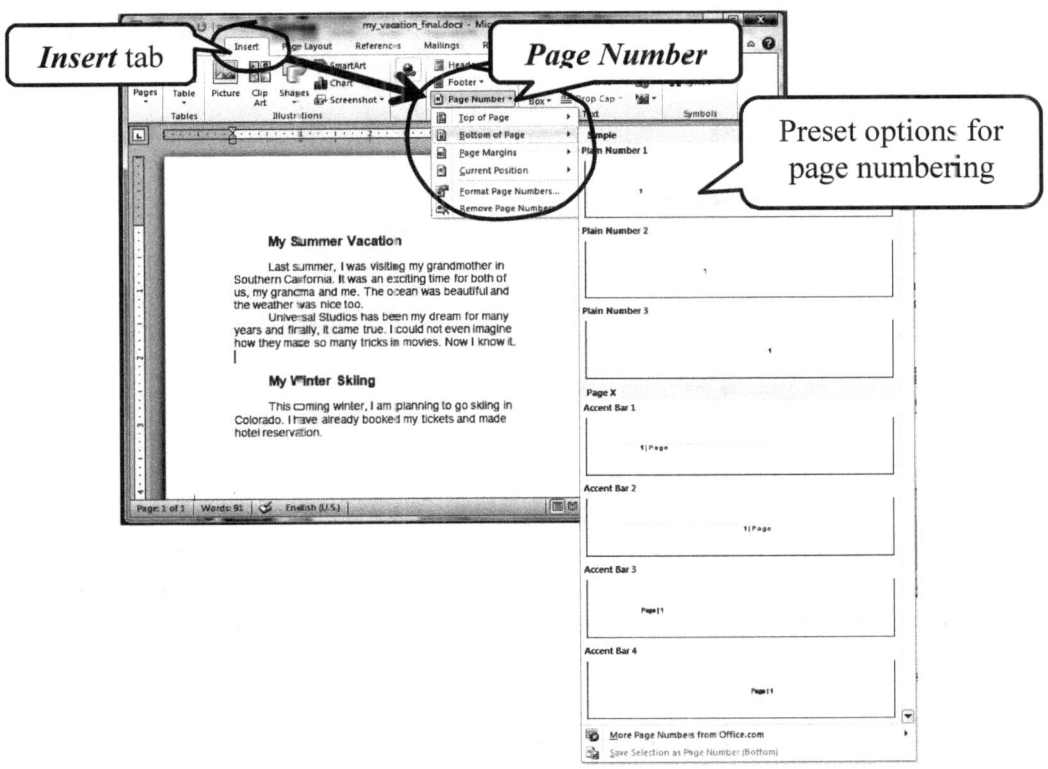

Figure 4-32: Preset page number formats

Another way to set page numbering is to do it directly from the already set headers or footers where you want the page number to appear. Select a field in the header, footer, or any other place on the page where you wish to see the page number, and click on feature **Quick Parts** in one of the tabs **Insert** or **Design**. Then choose option **Field** and select **Page** property from the list as shown in Figure 4-33.

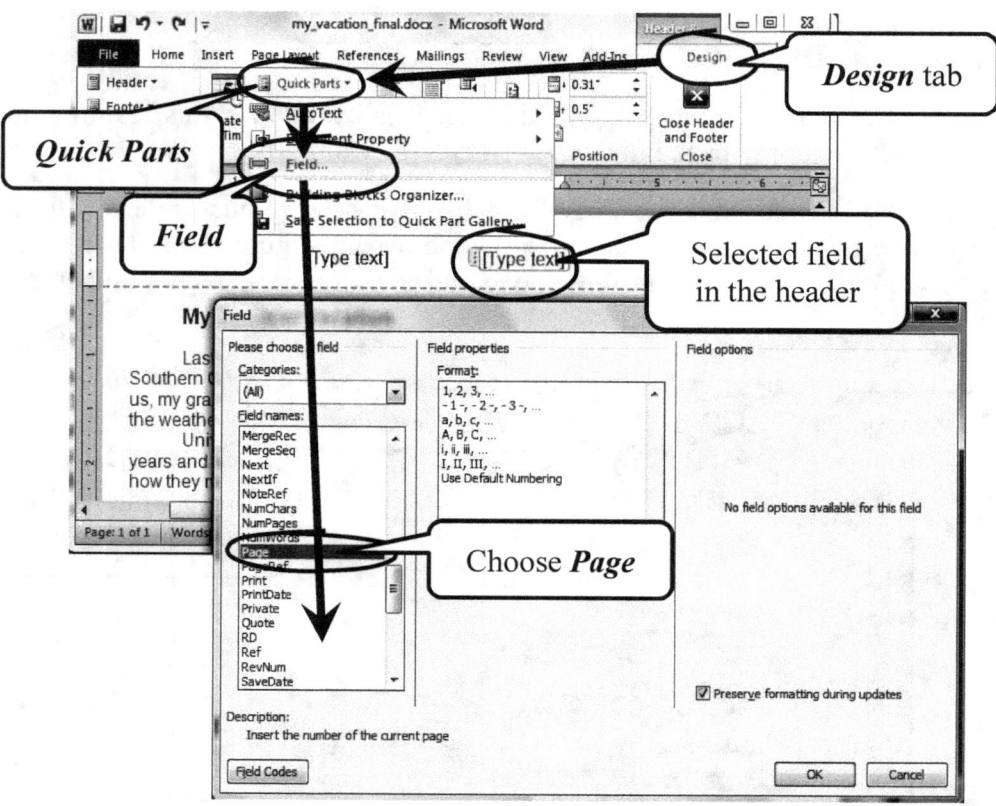

Figure 4-33: Setting up page number in a field

Sometimes it is very convenient to format page numbering like "Page 1 of 26" to show the current page as well as the total number of pages in the document. You can do this using feature **Quick Parts** similarly to setting page numbering. Suppose you have already set regular page numbering by following the procedure described above and illustrated in Figure 4-33. Current page number 1 appears in the selected field as shown in Figure 4-34. Type "Page" to the left of the current page number and "of" to the right of it, and then follow the same procedure as described above but choose property **NumPages** from the list instead of "Page" as in the previous case. Property **NumPages** shows the total number of pages in the document. In result you see "Page 1 of 26" in the header where number 1 is the current page number and number 26 is the total number of pages in the document. It is exactly what we wanted.

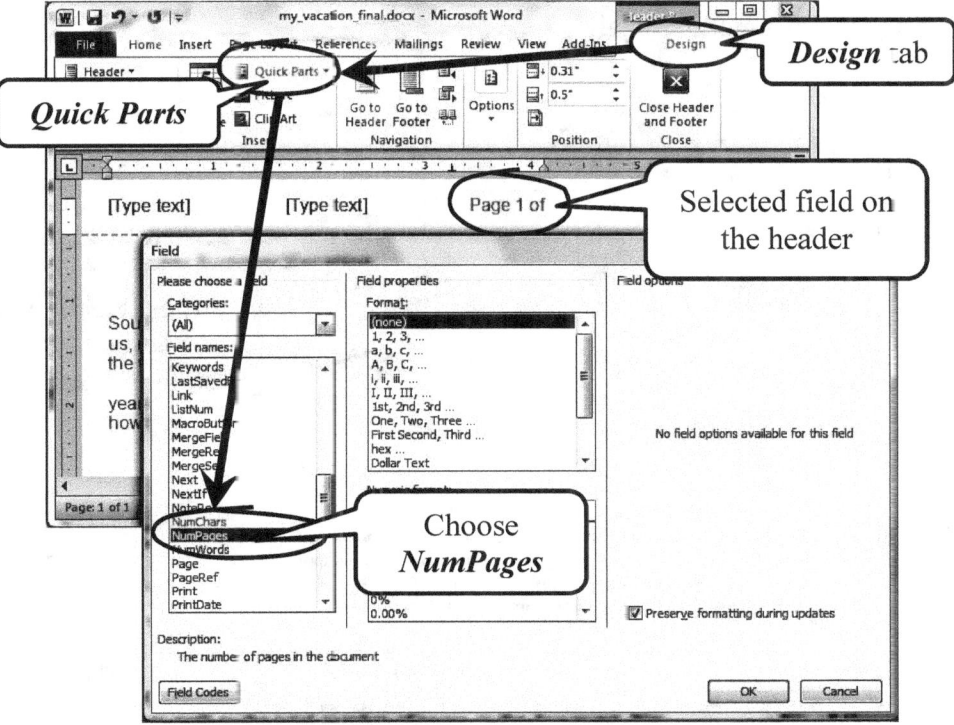

Figure 4-34: Setting up the total number of pages in the document

4.4 Style Hierarchy

4.4.1 How Style Hierarchy Works

Styles in Microsoft Word have a very interesting feature – style hierarchy. When creating a style, you have an option to either ***Create a New Style*** or ***Modify Style***, both of which work basically identically (Figure 4-35).

The name of a (new or modified) style and the style on which it is based defines a hierarchy of styles. The new or modified style inherits all properties of its base style except for any properties that were redefined. For example, in Figure 4-35 "Heading 1" style is based on "Normal" style and for this reason it inherits all properties of the "Normal" style. If we change the font size from 12 to 14 and make the font "bold" in the properties of "Heading 1", these are the only formatting properties that will be different from the base style "Normal". If we change any properties in style "Normal" which were not modified for "Heading 1", the change would automatically occur for "Heading 1". For example, when we defined style "Heading 1" we did not change the font, so it inherited the "Times New Roman" font face from the "Normal" style. Thus, if we change the font face in "Normal" from "Times New Roman" to "Arial", both styles—"Normal" and "Heading 1"—change to "Arial".

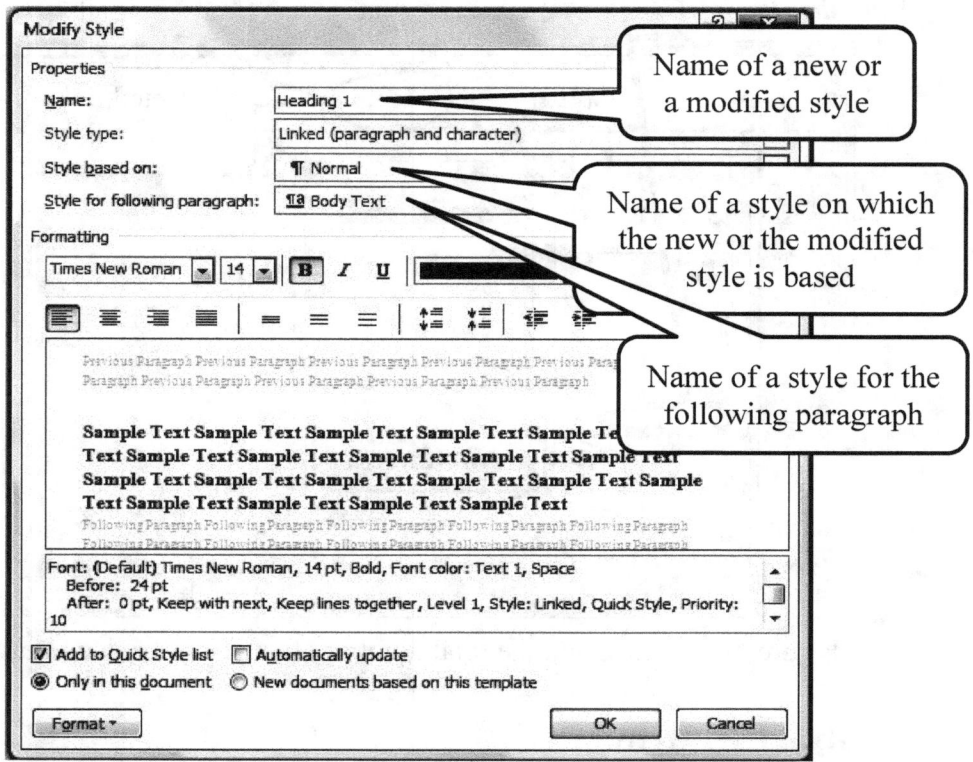

Figure 4-35: Basics of style hierarchy

The "Style for following paragraph" property sets the style for the next paragraph as soon as the user presses "Enter". For example, style "Body Text" may keep the same style for the next paragraph while style "Heading 1" may be set to switch to style "Body Text" for the following paragraph. In this case, if you write a heading and assign style "Heading 1", as soon as you press "Enter" on the keyboard the style for the next paragraph will automatically be set to "Body Text". This is a very convenient feature, so you don't need to manually switch styles from "Heading 1" to "Body Text" each time.

4.4.2   Style Hierarchy for a Document

It is recommended that you think about and develop a style hierarchy for your document. Just for example, if you write a research paper you may create a hierarchy of styles as shown in Figure 4-36.

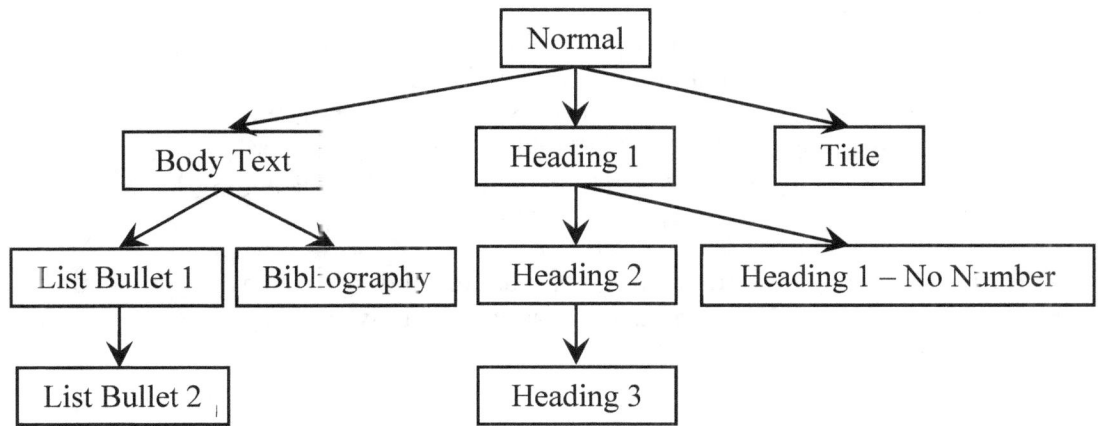

Figure 4-36: Sample Style Hierarchy of a Document

The following logic is used in the sample style hierarchy shown in Figure 4-36:

- All major style properties used in the document are set in style "Normal"
- Style "Body Text" is used for the main text in the document. We may change line spacing and text alignment in this style to match the desired document look and feel. All other properties will be inherited from style "Normal".
- Styles "Heading 1" and "Title" are based on "Normal" with changes in the font size, "regular" to "bold" font type, and some other properties. In both styles, "Heading 1" and "Title", the style for the following paragraph will be set to "Body Text" for convenience. The other properties will be inherited from style "Normal". We don't base it on style "Body Text" because we don't want to inherit the alignment and line spacing of that style.
- Styles "List Bullet 1" and "Bibliography" are based on style "Body Text" to inherit the main properties of the text in the document. Additionally to the properties inherited from "Body Text" we set bullets property for style "List Bullet 1" and property "Hanging" for style "Bibliography". The style for the following paragraph in "List Bullet 1" is set to "List Bullet 1" and in "Bibliography" to "Bibliography" for continuity of formatting. The other properties of "List Bullet 1" and "Bibliography" will be inherited from style "Body Text".
- Style "List Bullet 2" is based on style "List Bullet 1" to inherit all properties of this style including bullets. We may increase an indent and a bullet shape of this style to make a different type of bullet. The other properties of "List Bullet 2" will be inherited from "List Bullet 1".
- Similarly, style "Heading 2" is based on "Heading 3" and style "Heading 2"

is based on "Heading 1".

- Style "Heading 1" may have automatic numbering (described in the next section of this book) but we want a heading for the bibliography that is formatted exactly like "Heading 1" but not numbered. We may create a new style "Heading 1 – No Number" which is based on "Heading 1" but with the numbering feature disabled. The other properties of "Heading 1 – No Number" are inherited from style "Heading 1".

The example above provides a clear understanding of why style hierarchy is important and convenient. You can design a style hierarchy that is most suitable for you and better reflects your writing process.

4.5   Document Headings, Outline, and Table of Contents

Automated multilevel outline numbering for document headings and automated generation of table of contents are among the most attractive features of Microsoft Word and other advanced word processors. This feature offers so much convenience, saves so much time in document development and preparation, and ensures an outcome of very clean documents with proper numeration of sections. Thus the power of this feature is difficult to overestimate.

4.5.1   Document Headings

Imagine you are writing a paper, thesis, business plan, book, or any other document of a more or less complex structure that includes chapters, sub-chapters, and so on. As an example, let's examine the structure of this book that has three levels of numbered headings as shown in Figure 4-37. These levels are called "Heading 1" for level 1, Heading 2" for the level 2 and "Heading 3" for level 3. You want the headings of each level to have different font sizes and indents.

Imagine you are writing a long document with a complex structure. You are a very accurate person and therefore you carefully follow the three-level heading chapter numeration. However, while writing your document you come up with new ideas and so need to add new chapters or sub-chapters, move some around within your document, and even permanently remove some sections. While you definitely try your best to keep the consistent numeration of your headings at all levels, it is quite a challenge and it would be surprising if the final document did not have many inconsistencies with chapter, sub-chapter, and sub-sub-chapter numeration. In addition to this problem, the table of contents—which you have carefully matched with the document chapters and sub-chapters—also shows inconsistencies due to the multiple changes in the document structure. It is a very frustrating experience.

The good news is that modern word processors can apply these changes automatically. You just need to assign appropriate styles for headings of the appropriate levels, set up the appropriate font face, font size, indents, and other properties with styles, and associate the styles with the appropriate hierarchical outline heading numbering. If you also use an automated generation of the table of contents, it eliminates even a slim chance of any inconsistency as described above.

1 Level 1 heading for chapter
   1.1 Level 2 heading for sub-chapter
      1.1.1 Level 3 heading for sub-sub-chapter
      1.1.2 Level 3 heading for sub-sub-chapter
   1.2 Level 2 heading for sub-chapter
   1.3 Level 2 heading for sub-chapter
2 Level 1 heading for chapter
   2.1 Level 2 heading for sub-chapter
      2.1.1 Level 3 heading for sub-sub-chapter
      2.1.2 Level 3 heading for sub-sub-chapter
   2.2 Level 2 heading for sub-chapter

Figure 4-37: Three-level heading structure and hierarchical numbering

Level 1 heading for chapter
Level 2 heading for sub-chapter
Level 3 heading for sub-sub-chapter
Level 3 heading for sub-sub-chapter
Level 2 heading for sub-chapter
Level 2 heading for sub-chapter
Level 1 heading for chapter
Level 2 heading for sub-chapter
Level 2 heading for sub-chapter

Figure 4-38: Three-level headings with no structure

4.5.2   Automated Numbering for Document Headings

All heading of the document constitute the document outline. The document outline represents the structure of the document. Let's start with the plain headings that have yet no numbering and written with the same font size as shown in Figure 4-38.

To create automatically updated heading numbering, first of all, you have to assign the following styles to the structural elements of your document hierarchy as shown in Table 4-1.

You do not need to have an entire outline of headings when you start. One heading is enough to begin. As your writing progresses, you may add more headings of each level to you document later; just don't forget to assign the appropriate styles to them.

Table 4-1: Document hierarchy and the associated styles

Document Structural Element	Style
Level 1 heading (chapter)	Heading 1
Level 2 heading (sub-chapter)	Heading 2
Level 3 heading (sub-sub-chapter)	Heading 3
... and so on	... and so on

Now is the right time to set up the text properties to the styles for headings of different levels. Select the appropriate heading in the document, open the style pane as in Figure 4-10 in section0, right click on the appropriate style, and select "Modify" option to make all necessary changes to the text properties of the heading style as discussed above. You may change font color, face, size, spacing between lines and many other properties.

Once the heading styles are assigned and the major properties set, let's now set up multilevel outline numbering for the headings. In the previous versions of Microsoft Word (up to and including Word 2003) it was done in quite a logical way—by right clicking on the appropriate style and applying *Modify* → *Numbering* feature similarly to all other features[1]. In Word 2007 and 2010 this feature is no longer available for multilevel list numbering, so do not use the *Modify* → *Numbering* feature for this purpose. Instead switch to tab *Home* and click on the *Multilevel List* icon in the ribbon, and select the multilevel outline nested numeration option as shown in Figure 4-39.

---

[1] This comment reflects personal opinion of the author.

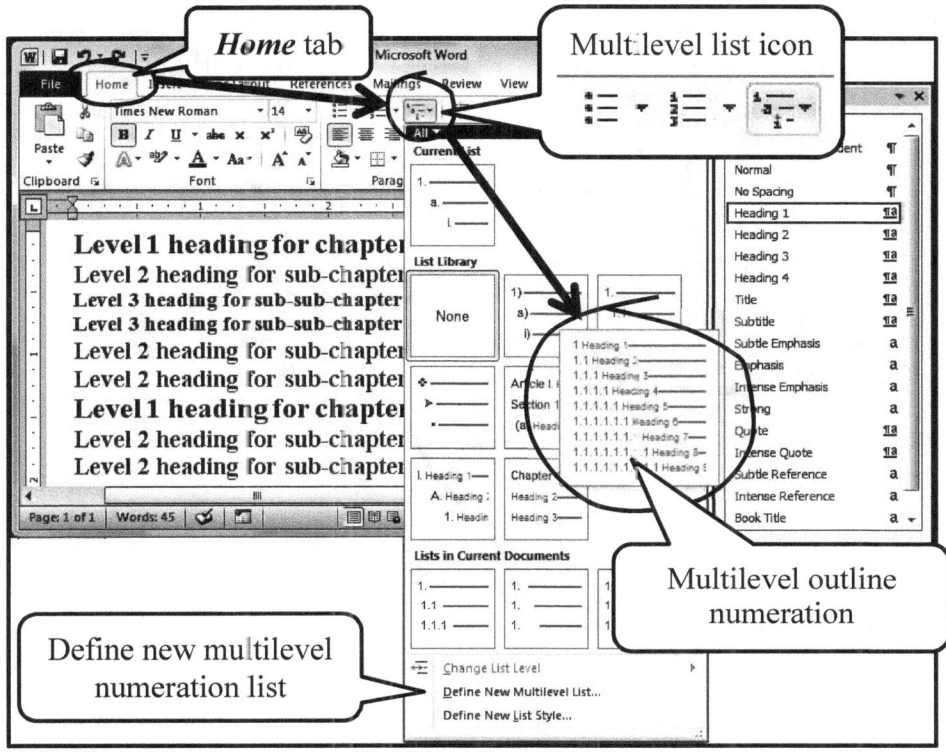

Figure 4-39: Setting up automatic hierarchical multilevel numeration for headings

As a result of following procedures described above, the headings get multilevel outlined numbering and font properties exactly as we wanted but the heading indents haven't yet been set (Figure 4-39). To set the desired indents to the heading lines, select a heading, right click on the appropriate style and choose the **Paragraph** option from the **Format** feature as shown in Figure 4-40.

This opens a **Paragraph** feature popup window as shown in Figure 4-41. Set up the parameters you wish and press **OK**. For example, for "Heading 2" style you wish to have a "left indentation" of 0.3" to see the numbering for heading 2 aligned with the title of heading 1 and a "Hanging" parameter of 0.4" to make sure that the title of heading 2 is aligned with the numbering of heading 3 (Figure 4-37). You may also want to set up an extra space before or after the heading line. You can do this by setting up the appropriate parameters in section **Spacing** as shown in Figure 4-41. You can then you set up the desired parameters for all headings you need in a similar way.

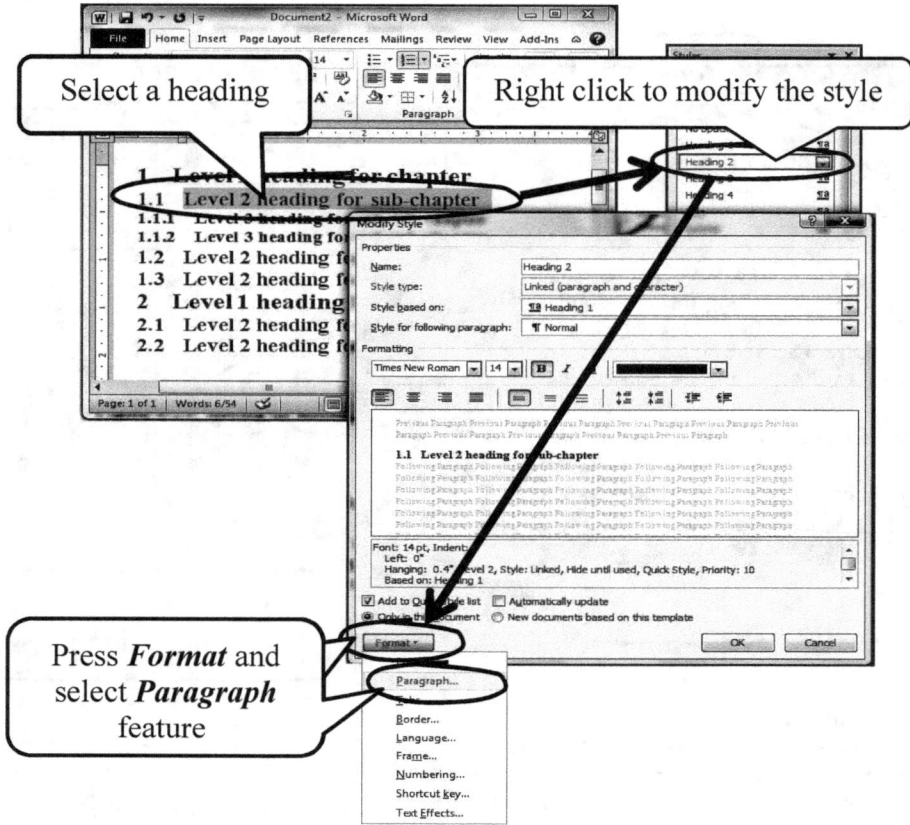

Figure 4-40: Three-level outline heading numbering

When you're finished, your headings will look exactly as you wanted (Figure 4-37). Actually, you can do much more than you've just done.

With the multilevel outline headings described above, you set up a multilevel structure of hierarchically numerated heading (sections, chapters) of your document. If you decide to add or remove a heading or move a heading within the document, the entire numbering structure will be automatically updated to match the changes, so you should have no concerns about breaking the consistency of numbering in the process of document development and editing.

4.5.3   Generating and Updating a Table of Contents

Creating a table of contents manually is very tedious and frustrating. First of all, you have to find and copy all headings used in the document into the table of contents, then match all page numbers for the headings. If by chance the document was later edited, headings were moved, new headings were added, existing headings removed, or the document text was changed in a way shifting existing headings to different pages, you have to make all these changes in table of contents again. Thus it is an enormous amount of work and there a high likelihood that something will be missing.

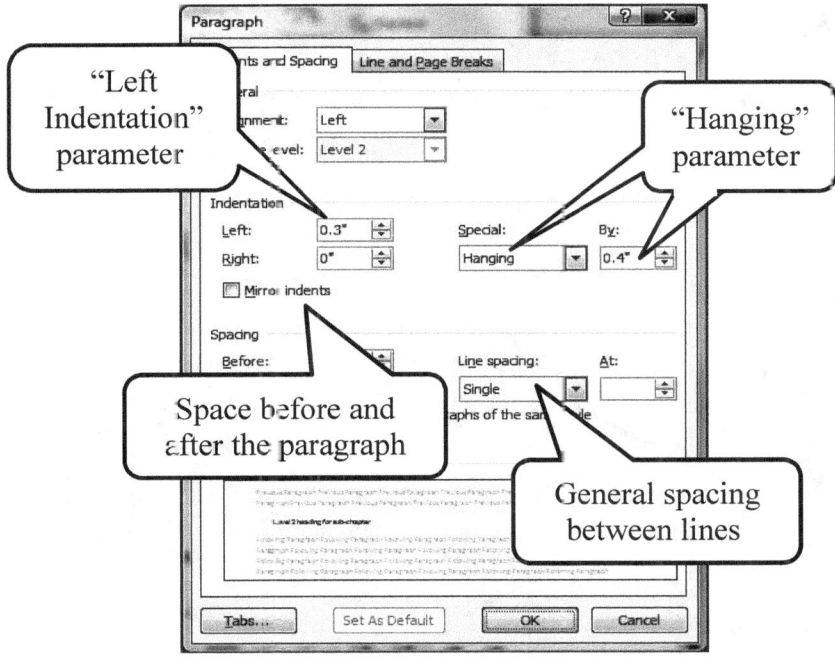

Figure 4-41: Setting up the paragraph properties

With Microsoft Word, you can do all this work automatically with just a single minute of your time. Let's start with the simplest case. Assume all headings in the document have been assigned to the appropriate heading styles, i.e. "Heading 1", "Heading 2", and so on. Place the cursor in the document in the position where you want to insert the table of contents, then navigate to "Reference" tab and then click on "Table of Contents" and choose "Insert Table of Contents" option as shown in Figure 4-42. This action opens a "Table of Contents" popup window. In this window select the number of levels in the table of contents and press the "Options" button. A "Table of Contents Options" popup window opens. In this window you can assign the styles by level as you wish the content be shown in the table of contents. For example, as you see in Figure 4-42, both styles "Heading 1" and "Heading 1 – No Number" will be shown on the same level of the table of contents. This means that all headings assigned to the style "Heading 1" and "Heading 1 – No Number" will be shown on the same level of the table of contents, so you have solved the problem of showing all headings of level 1 and bibliography heading on the same level in the table of contents.

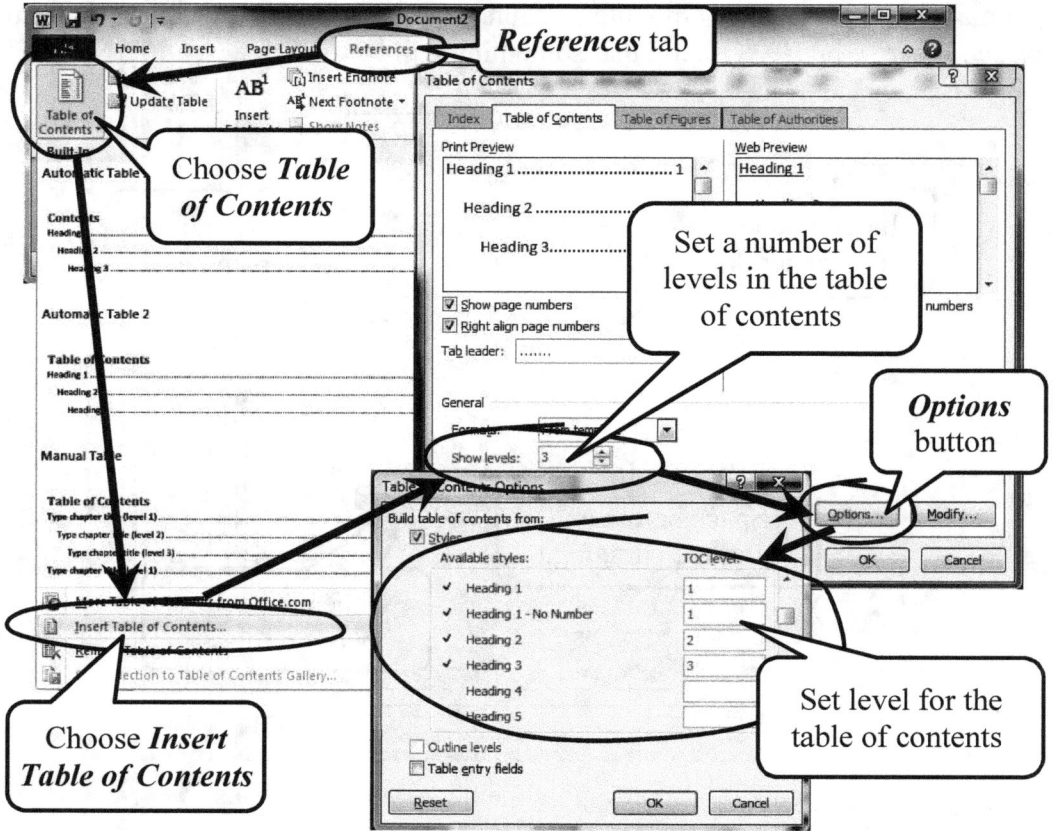

Figure 4-42: Building the table of contents

4.5.4   Updating a Table of Contents

Suppose you have already generated a table of contents for a document and keep developing the document. You made a number of changes to the document, added, removed, or moved some headings, and made some other changes to the document. There are several ways of updating the table of contents:

- You can find the *Update Table* feature next to the *Table of Content* feature in the ribbon of the *Home* tab. Click on this feature and a popup window appears offering you two options: *Update page numbers only* and *Update entire table*. Make your choice and press *OK*. It is advisable to choose *Update entire table* because it in that case the system updates much more information than page numbers.

- In *Home* tab select the entire document and press key *F9* on the keyboard. This results in the same action as with the previous case.

Questions and Exercises

Questions

1. What is Microsoft Word style?
2. Why use styles?
3. How do you assign a style to a portion of text in a document?
4. How do you find a style assigned to text?
5. How do you modify a style?
6. How do you create a new style?
7. How do you set tabs and text edges to a style?
8. How do you set line indent to a style?
9. How do you set the first line indent in a paragraph to the appropriate style?
10. What is text hanging and how do you set it to a style?
11. How do you set line spacing to a style?
12. How do you define a bulleted style?
13. How do you set a style for numbered list?
14. What are headers and footers?
15. How do you set a style for headers and footers?
16. What is hierarchy of styles?
17. Why is style hierarchy needed?
18. What is multilevel outline numbering?
19. How do you set a multilevel outline numbering to a document headings?
20. How do you generate a table of contents?
21. How do you update a table of content?

Exercises

1. Write your own document and incrementally keep setting and defining styles in it. Do not write anything without setting a style.
2. Generate a table of contents for the document.

5   Tables, Images, Drawings, and Objects

Many documents require tables, images, drawings, or other objects to be inserted into or created within the document.

5.1   Tables

5.1.1   Create / Delete Table

To generate a table, place the cursor in the position where you wish to have a table, navigate to the **Insert** tab and press the **Table** icon on the ribbon as shown in Figure 5-1. Then, select the table size and left click on the selection. A table of the specified size will be generated in the document.

To delete a table, select the entire table, right click on it and choose the **Delete Table** option in the popup list (Figure 5-2).

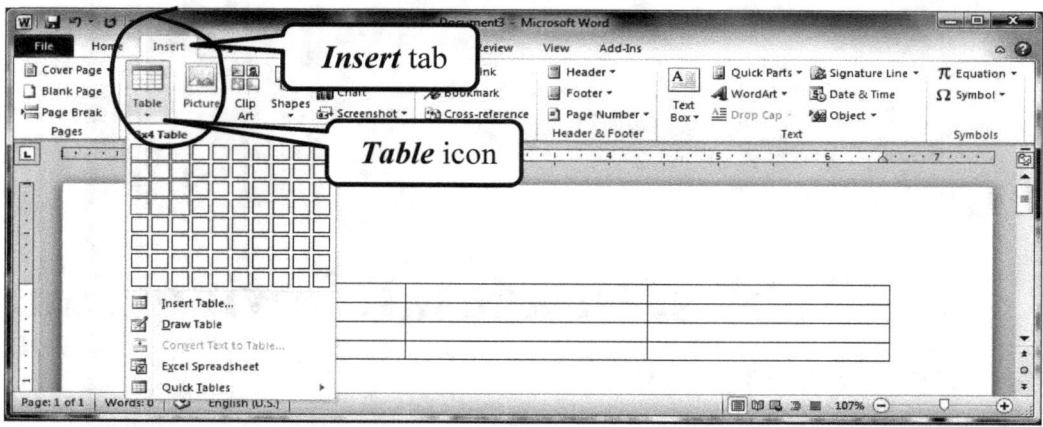

Figure 5-1: Insert table

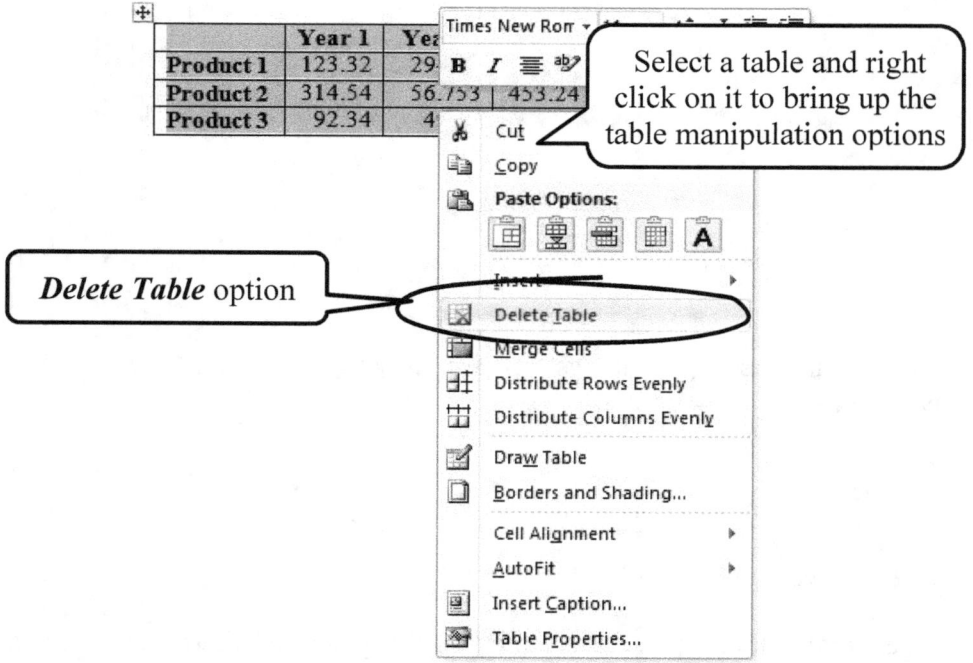

Figure 5-2: Delete table

5.1.2 Add / Remove Rows / Columns

If you come to the end of a table and want to add a new row, just place the cursor in the bottom-right cell of the table and press the *Tab* key.

In general, to add a cell, a row or a column to a table, position the cursor in the cell, row or column where you want the addition and right click to bring up the options list. Then, choose *Insert* and select the option you want from the choices as shown in Figure 5-3.

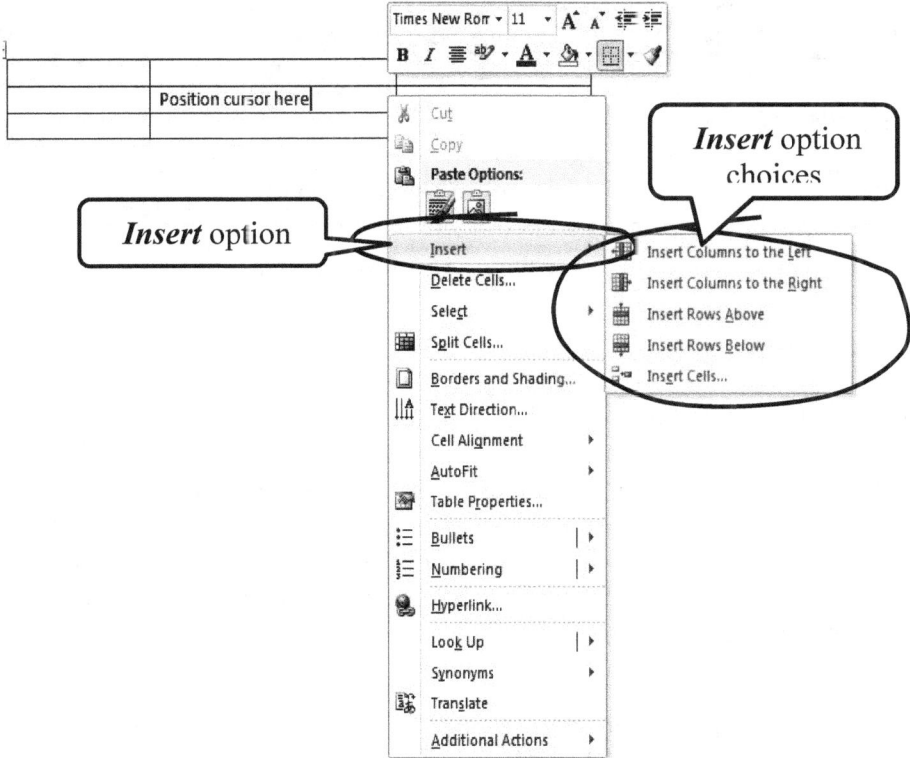

Figure 5-3: Add a row or column to a table

To delete a cell, a row, or a column from a table, select the element to delete and right click. A popup options list appears similar to the previous one shown in Figure 5-3. Make your choice and proceed.

5.1.3   Change Column Size

To change the column width, position the cursor on the column border and move it around until the cursor takes the shape of ✛ , then drag the boundary of the column to the size you want (Figure 5-4). You can achieve the same result by moving the column separator in the ruler. Both methods work identically.

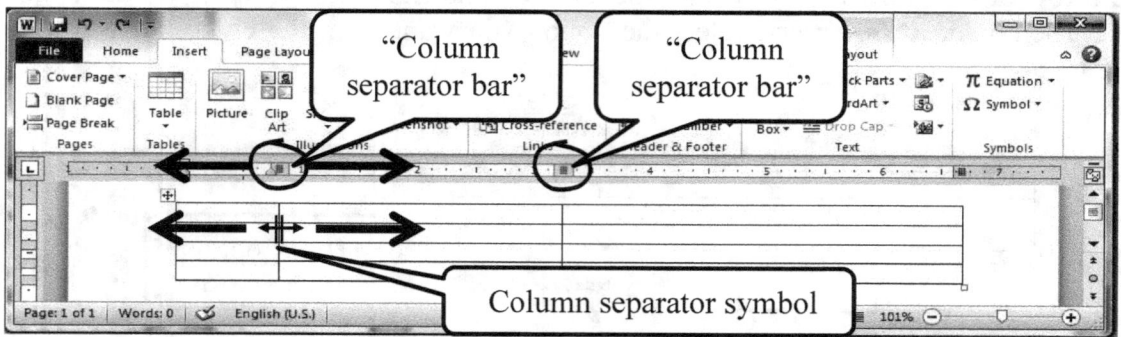

Figure 5-4: Change the column size

5.1.4   Merge and Split Cells

Sometimes it is necessary to merge cells in a table. For example, in table Figure 5-5 (a) the "Payment" cell is located just above the "Date" cell but it relates to both "Date" and "Amount"; in this case, it makes sense to merge the "Payment" cell with the empty cell to its right. To merge cells, select the cells you want merged, right click, and choose option *Merge Cells* as shown in Figure 5-5 (a). The two cells then merge into one, as shown in Figure 5-5 (b). A similar merge makes sense for the "Customer" cell as well, and is also demonstrated in Figure 5-5.

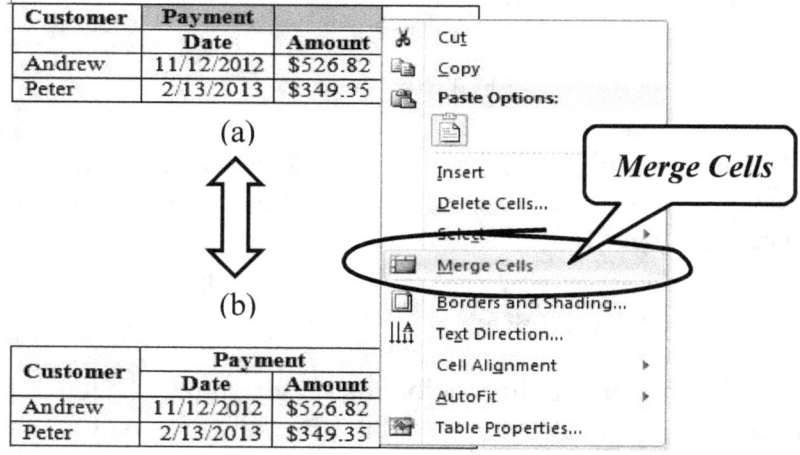

Figure 5-5: Merging table cells

To perform the opposite function—to split a cell, select it, right click on it, and choose the *Split* option as shown in Figure 5-6. This opens a popup control where you enter the number of rows and columns you want to split the cell into.

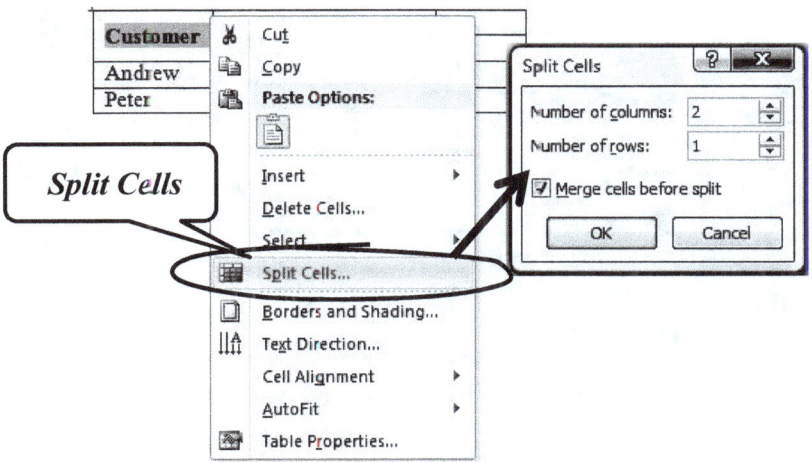

Figure 5-6: Split a cell

5.1.5 Styles for Table Content

It is recommended that you set up a style for tables that is different from the style used for text. This helps avoid formatting conflicts of indentation, line spacing, and others between the main text of the document and the tables in it. For example, let's say you set up an indent for the first line of every paragraph in the text and increase spacing between lines and/or paragraphs. Since practically every record in a table is a new paragraph, it would be look quite weird to apply the same style for tables as you do for the body of the document.

5.2   Images

5.2.1   Insert an Image

Images can be easily incorporated into a document either by using copy/paste or by inserting an image from a file. To insert an image from a file, navigate to the *Insert* tab and press on icon *Picture* as shown in Figure 5-7. This brings up the standard dialog box for opening files. Browse your files, find and select the image you want, and press *Open*.

To insert a clip art image navigate to *Insert* tab and press on icon *Clip Art* in the ribbon as shown in Figure 5-8. This brings up a clip art library. Browse the library, choose a clip art image, and then either click on the image or drag it to the document.

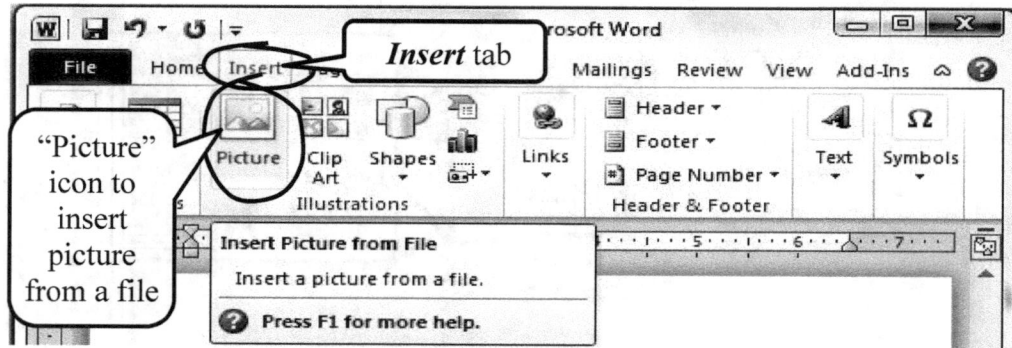

Figure 5-7: Insert picture from a file

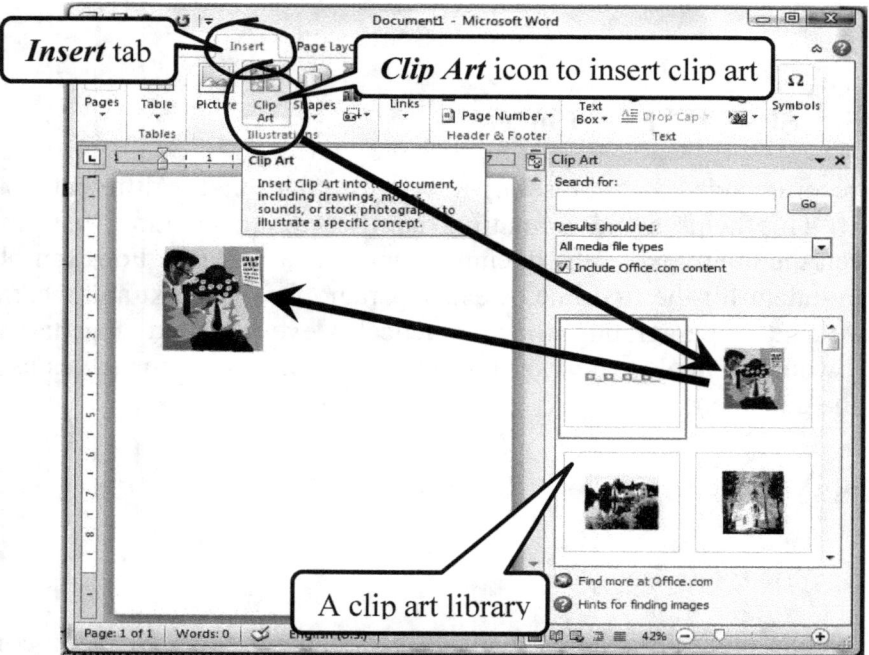

Figure 5-8: Insert clip art

5.2.2   Resizing an Image

The user can easily resize an image in the document by selecting the image, placing the cursor on one of the selection marks and dragging the mark in the desired direction for image resizing as shown in Figure 5-9.

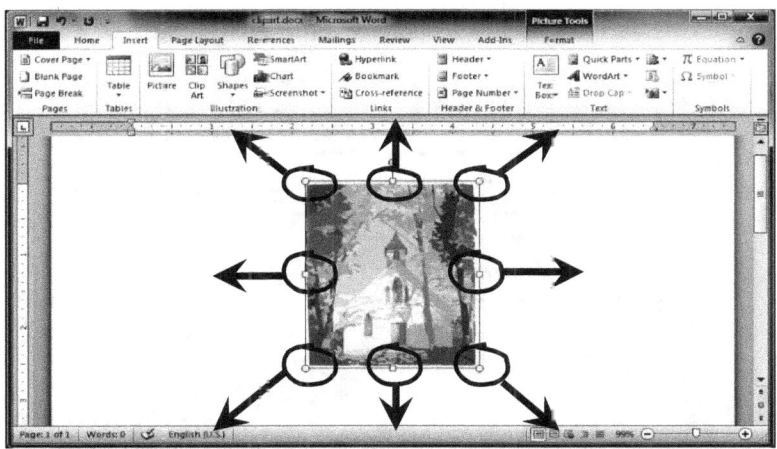

Figure 5-9: Resizing an image

5.2.3 Rotating an Image

A user can easily rotate an image in the document. Click on the image to select it, place the cursor on the mark, and rotate the image by moving the cursor as shown in Figure 5-10.

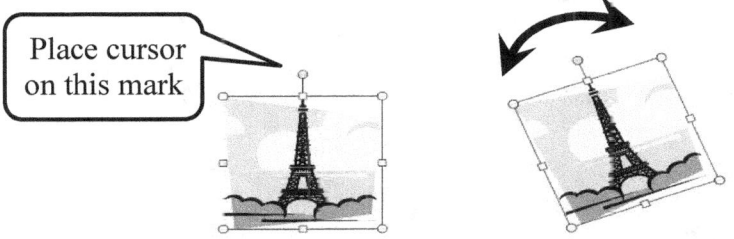

Figure 5-10: Free rotating of an image

There is another way to rotate an image. Select an image and navigate to the *Format* tab, which appears as soon as an image is selected. Then click on the *Rotate* icon and choose a rotation option from the popup rotation option list as shown in Figure 5-11.

5.2.4 Bringing Forward and Sending Backward

Sometimes images may overlap and it is important to control the order of appearance of the overlapping images. For example, if we want to switch the overlapping order for the images shown on the left side of Figure 4-16, we select the image on the top. This brings up the *Format* tab in the main menu. Navigate through the *Format* tab and choose the *Send Backward* option. This option sends the top image under the other image, switching the overlapping order as shown on the right side of Figure 4-16.

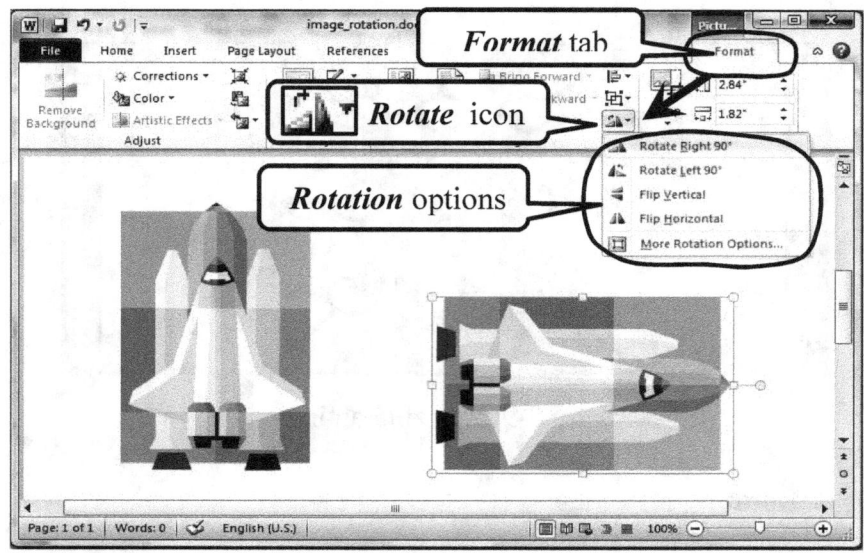

Figure 5-11: Rotating an image

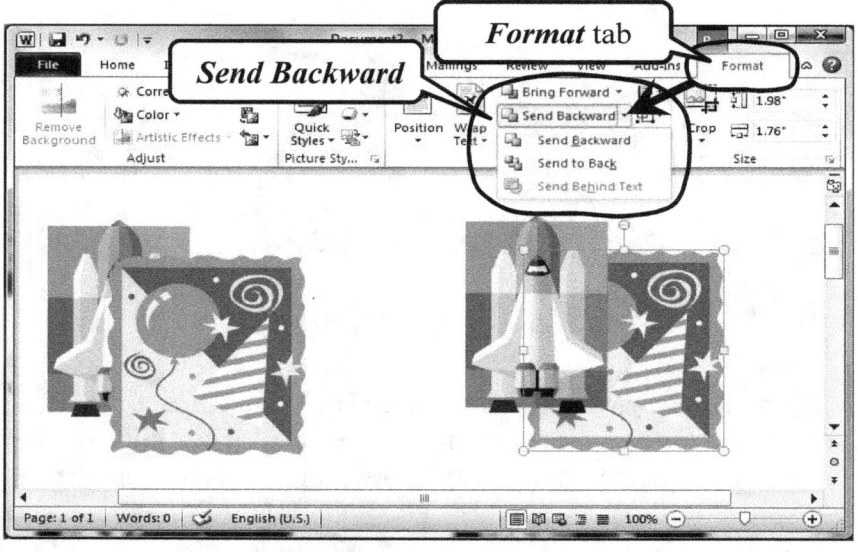

Figure 5-12: Send backward

Variations of **Bring Forward** and **Send Backward** options in **Format** tab are shown in Figure 5-13.

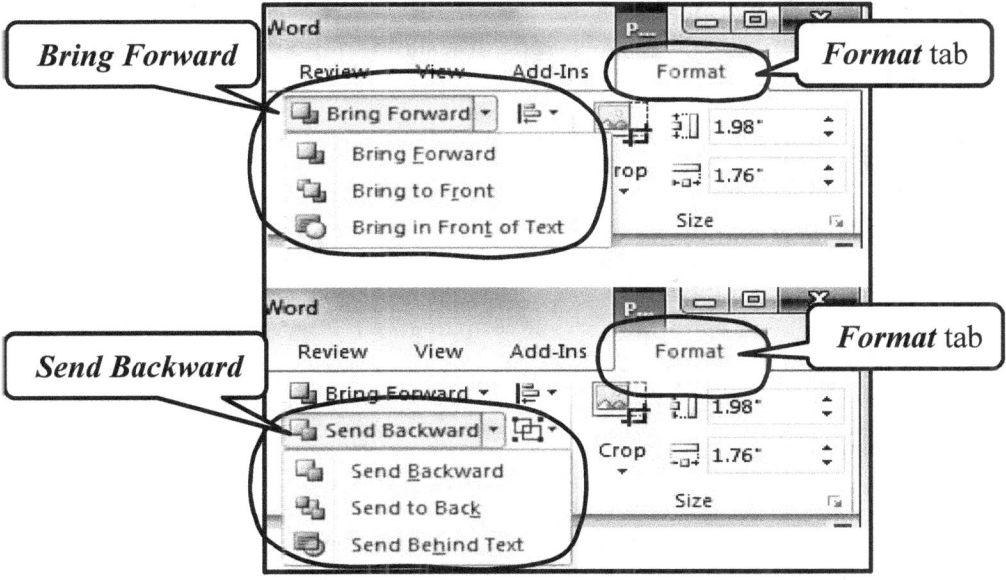

Figure 5-13: Forward / Backward menu

5.2.5   Text Wrapping

An inserted image can be placed in the document with a number of text wrapping options ():

- In line with text
- Square
- Tight
- Through
- Top and bottom
- Behind text
- In front of text

n line with text wrapping means the image will be treated as a character in line with other characters of the text regardless of the image size as show in Figure 5-14(a).

Tight wrapping means that the text wraps around the "white" (or empty) boundaries of the image as shown in Figure 5-14(c). Keep in mind that the image boundaries may not be rectangular. If the image does have a rectangular shape, you will see no difference between *Square* and *Tight* wrapping.

Through is similar to Tight wrapping but it also allows the text to go through other "white" (empty) areas of the image as shown in Figure 5-14(d).

Top and Bottom wrapping places the image between lines of text as shown in Figure 5-14(e). This kind of wrapping is good for stand-alone pictures, tables and other objects in the document text.

Behind Text wrapping places text on top of the image as shown in Figure 5-14(f), making the image part of the background.

In Front of Text wrapping places the image above text as shown in Figure 5-14(g), so it covers a portion of the text.

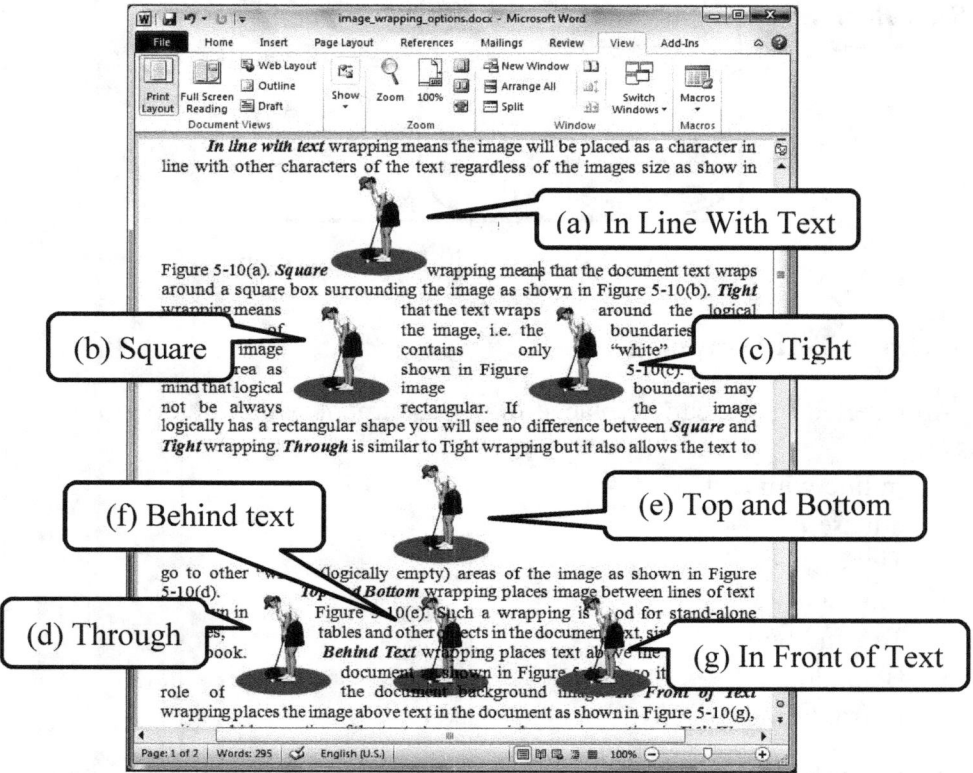

Figure 5-14: Image wrapping modes

To set any of the above wrapping options for an image, right click on the image, scroll down to *Wrap Text* and select the wrapping option from the list as shown in Figure 5-15. Clicking on "More Layout Options" brings up the popup control shown in Figure 5-16.

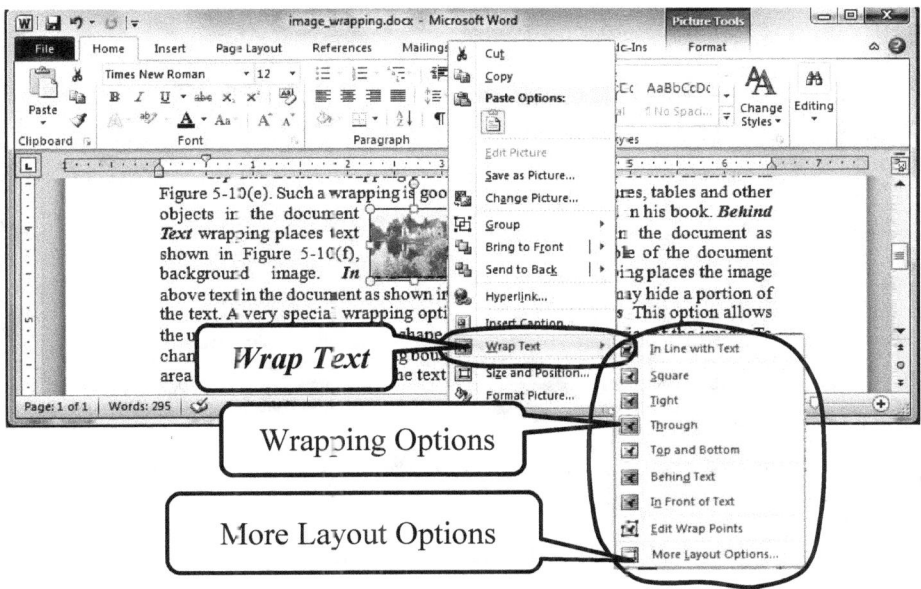

Figure 5-15: Setting wrapping option for an image

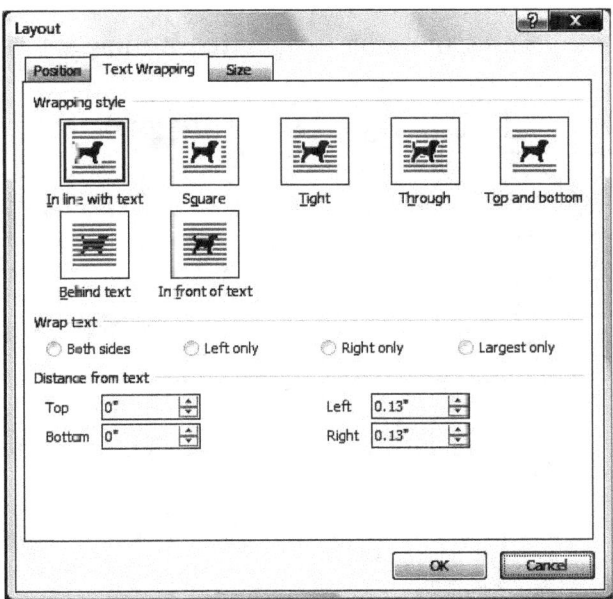

Figure 5-16: More wrapping options

Another interesting wrapping option is ***Edit Wrap Points***. This option allows the user to manually change the shape of the wrapping boundaries of the image. To change the shape of the wrapping boundaries the user has to drag the corners to the desired location in the text area as show in Figure 5-17.

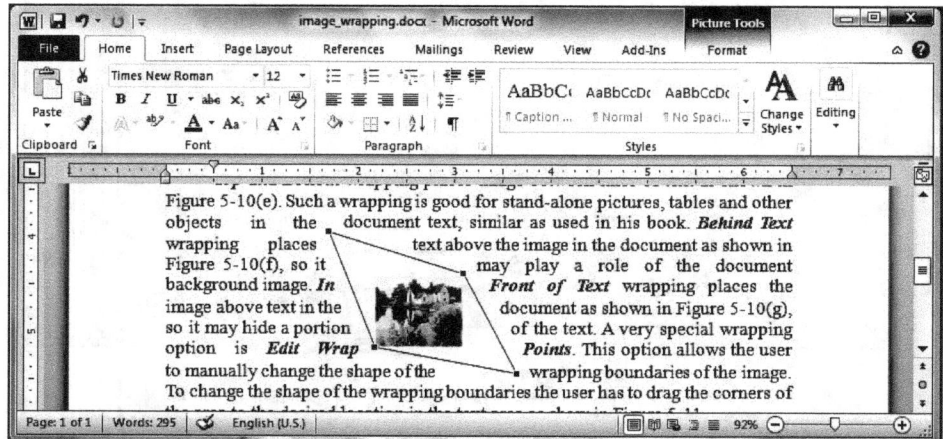

Figure 5-17: Edit wrap points

5.3   Drawing with Shapes

5.3.1   Inserting and Changing Properties of Shapes

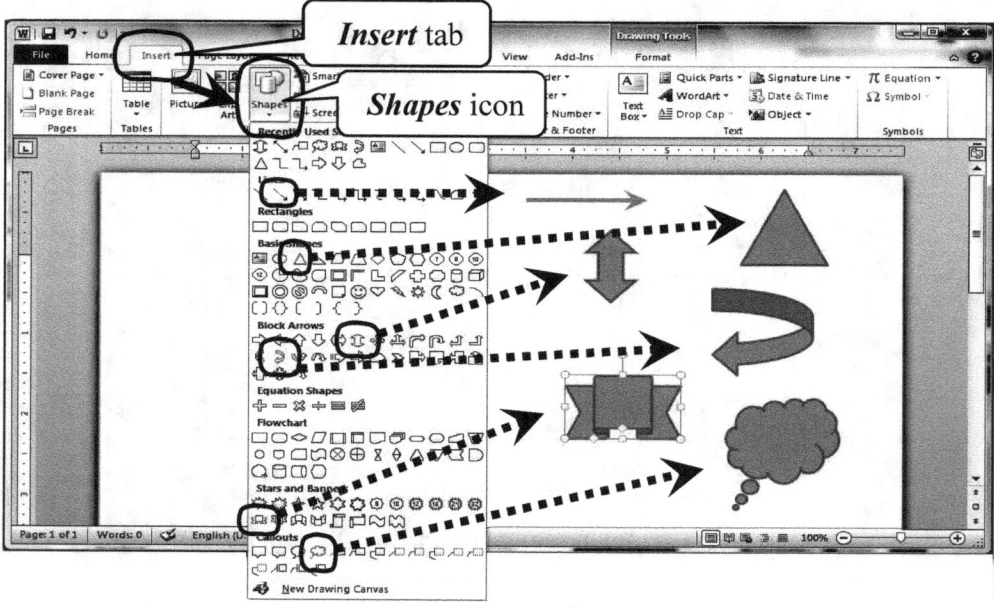

Figure 5-18: "Shapes" drawing tool

Microsoft Word has extensive drawing and schematic capabilities. To insert a drawing directly into the document, navigate to the ***Insert*** tab and open the drawing toolbar by choosing the ***Shapes*** icon as show in Figure 5-18. This brings up a shapes selection list.

To use a shape, select the one you want by clicking on it in the list and then click on the position in the document where you want the shape to appear as shown in Figure 5-18. Most shapes have properties that you can easily change. To change the properties, right click on the shape to open a shape management features list as shown in Figure 5-19.

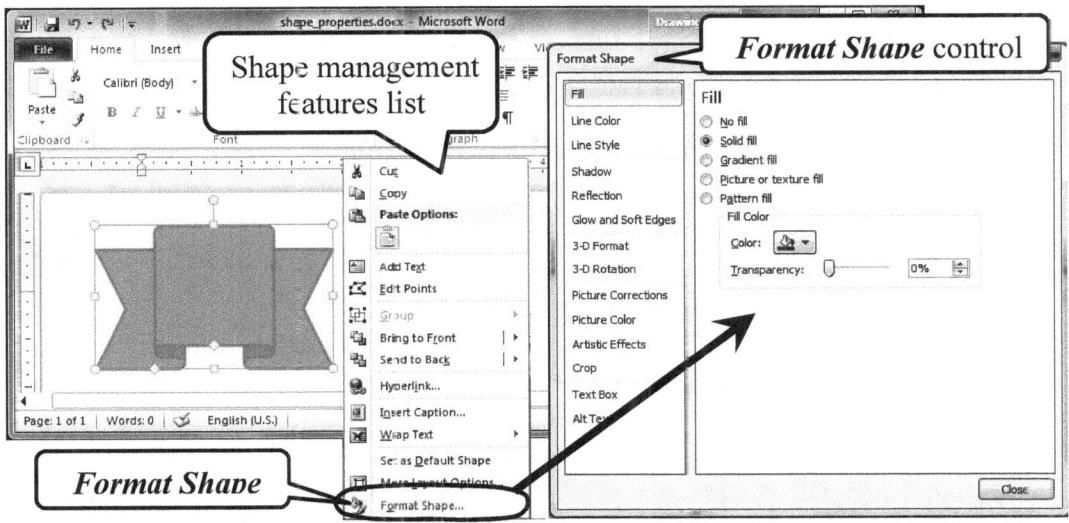

Figure 5-19: Shape features list and shape formatting control

You are already familiar with some of the features on the shape management list such as "Bring to Front", "Send to Back" and "Wrap Text". If you choose "Format Shape", the ***Format Shape*** control pops up (see Figure 5-19). For the sake of exercise, select the ***Fill*** property in the ***Format Shape*** control and play around with it—try changing the color and pattern of the shape's internal area. Figure 5-20 shows an example of setting a gradient color to the internal area of the shape.

You can change the color, width, and style of the shape contour line by selecting ***Line Color*** and ***Line Style*** properties in the ***Format Shape*** control as illustrated in Figure 5-21.

You can even write text in the internal area of a shape. Just place the cursor on the shape, left click on it, and type anything you want. Let's type the word "HELLO" as you see in Figure 5-21. You can adjust the font face, size and color of that text. To change the text properties, select the text inside the shape, navigate to the **Home** tab in the main menu, and change its properties using the text property section in the ribbon of the **Home** tab.

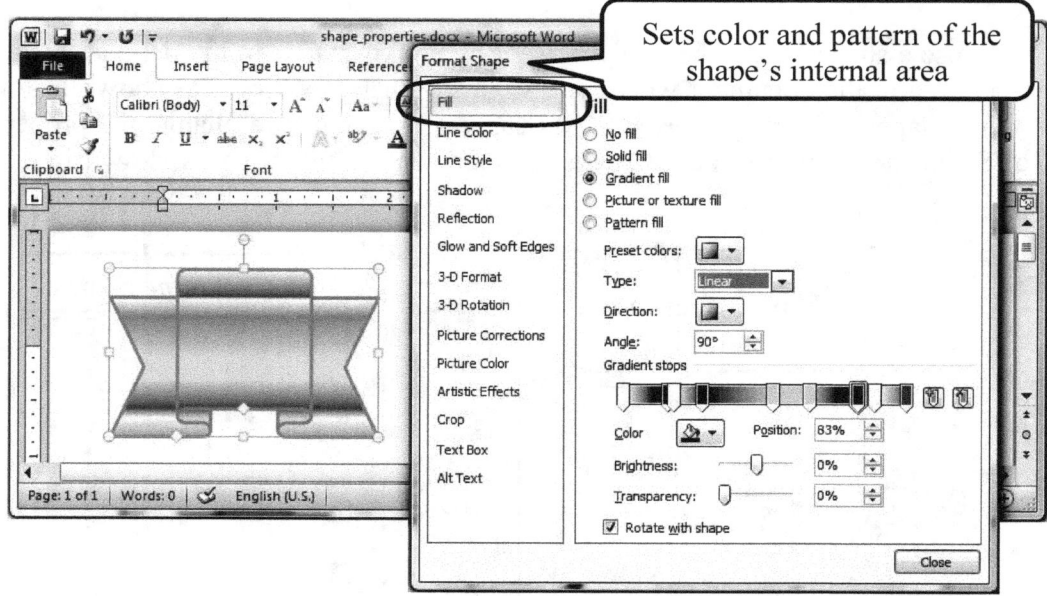

Figure 5-20: *Fill* property for shape

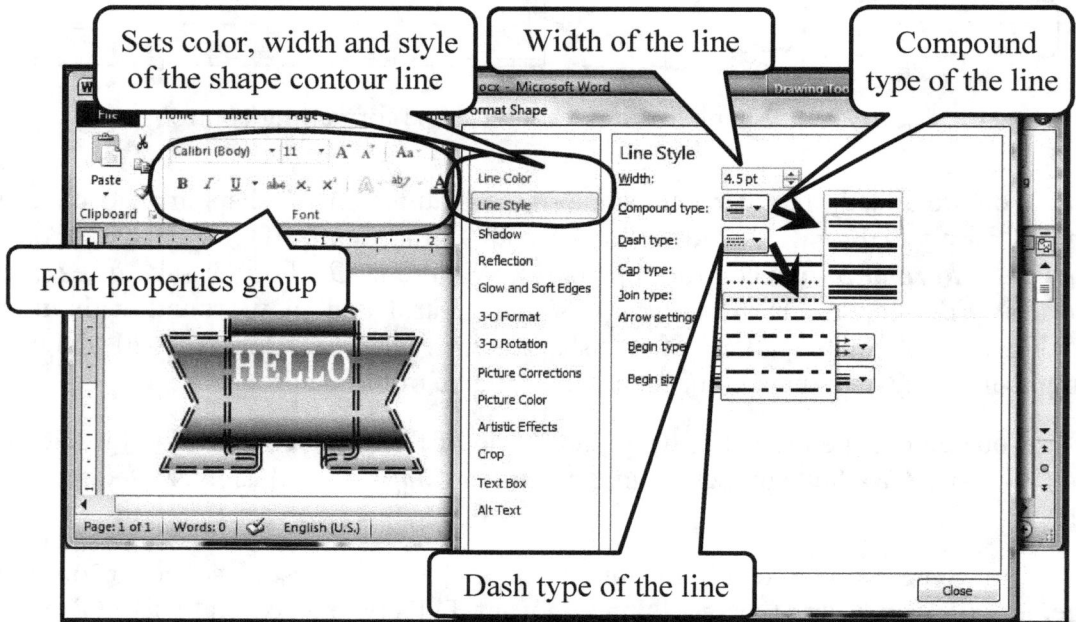

Figure 5-21: Setting shape contour line properties

Try a few other shape properties to learn how they work. Shapes can be managed in the same way as regular images, so you can rotate and resize shapes similarly to how you do it for images.

5.3.2 Shape Alignment

You may use a composition of several shapes or images in the document. Suppose you inserted them in a disorganized way like shown in Figure 5-22 but you want them to be better aligned and nicely distributed on the page. To align shapes or images select all objects which you want to manage by clicking on the objects one by one while keeping the *Shift* key pressed on the keyboard. The action of selecting objects automatically makes the *Format* tab to appear on the main menu. As the objects which you want to align are selected navigate to *Format* tab then left click on the *Alignment* icon in the ribbon, and choose the alignment option as shown in Figure 5-22.

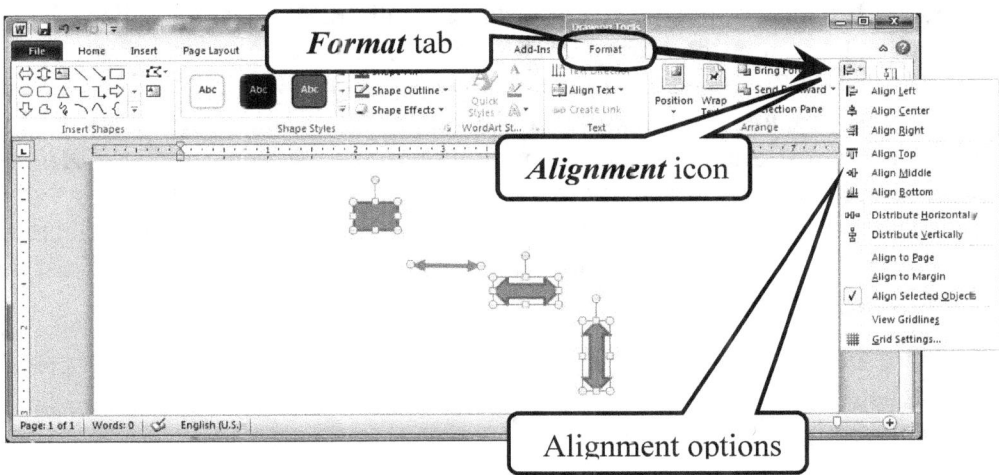

Figure 5-22: Drawings and alignment tool box

There are two kinds of alignment options for a group of objects:

- horizontal alignment
- vertical alignment

Horizontal alignment works in the horizontal direction aligning all selected objects relative to a certain vertical baseline. There are three major horizontal alignment options:

- align left
- align center

- align right

Align Left moves all selected objects horizontally to the position where their leftmost points touch a vertical baseline which goes through the leftmost point of all selected objects. *Align Center* moves all selected objects horizontally to the positions where their horizontally center points touch a baseline that goes through a horizontal center point between the leftmost and rightmost points among all selected objects. *Align Right* moves all selected objects horizontally to the positions where their rightmost points touch a vertical baseline which goes through the rightmost point of all selected objects. Al this sounds very complex but it is really easy; just do it once and you will figure it out.

Similarly there are three major vertical alignment options:
- align top
- align middle
- align bottom

Align Top moves all selected objects vertically to the position where their topmost points touch a horizontal baseline which goes through the topmost point of all selected objects. *Align Middle* moves all selected objects vertically to the positions where their vertically middle points touch a baseline that goes through a vertically middle point between the topmost and bottommost points among all selected objects. *Align Bottom* moves all selected objects vertically to the positions where their bottommost points touch a horizontal baseline which goes through the bottommost point of all selected objects. Similarly to vertical alignment it sounds very complex but it is really easy; just do it once and you will figure it out.

There are also two types of distribution:
- distribute vertically
- distribute horizontally

Distribute Vertically moves all selected objects—except the topmost and bottommost objects—so the objects become evenly distributed in the vertical direction. Similarly *Distribute Horizontally* moves all selected objects—except the leftmost and rightmost objects—so the objects become evenly distributed in the horizontal direction.

Figure 5-23 provides an example of horizontal and vertical alignments including *Align Left*, *Align Center*, *Align Right*, *Align Top*, *Align Middle*, and *Align Bottom*. The figure displays a composition of four scattered shapes in the left part of the figure while the right-hand side of the figure displays six versions of the same composition after the application of three vertical and three horizontal alignment options. The dashed vertical and horizontal lines represent the appropriate left, center, right, top, middle, and bottom baselines.

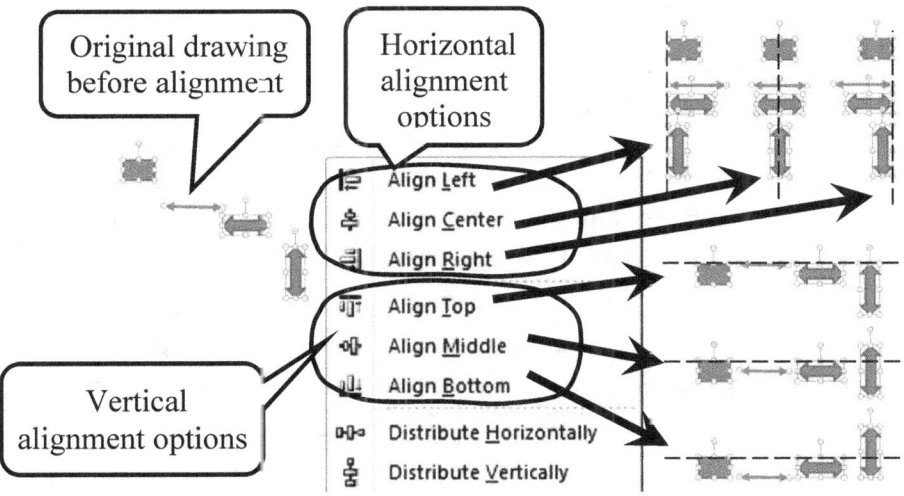

Figure 5-23: Alignment options

Figure 5-24 illustrates a horizontal distribution. The left-hand side of the figure shows the original composition of unevenly distributed objects. The right-hand side of the figure shows the same objects after application of the **Distribute Horizontally** option, where all the shapes become evenly distributed in the same space.

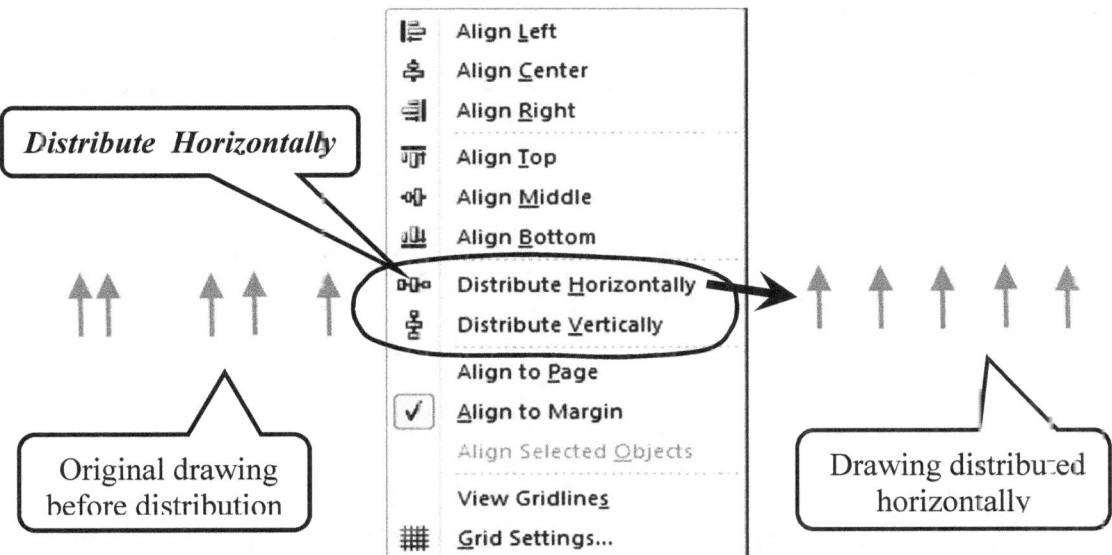

Figure 5-24: Horizontal distribution

5.3.3   Group / Ungroup

It is tedious to manage a composition of several shapes or images. Every time you need to copy, move, rotate, resize, or wrap the entire composition, you must make sure to select all the objects in that composition. It's easy to forget to select one of the objects, which means the entire operation will fail. Even if you have selected all the objects correctly, the outcome of some operations like rotation or resizing may disappoint you. In order to manage an entire composition as one object, you need to group them into a single object.

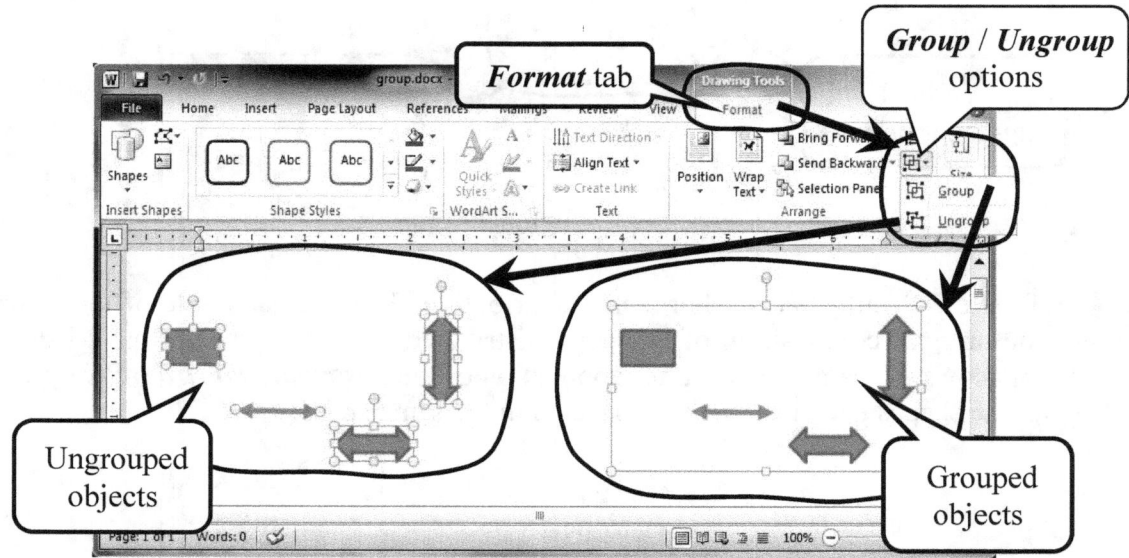

Figure 5-25: Group / Ungroup

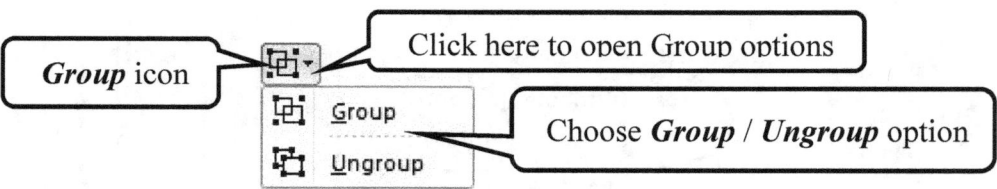

Figure 5-26: Group / Ungroup icon and options

To group a collection of shapes or images:
- select the shapes or images by clicking on each object while holding down the *Shift* key (Figure 5-25)
- navigate to the *Format* tab in the main menu (Figure 5-25)
- click on the inverse triangle to the right of the *Group* icon (Figure 5-25 and Figure 5-26)

- choose the *Group* option to group the shapes or images (Figure 5-25 and Figure 5-26).

To ungroup grouped shapes or images:
- select the group by clicking on it (Figure 5-25)
- navigate to the *Format* tab in the main menu (Figure 5-25)
- click on the inverse triangle to the right of the *Group* icon (Figure 5-25 and Figure 5-26)
- choose *Ungroup* option to ungroup it to separate shapes or images (Figure 5-25 and Figure 5-26)

5.4   Objects

5.4.1   The Role of Objects

Users can embed other applications—referred to as objects—into a Microsoft Word document. Embedded objects expand the functionality of Microsoft Word and make documents more powerful and functionally rich. Among the most popular objects are spreadsheets (Microsoft Excel), equations, and many others.

When an object is embedded in a Microsoft Word document, it looks static like an image does in a document. However, if the user double clicks on that object it engages the functionality of the embedded application so the user can change the content using that application.

Keep in mind that embedded objects significantly increase the size of Microsoft Word documents. The document size is important to be aware of when saving it or sending it electronically as an email attachment.

5.4.2   Inserting and Managing an Object

To insert an object, place the cursor where you want the object to appear. Then, navigate to the *Insert* tab in the main menu, go to the *Object* icon in the ribbon and select an object type from the popup list of available objects as shown in Figure 5-27. When the desired object is selected, press the *OK* button.

Inserting an object starts the application—you can then to use it to manage an image, develop a spreadsheet, build a chart, write an equation, and so on. Once you've developed the object, click somewhere in the Microsoft Word document outside the object working area and the object will be incorporated into the Microsoft Word document. To change the object, double click on it to open the application and make the change.

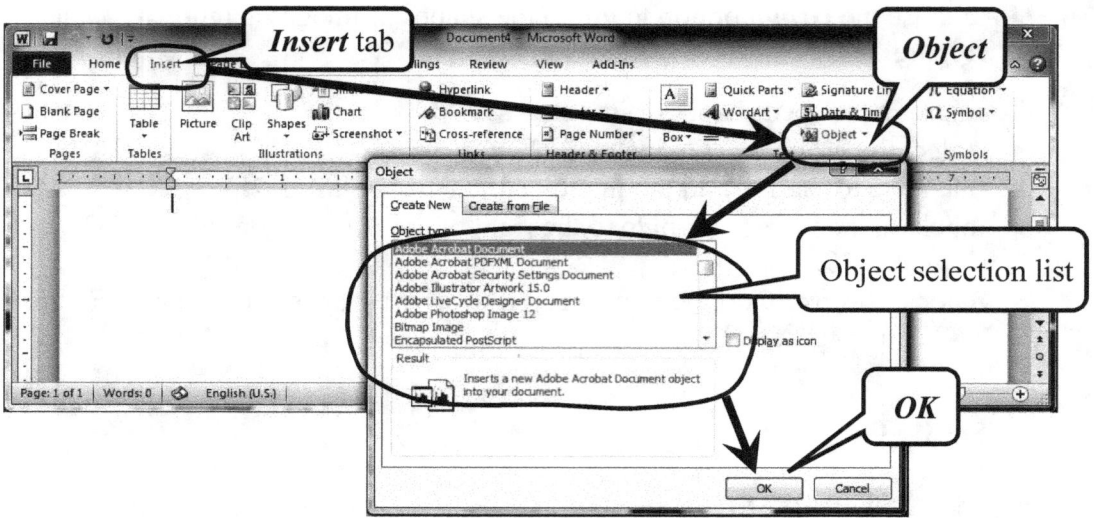

Figure 5-27: Inserting Objects

5.4.3   Equations

A variety of documents need equations. It is practically impossible to write a nontrivial equation by just using keyboard text.

Microsoft Equation 3.0

Microsoft Equation is a powerful application that allows users to write complex equations. To use this application, find and launch the "Microsoft Equation 3.0" object by following the procedure described above in section 5.4.2 and illustrated in Figure 5-27; i.e. navigate to the ***Insert*** tab, click on the ***Object*** icon, select Microsoft Equation 3.0 from the ***Object selection list*** in the ***Object*** popup window, and press the ***OK*** button in that window. You'll notice that the main menu changes because you temporarily switched applications from Microsoft Word to Microsoft Equation. You can also launch Microsoft Equation 3.0 by clicking on the equations developed by this application.

The ***Equation Tool*** (Figure 5-28) will pop up in the document. It contains a variety of equation formatting icons. Each icon represents a variety of symbols and formats. Clicking on an icon in the ***Equation Tool*** expands it into a variety of related icons. You can then select the function you need to insert it in the equation (Figure 5-28). The ***Equation Tool*** is quite intuitive, so you will easily figure out how to write equations. When your equation is ready, or any time you wish to insert it into the Microsoft Word document, simply click outside the equation frame anywhere in the Microsoft Word document. The applications will switch from Microsoft Equation to Microsoft Word and the equation you were working on will be incorporated into the Microsoft Word document as shown in Figure 5-29.

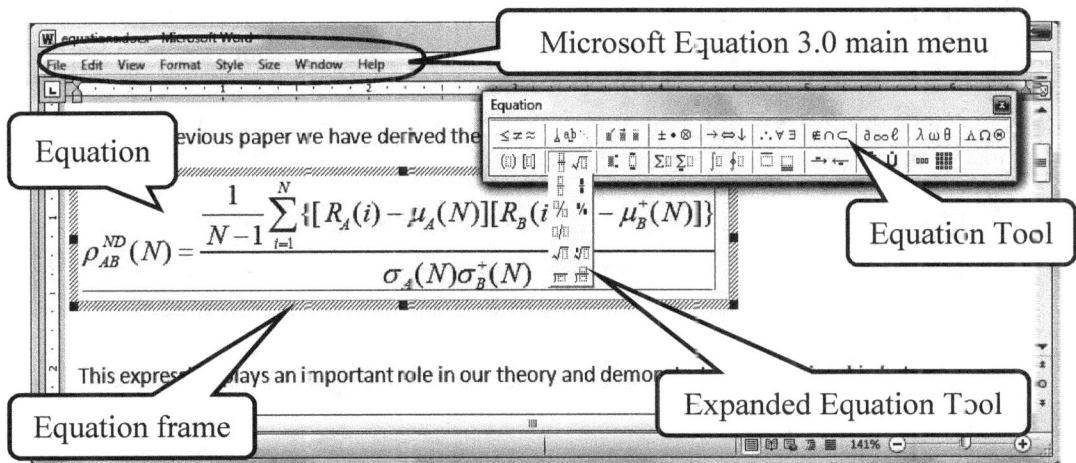

Figure 5-28: Equation tool in Microsoft Equation 3.0

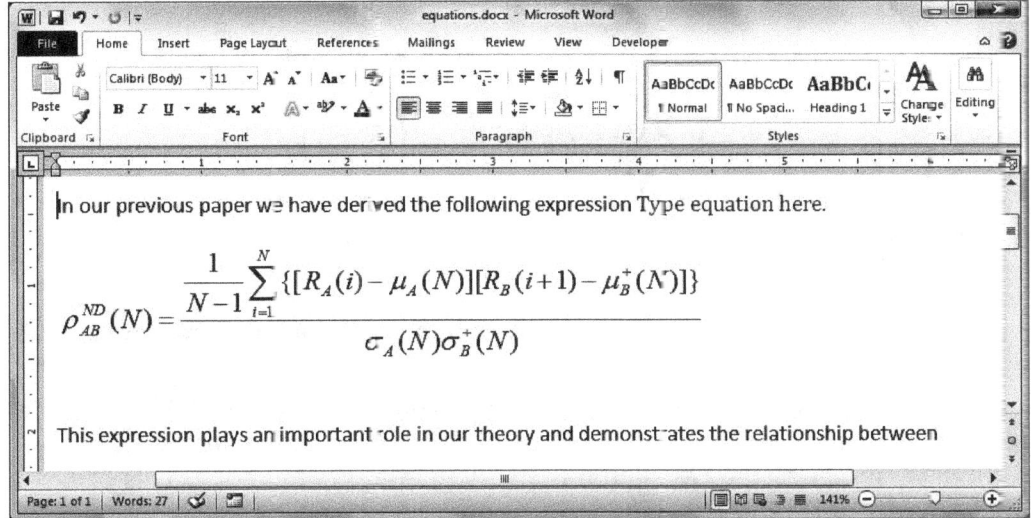

Figure 5-29: An equation inserted in the Microsoft Word document

Note that the user interface switched back to the Microsoft Word user interface as soon as you exited the Microsoft Equation application. To modify the equation, just double click on it. This brings back the Microsoft Equation application, where you'll see the Microsoft Equation Tool and Microsoft Equation main menu as in Figure 5-28.

Another Way of Writing Equations

There is another way of inserting equations into a Microsoft Word document. Navigate to the *Insert* tab in the main menu and click on the *Equation* icon in the ribbon as shown in Figure 5-30. This automatically opens the *Equation Tool* in the ribbon of the *Design* tab as shown in the same figure. The Equation Tool and the procedure of writing equations are very intuitive, so you can learn fast and start using the application in practically no time at all.

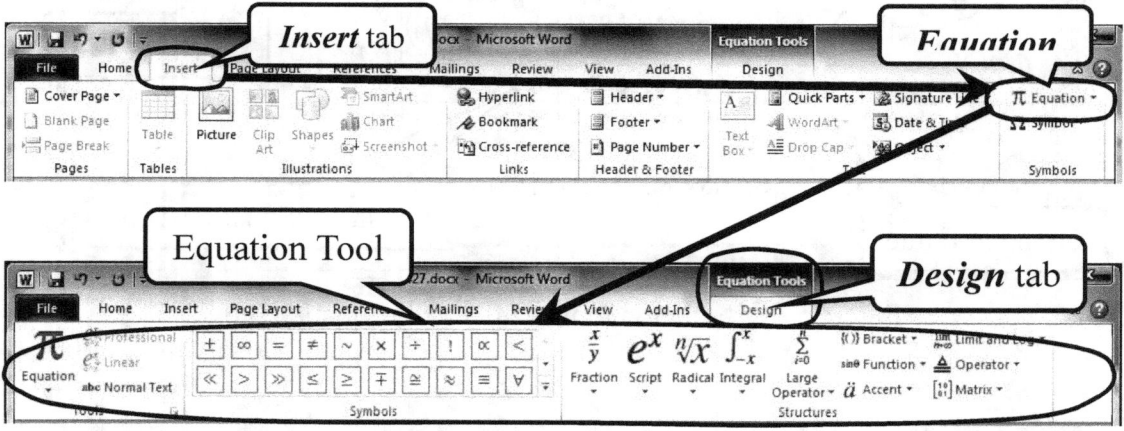

Figure 5-30: Microsoft Word Equation Tool

5.4.4   Embedding an Excel Object

Embedded Microsoft Excel objects enable users to present dynamic tables and charts in Microsoft Word documents, as well as modify the data and functionality of those tables and charts.

To insert a Microsoft Word Excel object into a Microsoft Word document follow the procedure described above in section 5.4.2 and illustrated in Figure 5-27. In other words, navigate to the *Insert* tab, click on the *Object* icon, select "Microsoft Excel Worksheet" or "Microsoft Excel Chart" from the *Object selection list* in the *Object* popup window, and press the *OK* button in that window (Figure 5-27). This brings up the Microsoft Excel application and its functionality as an embedded object. You can use the Excel application to build a worksheet or a chart and when it is ready click on the Word document outside the Excel work area. The results will be displayed in the Word document. To modify the tables or charts, double click on the object in the Word document. This brings back Excel where you can make modifications to the data, charts, or functionality (Figure 5-31 and Figure 5-32).

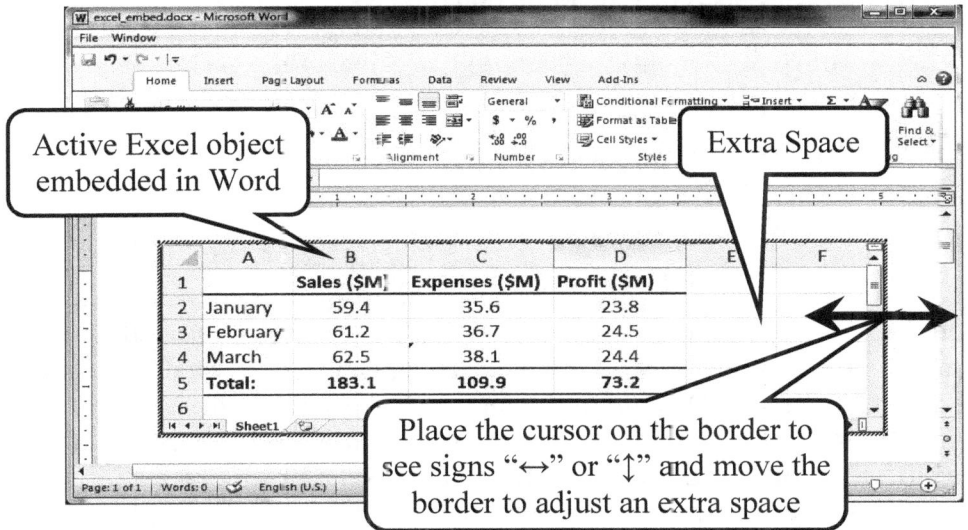

Figure 5-31: Active Excel object embedded in Word

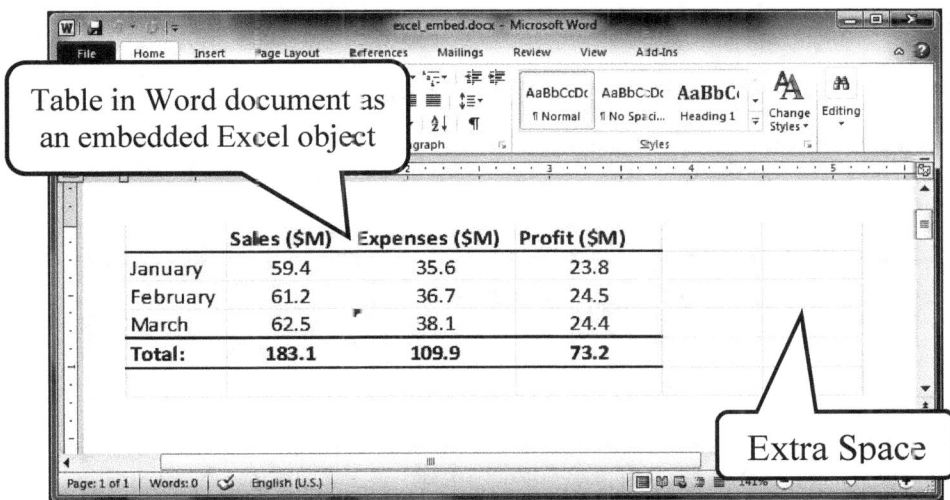

Figure 5-32: Table in Microsoft Word document as an embedded Microsoft Excel object

Sometimes an Excel object shows extra space (Figure 5-31 and Figure 5-32) which it is better remove. To adjust extra space in an object, double click on the object to bring it into active status, place the cursor on the active object border until you see signs "↔" (for vertical border) or "↕" (for horizontal border), and move the border by keeping the mouse button pressed to adjust for extra space (Figure 5-31).

Microsoft Excel Charts can be embedded in a similar way in a Microsoft Word document, as it is basically part of Excel functionality.

Refer to Chapters 9 and 10 for instructions on Microsoft Excel functionality.

5.5   Drawing Canvas

5.5.1   The Role of Drawing Canvas

When you draw shapes or place images, clip art or other objects in a Microsoft Word document, it is important to wrap the document text correctly around those objects. In some cases you may want to wrap around a composition of several objects together, which can be a challenge. One of the solutions to this problem is object grouping described in section 5.3.3 . Another, even more thorough, solution is to use canvas. The term canvas in Microsoft Word refers to a frame encapsulating all objects inside it. Thus if a canvas itself is placed in or moved within the document, all objects placed inside the canvas are placed or moved together preserving their positions and order within the canvas.

5.5.2   Inserting and Managing a Drawing Canvas

To insert a drawing canvas the user first has to place the cursor in the desired position in the document, then navigate to the *Insert* tab in the main menu, click on the *Shapes* icon in the ribbon and choose *New Drawing Canvas* in the expanded drawing tool choices as shown in Figure 5-33.

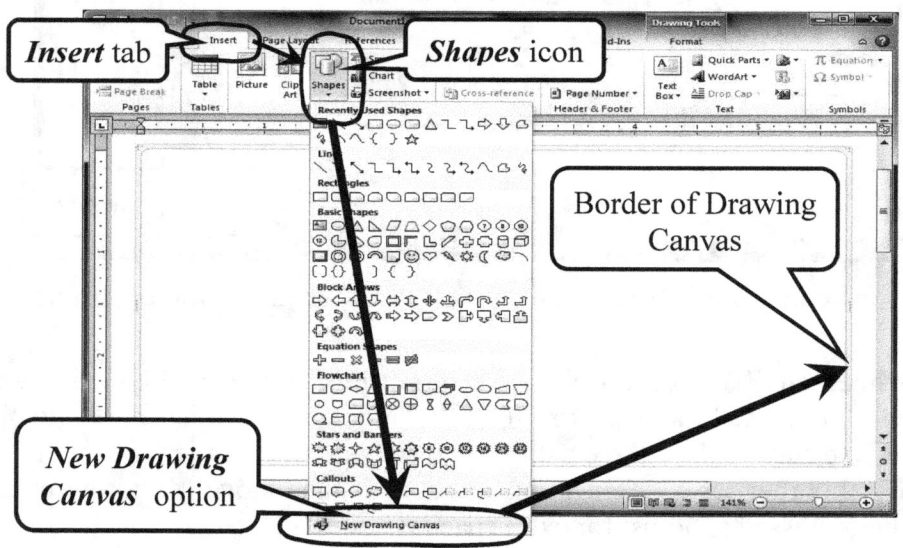

Figure 5-33: Inserting a drawing canvas

A new drawing canvas appears in the form of a grey rectangle in the document (Figure 5-33 and Figure 5-34).

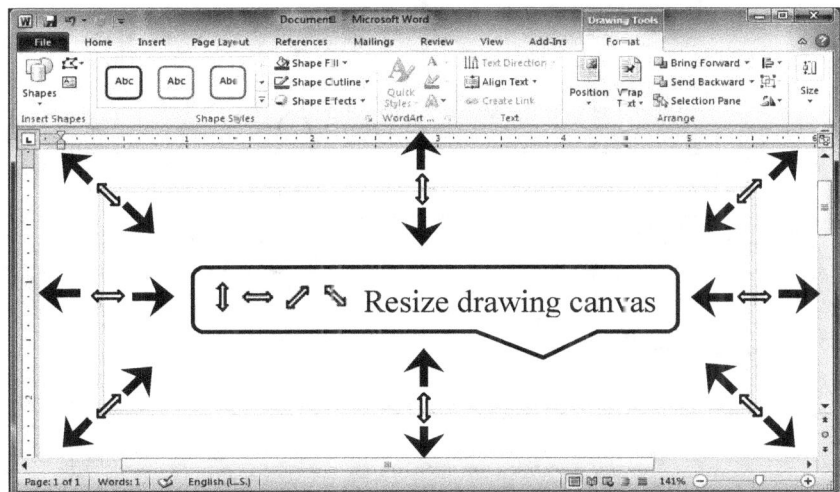

Figure 5-34: Managing a drawing canvas

To resize the drawing canvas the user positions the cursor over the corners or centers of the edges of the canvas. When the cursor changes shape into a vertical, horizontal, or tilted double arrow such as $\Updownarrow \Longleftrightarrow \nearrow \searrow$ this indicates the position is correct and the canvas is in resizing mode. Then, resize by clicking and dragging the edge or a corner of the canvas to the desired size as illustrated in Figure 5-34. Text wrapping can be done around a drawing canvas in the same way as for images described above (Figure 5-14).

The user can insert shapes, images or groups of objects (shapes and images) into a drawing canvas by following the same procedures as described above for inserting images and shapes directly into a document (Figure 5-35).

If you right click on a drawing canvas it opens options to *Fit* the drawing canvas to the objects inside, *Expand* the canvas and *Scale Drawing*. You will easily figure out how these features work.

5.6   Captions and Automated Numbering

Most tables and figures in documents are supposed to have captions and be numbered, and equations may also be numbered. If you manually entered table or figure captions or manually numbered tables, figures and equations, your document could be in trouble. Adding, removing, or just moving a table, figure or equation to a new location in the document may break the natural numbering order. Restoring this order is often a challenge, particularly for large documents.

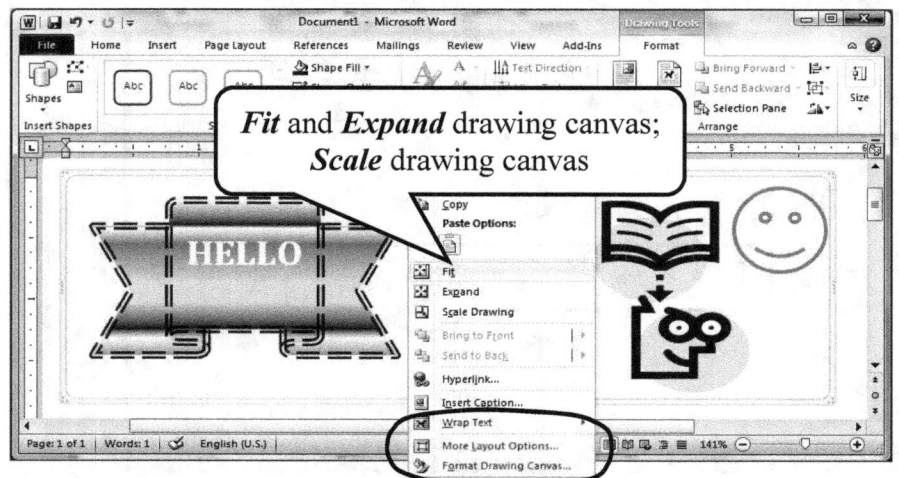

Figure 5-35: Managing a drawing canvas

Microsoft Word has an automated solution to this problem. Do not type a caption and its number manually. Instead use automatic caption insertion that guarantees consistent numbering in all cases.

5.6.1   Insert a Caption

To insert a caption for a table, figure or equation, select the relevant item or just position the cursor at the location where you want to insert the caption. Navigate to the **References** tab in the main menu, click on **Insert Caption** in the menu ribbon as shown in Figure 5-36. This action brings up a "Caption" popup control window. In that window choose a label (Equation, Figure, or Table) for the caption, a position for the label (above or below the item), type the caption and click **OK** in the control window. The caption then appears at the selected position in the document.

5.6.2   Caption Numbering and Other Properties

A principal difference between captions inserted as described above from captions inserted by manually typing it is the automated numbering. Captions you enter via **Insert Caption** will automatically adjust the numbering to reflect any changes made in the document. This way, you no longer have to deal with the headache of manually renumbering captions. Another extraordinary advantage of automated captions is automated cross-referencing which is described in Chapter 6.

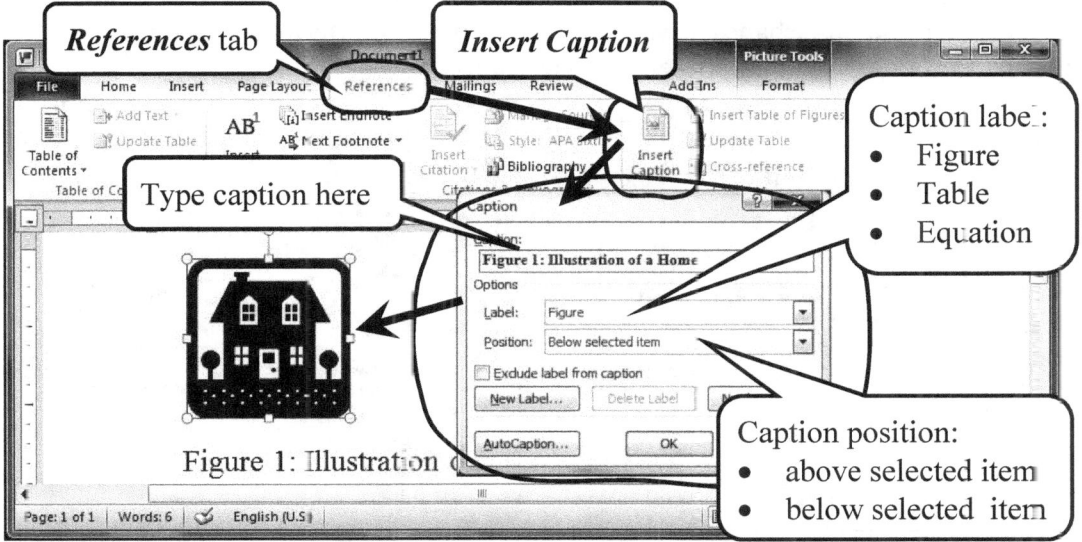

Figure 5-36: Inserting caption for a figure

The caption control window opens with **References → Insert Caption** and allows the user to configure captions the way the user wants. Figure 5-37 shows a variety of configuration options available for captions.

As described above, the user can choose between captions for equations, figures, or tables as shown in Figure 5-36 and Figure 5-37(a). Similarly the user can choose whether to place a caption below or above the item (Figure 5-36 and Figure 5-37(b)). The user can also control whether to exclude the label from the caption, i.e. to show only the number (Figure 5-37(c)). This option is very convenient for equations. The user can also choose to show sequential caption numbering for the entire document or start from one at every chapter and include the chapter number as part of the numbering (Figure 5-37(d)). For example, images in this book are numbered with the "include chapter number" option selected as shown in Figure 5-37(d).

5.6.3   Styles for Captions

Captions, as with any text items, follow a certain style (see Chapter 4). There is a preset default style for captions, so all captions if inserted in the way described above will appear with the default style "Caption". However, users can change the style for captions. Typically, captions for tables are placed above the tables, captions for figures are placed below the figures, and captions for equations are placed to the right of equations. The caption style may also differ by the line spacing before and after the caption. To meet these requirements and keep captions consistent, it is recommended that you define new styles for each of those categories of captions to reflect the desired differences. On the other hand, it would be good to base all those styles on the base style "Caption" to keep up with all properties of captions.

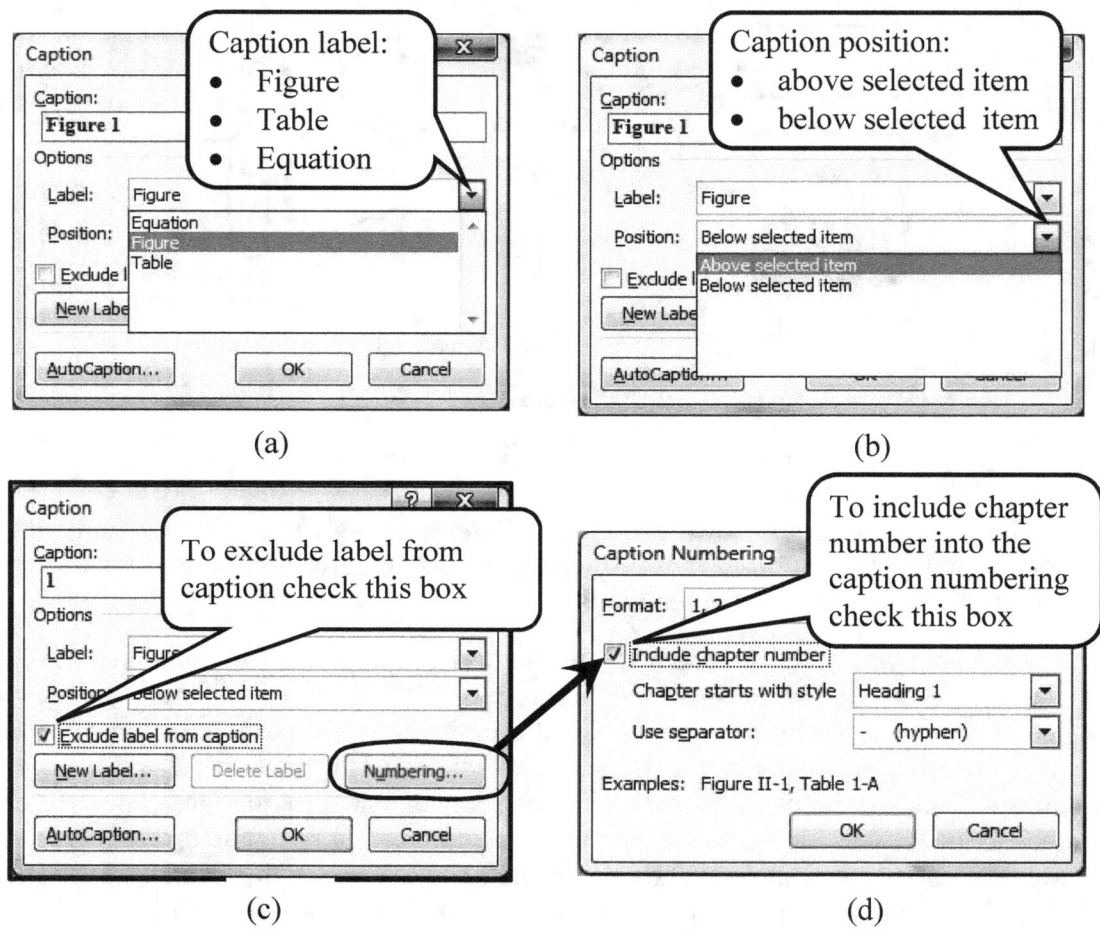

Figure 5-37: Caption configuration options

5.6.4   Updating Caption Numbering

With properly set headings, their numbering is automatically changed and instantly updated to reflect any added, removed or changed headings. While caption numbering is also automatically changed, it is not automatically reflected in the document. To see the numbering changes for a single caption, the user has to select the caption and press key F9. To update the numbering for all captions, the user has to select the entire document by navigating to the **Home** tab, pressing on icon **Select,** choosing the **Select All** option as shown in Figure 5-38, and then pressing the **F9** key. This updates all references in the document including captions. "Select All" can be also accomplished by pressing **Ctrl-A** on the keyboard.

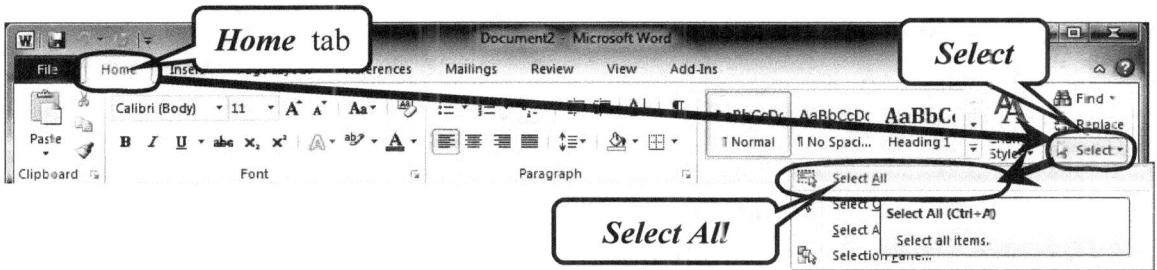

Figure 5-38: Select all

Questions and Exercises

Questions

1. How do you insert a table in a document?
2. How do you delete a table from a document?
3. How do you resize columns in a table?
4. How do you merge adjacent cells in a table?
5. How do you split a cell in a table?
6. What kind(s) of style(s) should be assigned to the table content?
7. How do you insert an image in a document?
8. How do you resize an image?
9. How do you rotate an image?
10. How do you bring an image forward or backward in a composition of overlapping images?
11. What is text wrapping around an image?
12. What types of text wrapping do you know?
13. How do you set text wrapping?
14. How do you draw a shape?
15. What properties of a shape do you know?
16. How do you change the properties of a shape?
17. What is shape alignment?

18. What types of alignment do you know and how do they work?
19. What is grouping?
20. How does grouping / ungrouping work?
21. How do you insert an object in a document?
22. What types of objects do you remember?
23. How do objects work?
24. What is a drawing canvas and why is it needed?
25. How do you insert a drawing canvas?
26. How do you resize a drawing canvas?
27. How do you insert items into a canvas?
28. What is a caption?
29. Why is automated caption important?
30. How do you insert a caption?
31. What types of captions do you know?
32. How do you achieve automated numbering for captions?
33. Why may different types of captions be assigned to different styles?
34. What style should be used as a base for all caption styles?
35. How does automated caption numbering work?
36. How do you update caption numbering?

Exercises

4. Develop a document and include a couple of tables and figures in it. Some figures should be composed of a single image or shape but some should be a composition of various images and shapes.

5. Resize a table column, add a new column, and delete a row.

6. Merge a couple of adjacent cells in a table. Then split them back.

7. Insert a number of shapes and change some of their properties. Group the shapes. Then ungroup them.

8. Insert a drawing canvas and insert an image and a couple of shapes into it. Then change the text wrapping for the canvas and move it around the document. Watch how the items inside the canvas respond.

9. Insert captions for some tables and figures. Insert a new image between two existing images and add a caption to it. Update the numbering by selecting the entire document and pressing *F9* on the keyboard.

6   Referencing and Updating

6.1   Cross-References

By now you should know how to write a document with dynamically numbered headings and captions of all kinds. Thus we can presume that all chapters and subchapters, equations, figures, and tables in your document are correctly styled and numbered. The text of a document frequently cites a heading, equation, figure or table within the document. For example, one may write

- … as described in Chapter 5 …
- … the problem was addressed in section 3.2 …
- … as shown in Figure 7 …
- … Eq. (12) clearly explains …
- … it becomes evident from Table 3 …

Imagine you made such citations in the text by explicitly typing the number of the chapter, subchapter, figure, equation, or table. It looks fine until the numbering changes due to the addition, deletion or repositioning of existing items. In that case, citations you made would no longer be correct and you would have to spend time manually fixing all citation numbering.

There is another way to solve this problem or, more accurately, to prevent this problem completely: use automatic cross-references instead of typing them manually.

To make an automatic cross-reference, navigate to the **References** tab in the main menu and click on the **Cross-reference** icon in the ribbon as shown in Figure 6-1. This brings up a cross-reference popup control window. In that window choose a Reference Type ("Bookmark", "Footnote", "Endnote", "Equation", "Figure", "Heading", "Table", etc) by making a choice in the drop-down selection box as well as the form in which the cross-reference will appear in the document. The form of the cross-reference depends on the cross-reference type. For example, if you select the reference type "Figure", then the drop-down list of "Forms of cross references" includes the options "Entire caption", "Only label and number", "Only caption text", "Page number" and "Above / Below".

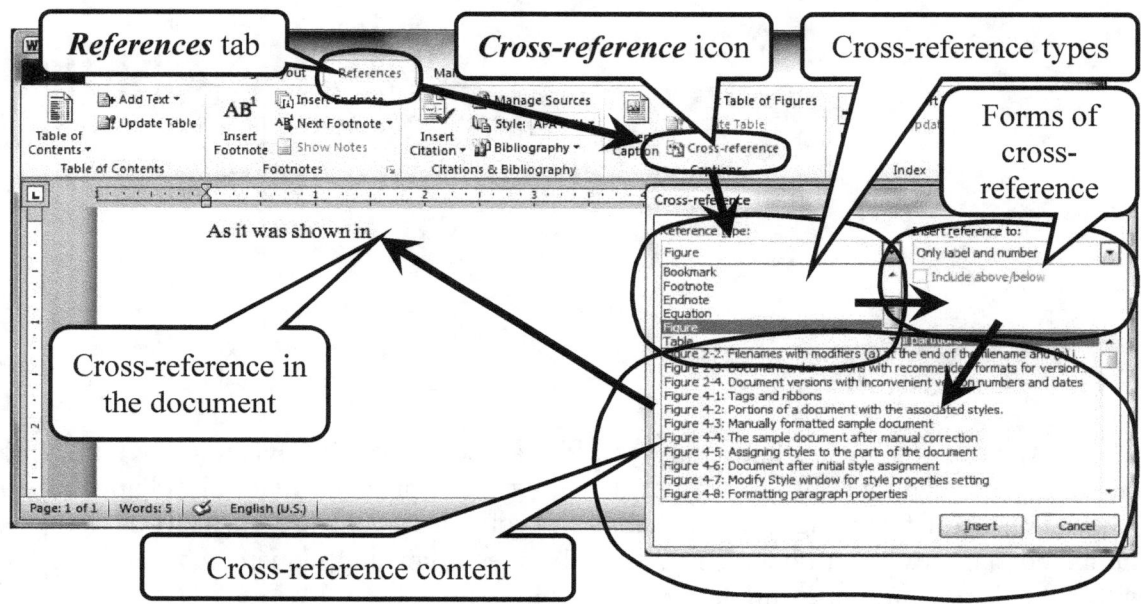

Figure 6-1: Inserting cross-references

Once the cross-references are inserted as described above, they become dynamic and will be updated if the content or numbering of the appropriate items changes. However, these cross-references don't show up automatically in the document and should be forced by the user. To update the cross-references, you can either

- select the appropriate cross-reference and press **F9** for a partial update, or
- select the entire document by pressing **Ctrl-A** and then **F9** (as described in section 5.6.4 for total update of the document).

6.2   Bibliography and Citations

A bibliography is a list of information sources used in a document typically placed at the end of a document. Citations are placed throughout the body of the document and refer the reader to the appropriate bibliography entry each time that source is cited. There are different standards for bibliographies and citations, and the requirements differ depending on the publisher or organization.

6.2.1   Inserting Citations

You can do citations and a bibliography by manually typing all of the entries into the document. This should not cause a problem if you are sure which citation style (referred to as publishers styles[2]) has to be used and you are not going to change the citation standard during the document development. However, if the citation style in your document may need to be changed, then you have to go through the entire document changing the format of all the citations and the entire bibliography.

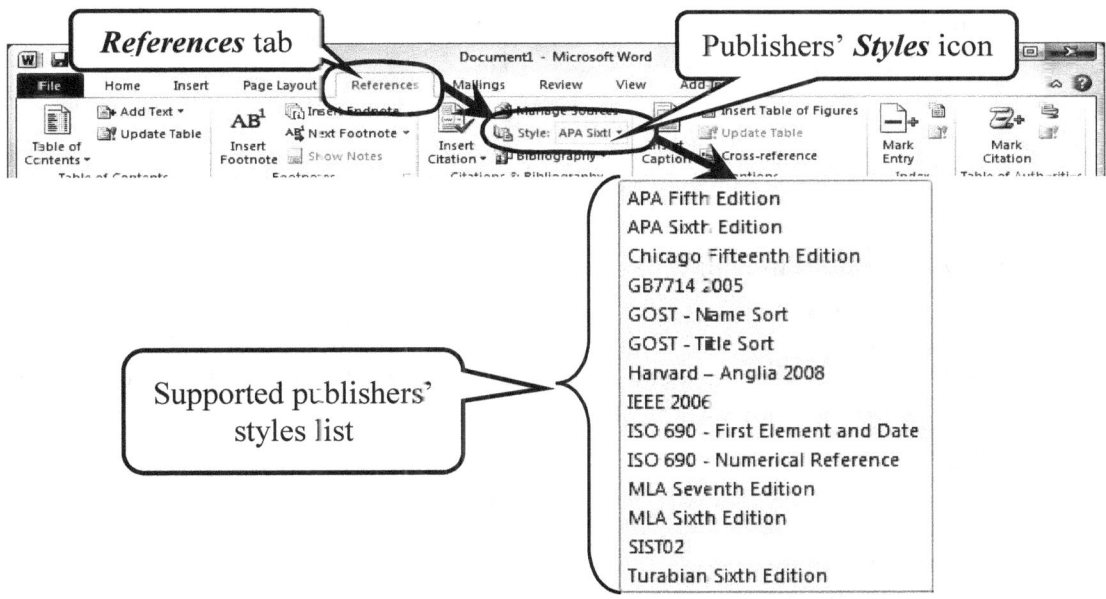

Figure 6-2: Setting up publishers' style

Using Microsoft Word functionality to handle the bibliography and citations helps avoid this problem. Microsoft Word 2010 supports the citation styles shown in Figure

---

[2]   Please do not confuse Microsoft Word styles with publisher styles; they are quite different things.

6-2. To set a citation style, navigate to the **References** tab in the main menu, click on the **Styles** icon in the menu ribbon and choose a citation style from the list of supported styles (Figure 6-2).

Let's go through the process of making citations and building a bibliography. Imagine you are writing a document that requires a reference to an information source. You want to provide a citation in the text (Figure 6-3) and include it in your bibliography using APA style[3] (Figure 6-4).

… as it was shown in the previous analysis (Smith & Duncan, 2012) …

Figure 6-3: Citation using APA style

Smith A.P. & Duncan, J.D. (2012). Analysis of Business Perspectives, *J. Business Management*, 14(3) 18-23.

Figure 6-4: Bibliography using APA style

When you come to the point in the document where you want to insert a citation (Figure 6-3), first you have to choose a citation style by following the procedure described above and illustrated in Figure 6-2. To insert a citation navigate to the **References** tab in the main menu, choose the **Insert Citation** icon in the ribbon and use one of the three options as shown in Figure 6-5.

The three options are:

- use existing source
- add new source
- add new placeholder

Option 1 "Use existing source" allows the user to use a source that has already been inserted in the document. To use this option, just click on a source displayed in the top portion of the options and the appropriate citation will be placed in the location of the

---

[3]   APA and other publishers' style are document writing standards rather than Microsoft Word styles.

cursor.

Option 2 "Add new source" allows the user to add a new source. This option brings up a popup control from which the user chooses a citation type and enters bibliographic information on that source (Figure 6-6). To choose a citation type, click on the inverted triangle icon to open a list of types of sources. Select the type of source you want to add and press **OK**. The user interface will adjust to the chosen source type.

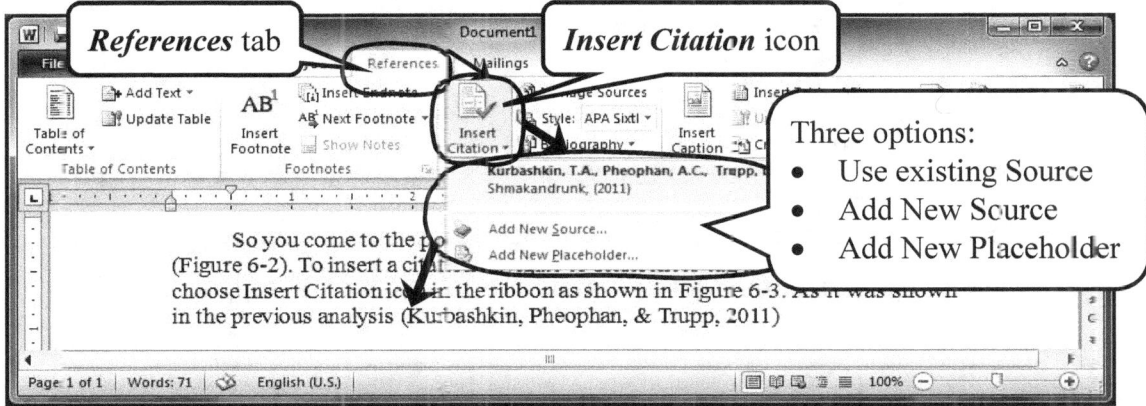

Figure 6-5: Inserting Citation

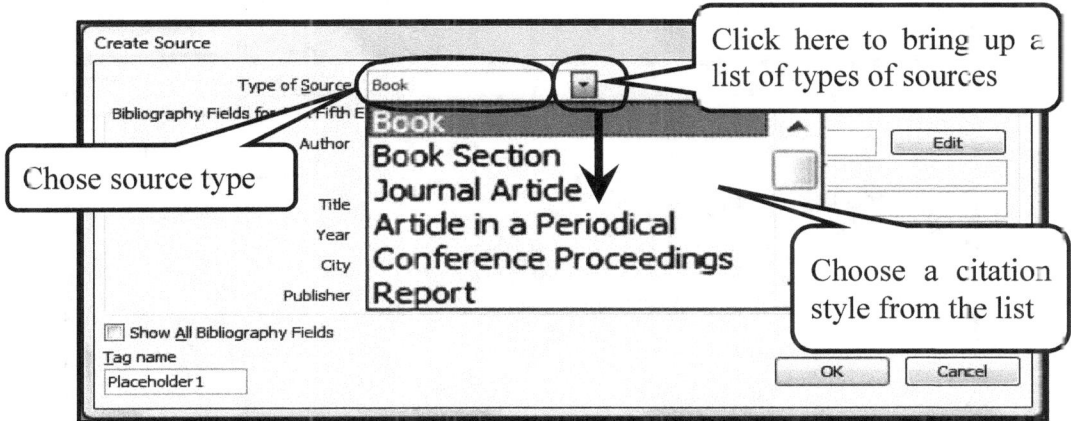

Figure 6-6: Add a new source for citation

For illustration, Figure 6-7 shows a form for inserting a journal publication as a source. This information will be used for both the citations and the bibliography. Pressing the **OK** button inserts the appropriate citation in the document at the position of the cursor.

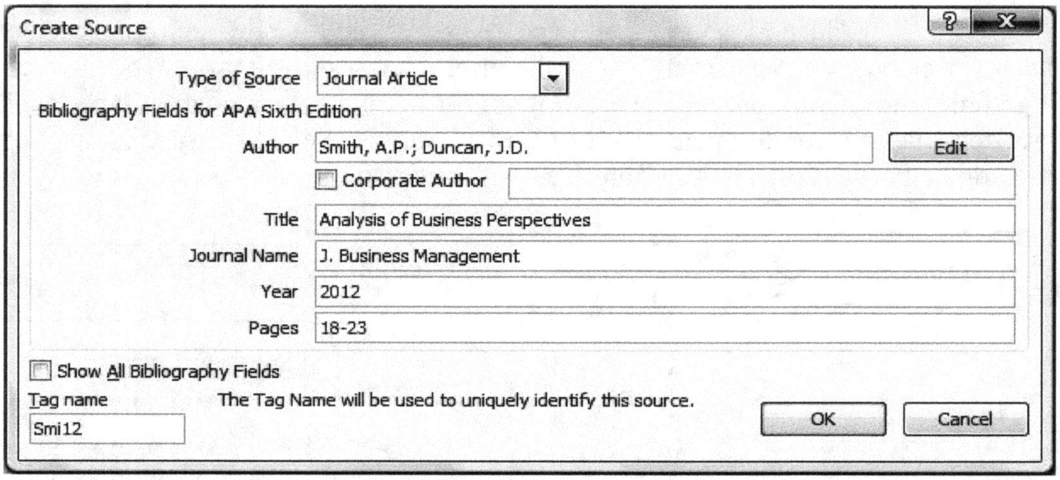

Figure 6-7: Add a new source (a journal article) for citation

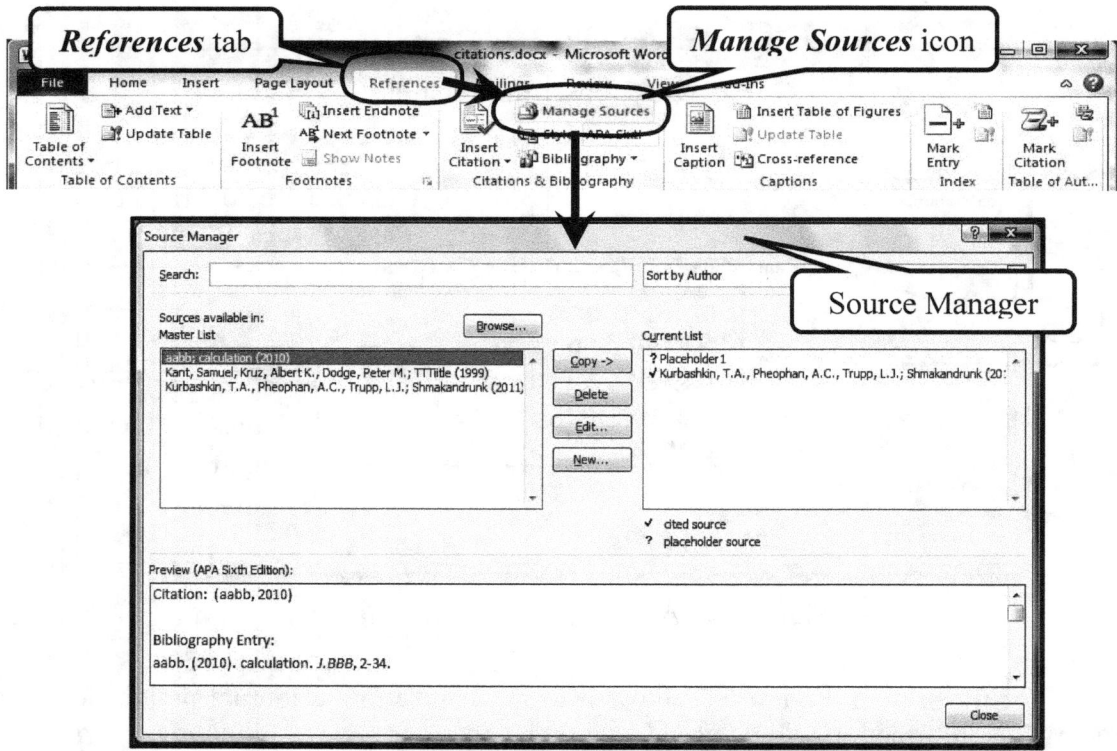

Figure 6-8: Source Management

Option 3 "Add new placeholder" adds a citation placeholder at the position of the cursor. The placeholder is just an "empty" citation which can be filled out later. Clicking on the inverse triangle expansion sign at the "Placeholder" offers options to remove, edit citation, edit source, and others.

6.2.2   Managing Sources

The user can manage sources inserted in the document or saved in another file. To do so, navigate to the ***References*** tab in the main menu and click on the ***Manage Sources*** icon in the ribbon (Figure 6-8). This brings up the "Source Manager" popup control. Using Source Manager allows the user to use old sources stored in some other file (option ***Browse***), copy, delete, edit, and add new sources to the document. Source Management is very intuitive, so it takes practically no time to become familiar and comfortable with it.

6.2.3   Bibliography

The user can generate a bibliography listing the resources used in the document by navigating to the ***References*** tab and clicking on the ***Bibliography*** icon (Figure 6-9). The icon expands a list of options, one of which is ***Insert Bibliography***. When you choose this option it generates a bibliography at the end of the document.

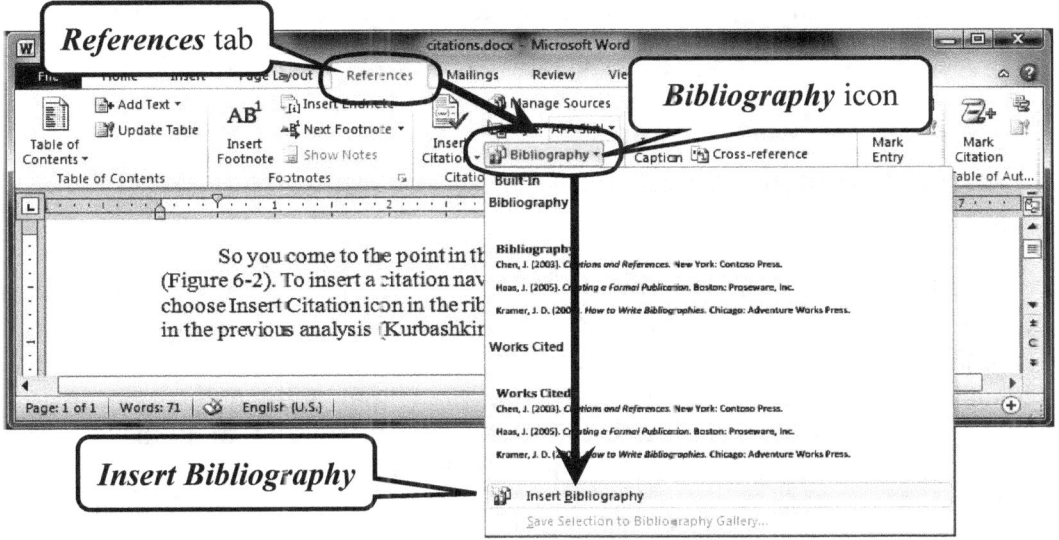

Figure 6-9: Inserting bibliography

6.2.4   Choosing Citation and Bibliography Styles

One great advantage of using the automated citation and bibliography creation described above is the flexibility of switching between a variety of citation and bibliography styles. To change a citation style, navigate to the **References** tab in the main menu and click on the **Style** icon in the ribbon (Figure 6-10).

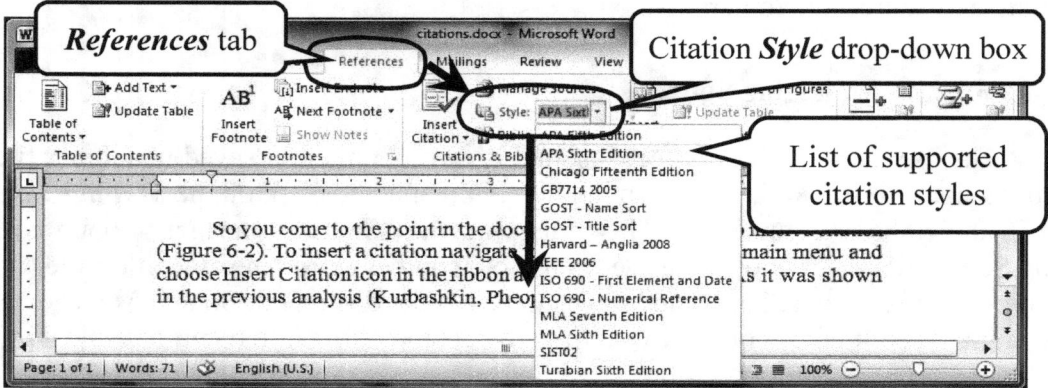

Figure 6-10: Changing citation and bibliography styles

Choose from a popup list a citation style you want to use in the document. Choose the citation and bibliography style you want to use from the popup list. As soon as the style is chosen, all citations and the bibliography will automatically change to that style. This is a great convenience, particularly if you suddenly learn that your publisher requires a style different than one you have used throughout the document. In this case, not a problem at all— just choose the right style and fix the problem with the click of a button.

6.3   Footnotes and Endnotes

6.3.1   Footnotes

Sometimes a citation is needed which does not fit into the main text, or you want the citation source to be easily seen on the same page where the citation is made. In such cases, a citation and its source can be added as a footnote similar to the one you see for this sentence. A footnote also can be used to make a comment about a certain part of the document, like the one you see for this sentence[4]. To insert a footnote, navigate to the **References** tab in the main menu and click on the **Insert Footnote** icon in the menu ribbon (Figure 6-11). A footnote mark appears at the position of the cursor and a space to write the footnote becomes available at the bottom of the page. Enter the source or comment in the footnote space as illustrated in Figure 6-11.

---

[4] The footnote is placed at the foot of the same page where the footnote citation is made.

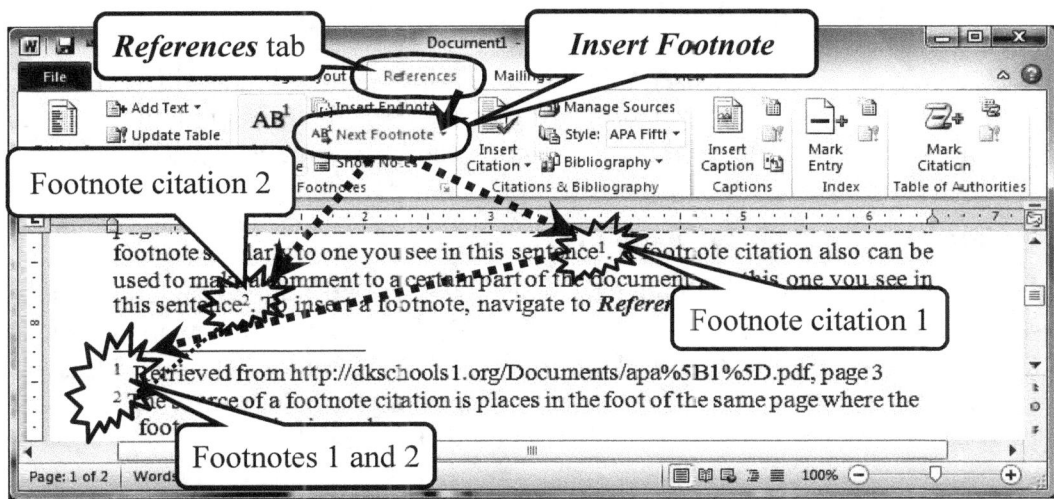

Figure 6-11: Inserting a footnote

6.3.2   Endnotes

Endnotes are similar to footnotes. The only difference is that all endnotes are located at the end of the document rather than on the same page where the footnote citation occurs in the document.

6.4   Index

An index is a list of keywords used in the document along with the page numbers where these keywords appear. Many books, large reports, and other documents have an index to help readers find keywords. A keyword may be a separate word, a combination of words, or a combination of symbols. The notion of an index is similar to the notion of table of contents in that it provides the reader with a quick way to locate information by topic.

- A *table of contents* is a list of major headings of the document with the appropriate pages. In other words, a table of contents helps navigate within the structure of the document.
- An *index* is a list of keywords in the document with the pages where these keywords occur. In other words, an index helps navigate within the keywords in the document.

6.4.1   Marking Index Entries

To create an index, the user first has to mark the entries that will be included in the index; each entry is a term or a keyword that the user identifies as important enough to be useful. Once the entries are marked an index can be automatically generated.

Marking Index Entries Manually

Suppose you want to include the word "style" in the index and that this word shows up on pages 8, 11, 14, 17, and 21. First find and select that word as shown in Figure 6-12. Then, navigate to the *References* tab in the main menu and click on the *Mark Entry* icon in the ribbon. This brings up the "Mark Index Entry" popup control with the selected keyword in the "Main Entry" field (Figure 6-12).

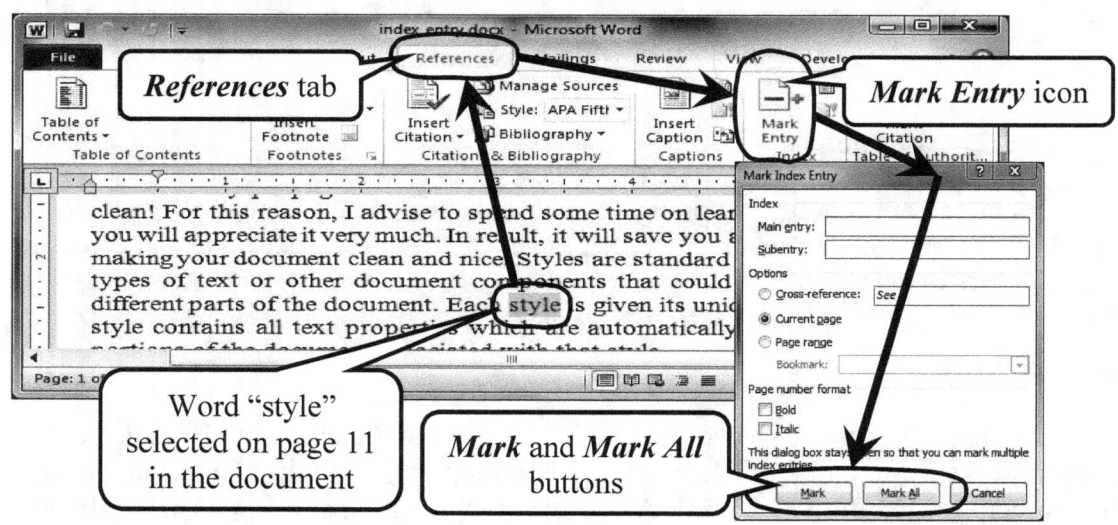

Figure 6-12: Marking an entry for the document index

Now you have two choices: to press either the *Mark* or *Mark All* button in the "Mark Index Entry" popup control.
- If you press the *Mark* button the index will show this particular entry only on that particular page where you selected it. In would mean page 11 in Figure 6-12.
- If you press the *Mark All* button, the index will scan the entire document for that particular keyword and show it along with all the page numbers where the keyword can be found in the document.

After the first index entry is marked you can go back to the document and select another entry. With each added entry you do not need to navigate to the *References* tab in the main menu and click on the *Mark Entry* icon in the ribbon. Once the term is selected, you just press the "Mark Index Entry" popup control (Figure 6-12) and mark the entry. You can continue marking new index entries without closing the "Mark Index Entry" popup control.

AutoMarking Index Entries

Instead of browsing the document and marking entries manually, you also have the option to create a separate file of keywords to include in the index. This separate text file could be a Microsoft Word file or a plain text (Notepad) file. All entries should be made one entry per line without punctuation and saved under any name you like. Suppose you list the following keywords in plain text file "index_entries.txt" as shown in Figure 6-13.

```
planet
satellite
star
orbital plane
```

Figure 6-13: An example of index entries stored in a separate file "index_entries.txt"

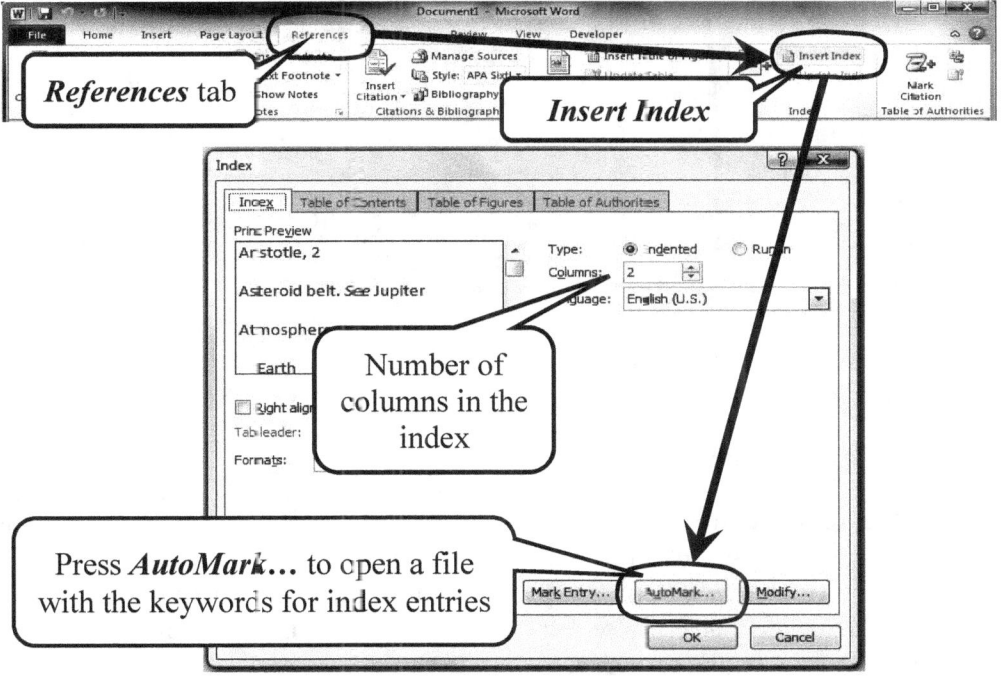

Figure 6-14: AutoMark index entries

The file should contain no symbols, nor words other than those keywords intended for the index.

To mark the keywords stored in a separate file, you have to use the ***AutoMarking*** option. To do so, navigate to the ***References*** tab in the main menu and press on the ***Insert Index*** icon from the Index group in the ribbon as shown in Figure 6-14.

This brings up the "Index" popup dialog box where you have to press on ***AutoMark …*** button (Figure 6-14). This brings up the "Open Index AutoMark File" box (Figure 6-15). Navigate in that box to the folder where the file is located, choose the file type you need and select the file to open. If you are not sure about the file type choose the option of ***All Files*** (*.*).

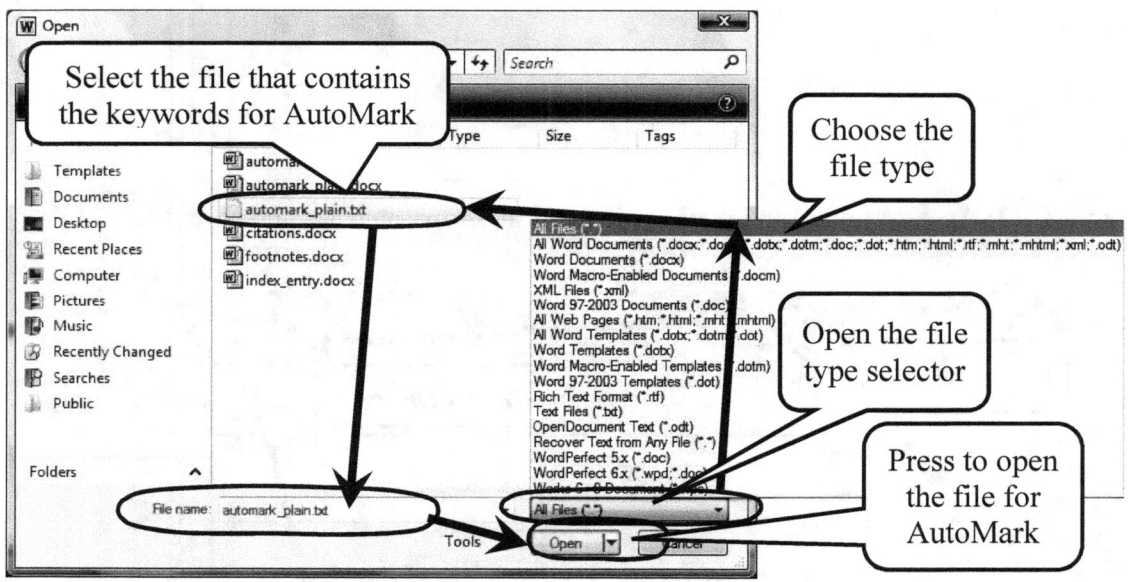

Figure 6-15: Opening a keyword file

6.4.2   Generating an Index

Once the index entries are marked as described above, you can generate the document index by navigating to the ***References*** tab in the main menu and pressing the ***Insert Index*** icon from the Index group in the ribbon as shown in Figure 6-16. This brings up the ***Index*** dialog box where you can choose options for the index (for example the number of columns) and press ***OK*** to generate the index (Figure 6-16).

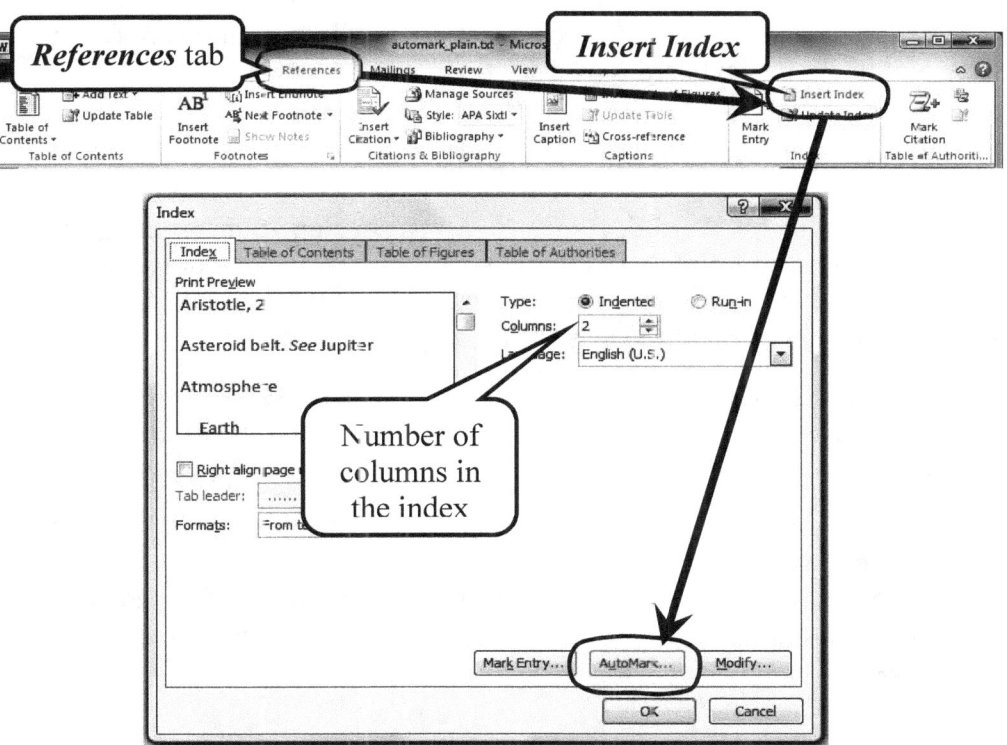

Figure 6-16: Inserting an index in the document

If you need to add new entries to the index, simply mark new entries as described above and illustrated in Figure 6-12 and update the existing index.

6.4.3   Updating an Index

As your document keeps evolving, its index will need to be updated because pages of the marked index entries may change, new entries may be marked, or some entries may have been removed. To update the index, select the index you would like to update, navigate to the *References* tab in the main menu and press on the *Update Index* icon from the Index group in the ribbon as shown in Figure 6-17.

Figure 6-17: Updating an index

You can update an index also selecting the index and simply pressing *F9* functional button on the keyboard.

6.5   Keeping Your Document Up-To-Date

As your Microsoft Word document is being developed, many things may get out of sync. Among them are outline numbering, figures, tables, equations, other numbered items, cross-references, table of contents, index, and many others. There are two ways to update your document to keep it in sync: local or global.

To update a feature or a number of features in your document (for example, figure numeration or a cross-reference) select the appropriate portion of the document and click F9 on the keyboard.

To update the entire document, including all features in it, select the entire document by pressing Ctrl-A on the keyboard and then F9. You will be asked if you want to update the entire table of contents or just the page numbers. It is recommended that you update the entire table of contents just in case. The entire document will be updated and all features will again be in sync.

Questions and Exercises

Questions

1.   Why is setting automated cross-referencing so important?
2.   How do you set automated cross-referencing?
3.   What is a citation?
4.   What is a bibliography?
5.   What is the difference between a bibliography and a citation?
6.   How do you insert a citation in a document?
7.   What is a citation style?
8.   How do you manage citation sources?
9.   How do you insert bibliography into the document?
10. How do you choose or change a citation style?
11. What is a footnote?
12. What is an endnote?
13. What is the difference between a bibliography and footnotes?
14. What is the difference between footnotes and endnotes?

15. How do you insert a footnote?
16. How do you insert an endnote?
17. What is a document index?
18. How do you mark index entries in a document?
19. How do you AutoMark index entries from a file with keywords?
20. How do you generate an index?
21. How do you update an index?
22. How do you update a document so that it is in sync?

Exercises

1. Write a document with several headings, figures, and tables. Then, set the heading structure and automated heading numbering and set captions for the figures and tables as described above in sub-chapters 4.5 and0of this book. Finally, make cross-references to certain headings, figures and tables in the document text.

2. Use the same document as developed for the previous exercise and insert citations of three sources and a bibliography using the technique discussed in section 6.2 .

3. Use the same document as developed for the previous exercise and insert footnotes and endnotes using the technique discussed in section 6.2 .

4. Use the same document as developed for the previous exercise and mark index entries and generate an index using the technique discussed in section 6.2 .

5. Use the same document as developed for the previous exercise and add an extra heading, remove the first figure, and add one table along with a caption placing it before the first table. These operations certainly make your document out of sync. Bring the document back in sync and update all features by using the technique discussed in section 6.5 .

7 Collaborative Document Development

7.1 Collaboration in Document Development

If you develop a document collaboratively with other people or review documents developed by someone else, it is helpful to be able to leave comments about parts of the document and to make changes in the document in such a way that they will be easily found reviewed, accepted or rejected by other participants. Microsoft Word provides functions for such operations.

7.2 Making and Deleting Comments

To insert a comment, select the portion of the text that you want to comment on, navigate to the ***Review*** tab and click on ***New Comment*** in the "Comments" section in the ribbon as shown in Figure 7-1. This brings up an area for a comment on the right-hand side of the document as shown in the same figure. Type your comment in the space provided.

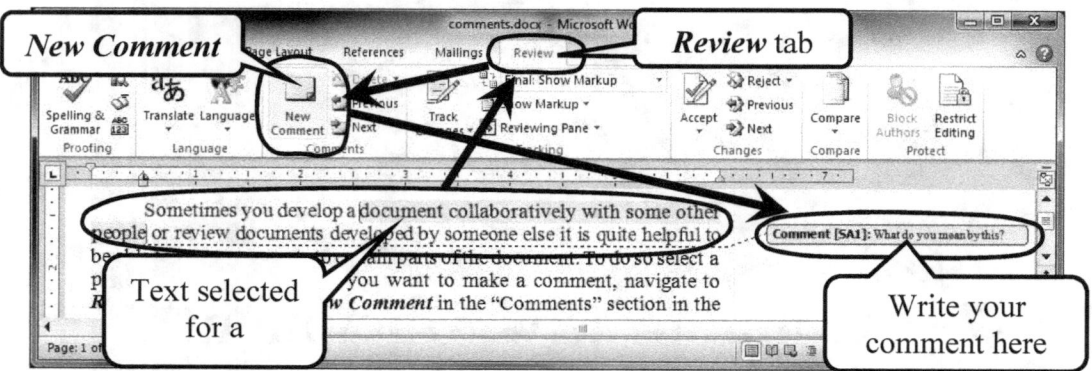

Figure 7-1: Inserting a comment

To edit a comment, simply click on the comment in the document and edit its text. To remove an existing comment, right click on the comment and choose **Delete Comment** option from the popup menu.

7.3   Tracking Changes in the Document

7.3.1   "Track Changes" Mode On/Off

In collaborative document development it is important to make changes in the document in such a way that the other party can easily find the changes, review them, and accept or reject them. This functionality is called "track changes". To turn the "track changes" mode on and off, navigate to the **Review** tab and click on the Track Changes icon in the "Tracking" group in the ribbon as shown in Figure 7-2.

Figure 7-2: Turning track changes mode on and off

It is important to turn the "track changes" mode off after the document review is complete to avoid occasional marks of this mode in the final document.

7.3.2   Making Changes in "Track Changes" Mode

Modify the document text and use formatting operations as you normally would.

The only difference you'll notice when using the Track Changes mode is that all the changes you make will be explicitly displayed in the document as shown in Figure 7-3.

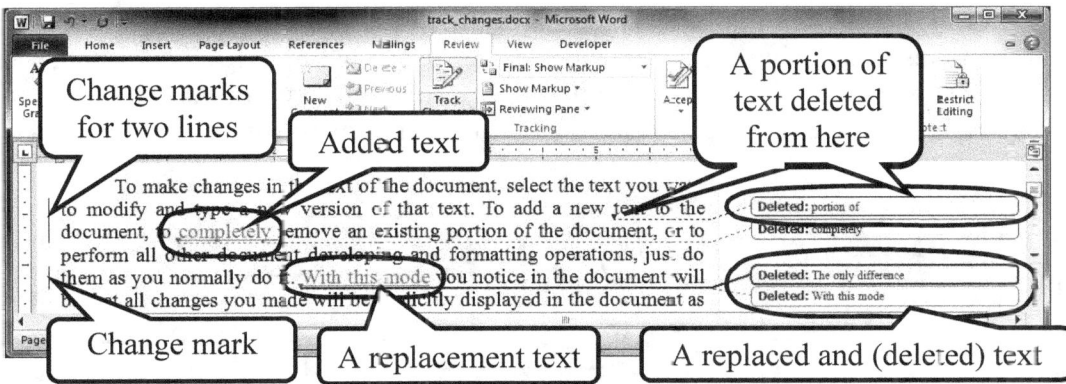

Figure 7-3: Working in the track changes mode with deleted text shown in balloons

In the track changes mode, each deleted portion of text is displayed on the right margin of the document and each added or modified portion of text is shown in a different color to the text to make it easily visible. Also each line of the document where any changes are made is marked by a change mark on the left margin of the document next to the appropriate line (Figure 7-3).

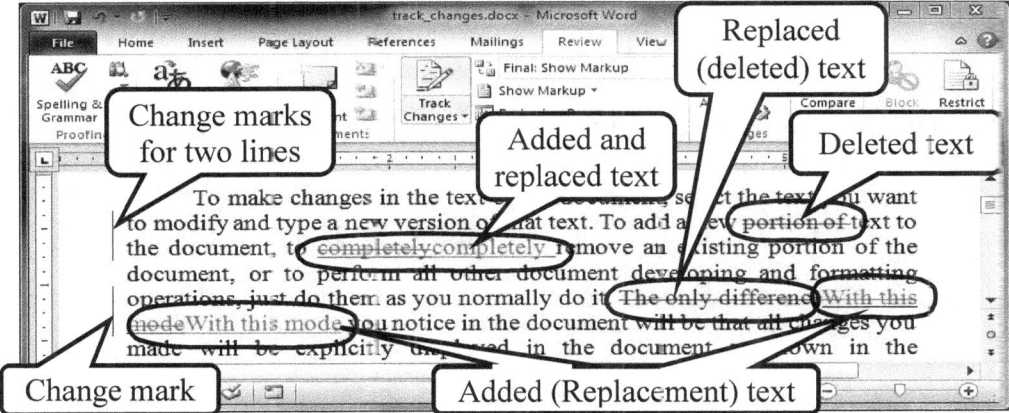

Figure 7-4: Working in the track changes mode with deleted text shown inline

7.3.3   Track Changes Options and Configuration

The user can control the track changes options and configuration by navigating to the **Review** tab in the main menu and using the appropriate option from the "Tracking" group (Figure 7-7). The user can also switch between different configurations at any time.

For example, the user may prefer to see the deleted text inline in the form of a strike-through text (Figure 7-4) rather than in balloons (Figure 7-3).

To switch between two configurations—for example, from showing the deleted text in balloons to showing it inline—the user has to navigate to the *Review* tab, then to *Show Markup* in the "Tracking" group in the ribbon, then to *Balloons* in the popup option menu, and finally select between these two options as illustrated in Figure 7-5.

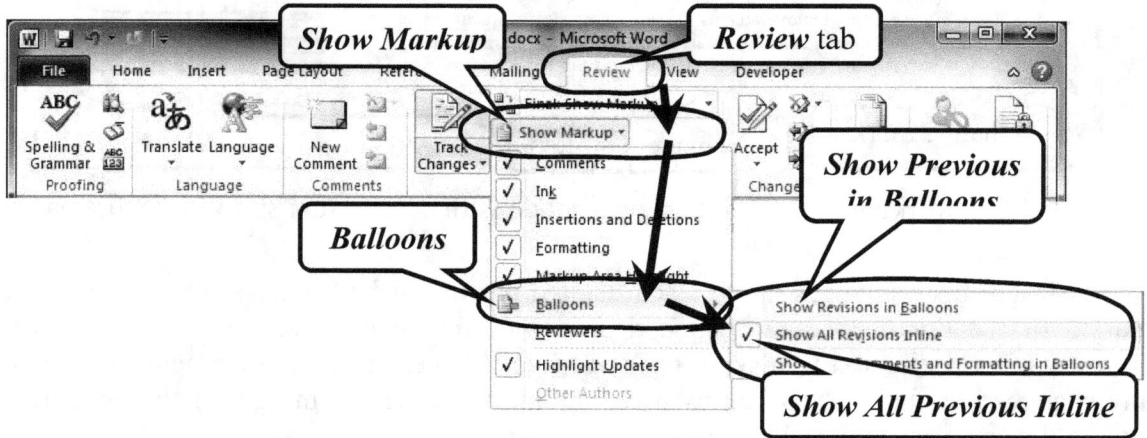

Figure 7-5: Configuration switch between "balloons" and "inline"

7.3.4   Accepting and Rejecting the Changes

Suppose you send a document to your colleague for review. Your colleague places comments, makes appropriate changes in the track changes mode, and sends it back to you. This edited version has your colleague's comments and corrections, which you can easily find because they are clearly identified in the track changes mode.

To review, delete existing, and make new comments follow the procedure described in section 7.2 above.

When you review each change made to your document, you can "accept change" if you like, otherwise you can "reject change" which will return this part of the document to its original form.

To find changes made to your document you can either locate them visually by scrolling through or use the automated search of changes feature shown in Figure 7-6. To find changes automatically, navigate to the *Review* tab and click on the *Next* or *Previous* options in the "Changes" group in the ribbon. This brings you to the next or previous change in the document.

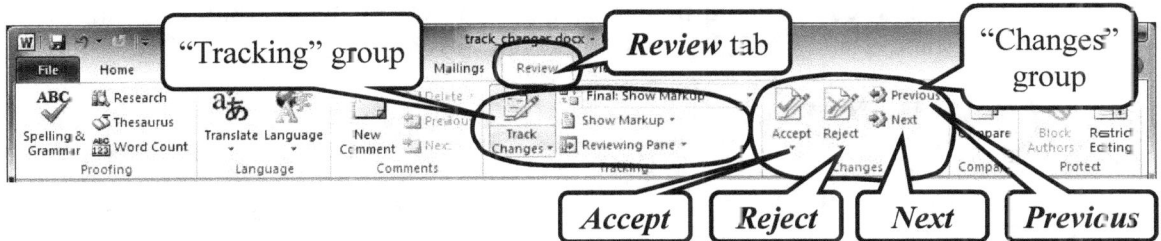

Figure 7-6: Track changes actions and options

To accept or reject the change you can either click on the icon **Accept** or **Reject** in the "Changes" group in the ribbon of the **Review** tab (Figure 7-6) or just right click on the appropriate change and choose the appropriate action **Accept…** or **Reject…** from the pop up menu (Figure 7-7).

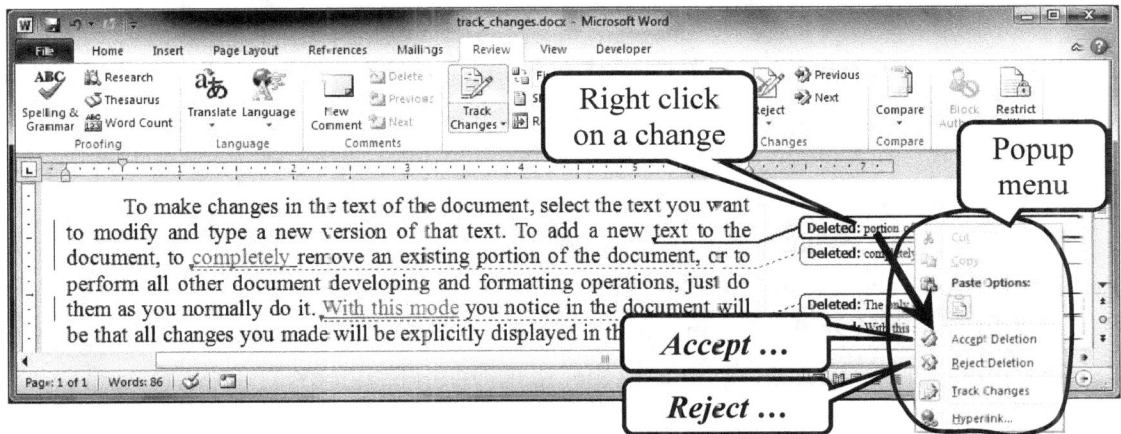

Figure 7-7: *Accept* or *Reject* changes

Accepting a change means that the change stays in the document and is no longer marked as a change. Rejecting a change means that the change is removed from the document without a track.

7.3.5   To Finalize the Document

When the document review is over you have to prepare the final version. It will look unprofessional to leave any tracks of past reviews in the final document.

To finalize your review and clean up the document, use option **Final** from the "Tracking" group in the ribbon of the **Review** tab as shown in Figure 7-8. Also, it would not be appropriate to submit your final document with the track changes mode turned on.

For this reason, it is recommended that you turn the track changes mode off in the final version as described in section 7.3.1 and illustrated in Figure 7-2 above.

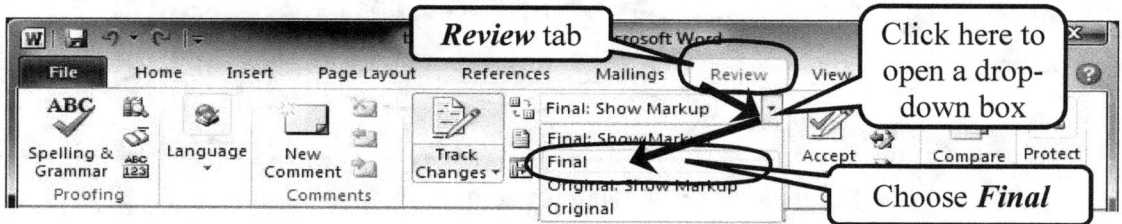

Figure 7-8: Setting the final version of the document

Questions and Exercises

Questions

1. How do you insert a comment in the document?
2. How do you delete a comment in the document?
3. What is the "track changes" mode?
4. How do you turn the track changes mode on / off?
5. How do you make changes in the document?
6. How do you accept or reject changes?
7. How do you finalize the document?
8. How do you use different options in the track changes mode?

Exercises

1. Use any Microsoft Word document and place comments in the document.
2. Use the same document, turn the track changes mode on, and make changes in the document. Accept some changes and reject some of them. Finalize the document by cleaning it up and turning the track changes mode off.

8   Document Templates

8.1   The Concept of Templates

Many documents you use in business or at home have similar or even identical layouts, differing only in their content. A couple of good examples are company letterhead and a fax cover page. Some companies and individuals use a specific design and layout for their stationary. In such cases, it is quite unproductive and time consuming to develop letterhead or a fax cover page from scratch every time you need. For this reason, one can develop and use a template that contains the preset design of the document. With templates the user has only to enter the unique content. In other words, a template is a preset framework for the document. In the case of a fax letter cover page, the unique content is the addressee name, addressee company name, mailing address, fax and phone number, date and number of pages in the fax, and a note.

Thus, you may develop and save an "empty" document that has a layout with default fonts and styles, and images and use this framework for writing all documents of this type. However, if you do this just by reusing the "empty" document or an old document, you must be careful not to save the new document and overwrite the framework document or you risk making unwanted changes to the framework of the "empty" document.

The concept of templates goes far beyond the simplistic definition and the usage given above. A template should be safe from occasional modifications and it has the potential to drive the user in the process of filling it out. Templates normally have a different file extension than actual documents. For example, in Microsoft Word 2010 templates have extension ".dotx" while actual documents have extension ".docx" to distinguish them.

To open a new document with a structure predefined in a template, the user may either click on the template in the file manager (file explorer) or use Word menu *File* ⟶ *New* and then choose the needed template. The newly opened document will look exactly like the template and will use all styles setup in the template, however, it will be a Word document rather than the template. So, when the user saves this document it will be saved as a new document and the template remains unchanged.

To create a template, the user has to follow a special procedure which is quite similar in the most word processing application; maybe different by just some minor details.

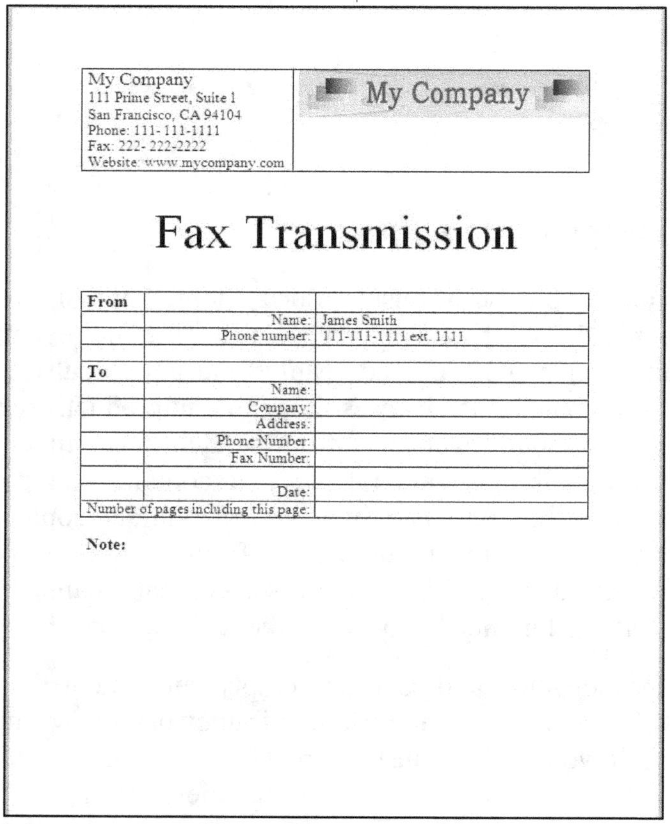

Figure 8-1: An initial fax cover page "empty" document with default text and images

In this chapter, we will go through the process and methodology of creating and using simple templates.

8.2   Creating a Simple Template

Let's create a template for a fax cover page. To create a template, open a new Word document and create an "empty" document that looks as you wish. Set all styles, work out the document layout and add all default text and images you would like in the document.

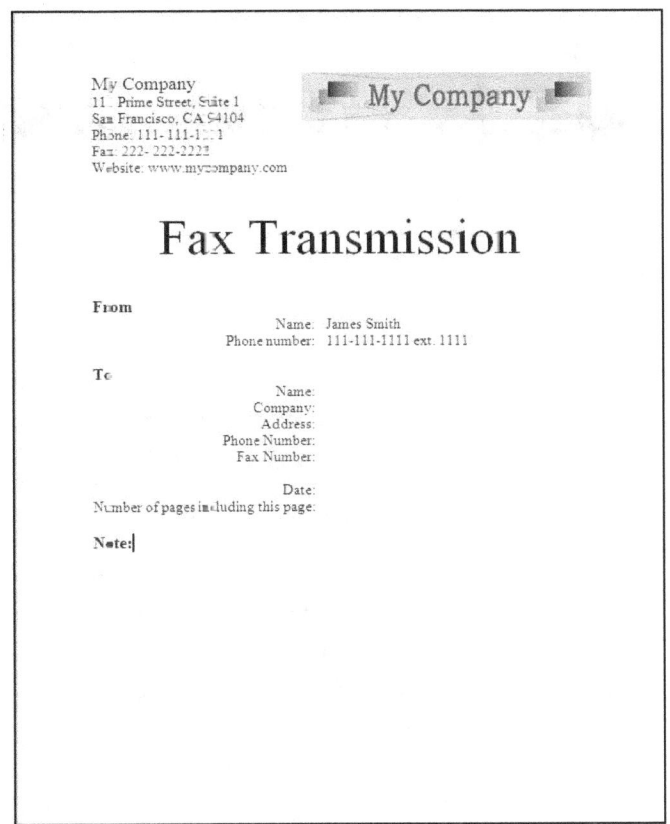

Figure 8-2: A fax cover page template without hints and adjusted information

Figure 8-1 shows an "empty" fax cover page for a company; it has default text and image. For the proper layout the document uses tables. The use of tables is advisable in this case to prevent the document layout from corrupting if any information is entered later that takes more space than a single line. Using tables prevents this situation and ensures that the layout is handled properly. In the actual "empty" document the table borders are removed to make the document look nicer. So let's remove the table borders from the "empty" document by selecting one table at a time, right clicking on the table, choosing "Borders and Shading" from the popup menu and removing the borders. This results in the "empty" document as shown in Figure 8-2.

To make a template from the "empty" document, the user has to save the document as a template. To do so, navigate to *File* $\rightarrow$ *Save As* and select the "Word Template (*.dotx)" option from the drop down box in the "Save as type" section as shown in Figure 8-3. Then navigate to the desired folder, enter the desired template name, and click the *OK* button to save the template.

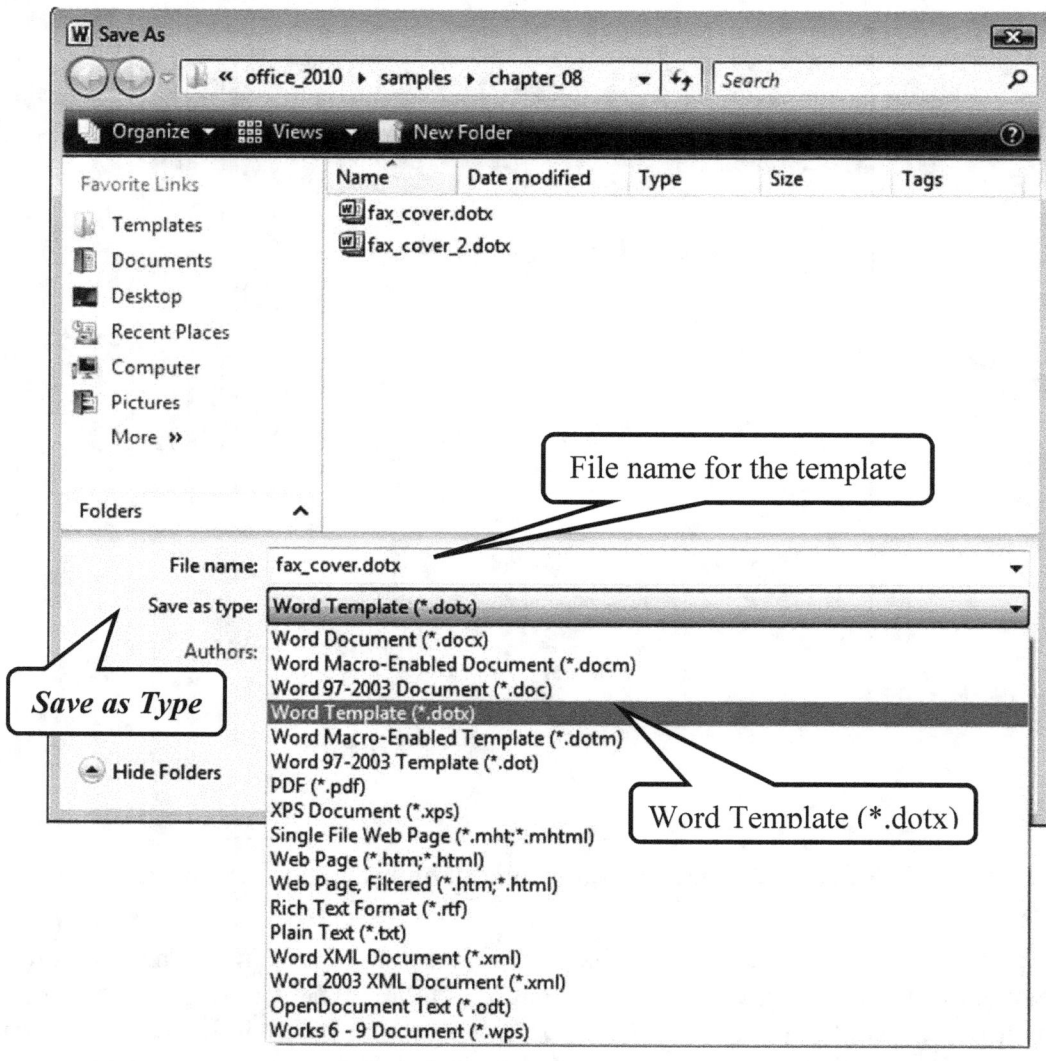

Figure 8-3: Saving document as a template

In result, when the user opens a template a Word document with a preset layout and content comes up, so the user just needs to add specific content to complete the document. With this technology, there is no way the user will change the template by mistake. If the user wants to change the template, the user has to go through the procedure described above in this section.

8.3 Creating a Template with Dynamic Information and Text Field Hints

8.3.1 Setting up Developer Menu Tab

The preset content in the template shown in Figure 8-2 is static; this means that whenever the user opens the template the preset content comes up the same, unchanged. To complete the document the user has only to add specific content to the document that was not preset in the template. It is clear that the addressee name, company name, address, phone and fax numbers, total number of pages in the fax, and notes differ from document to document and cannot be preset. However, the date in the fax cover page is normally the current date and could be automatically generated by the computer. It is also important to provide hints to the user so as not to forget to enter the addressee name, company name, address, phone and fax numbers, total number of pages in the fax, and notes.

To make this more advanced template takes a little more effort. First of all, you have to modify the main menu in Microsoft Word by adding the *Developer* tab to use the template development functionality. To do so, click on the *File* tab in the main menu and then select *Options*. In the *Word Options* dialog window check the *Developer* menu tab in the *Customize the* ribbon pane as show in Figure 8-4.

8.3.2 Inserting Current Date

To insert the current date function in a template, for example, in the fax cover page template (Figure 8-2), follow the instructions shown in Figure 8-5. Position the cursor where you want to insert that function, navigate to the *Insert* tab in the main menu, click on *Quick Parts* in the *Text* group of the ribbon, choose *Field* from the popup menu, select *Data* category from the *Field names* and select a desired format for the date in the *Fields* dialog window, and click the *OK* button.

The current date will now be displayed in the template. If you save this document as a template this functionality will be available for all documents opened from this template and the current date will be displayed in the specified position.

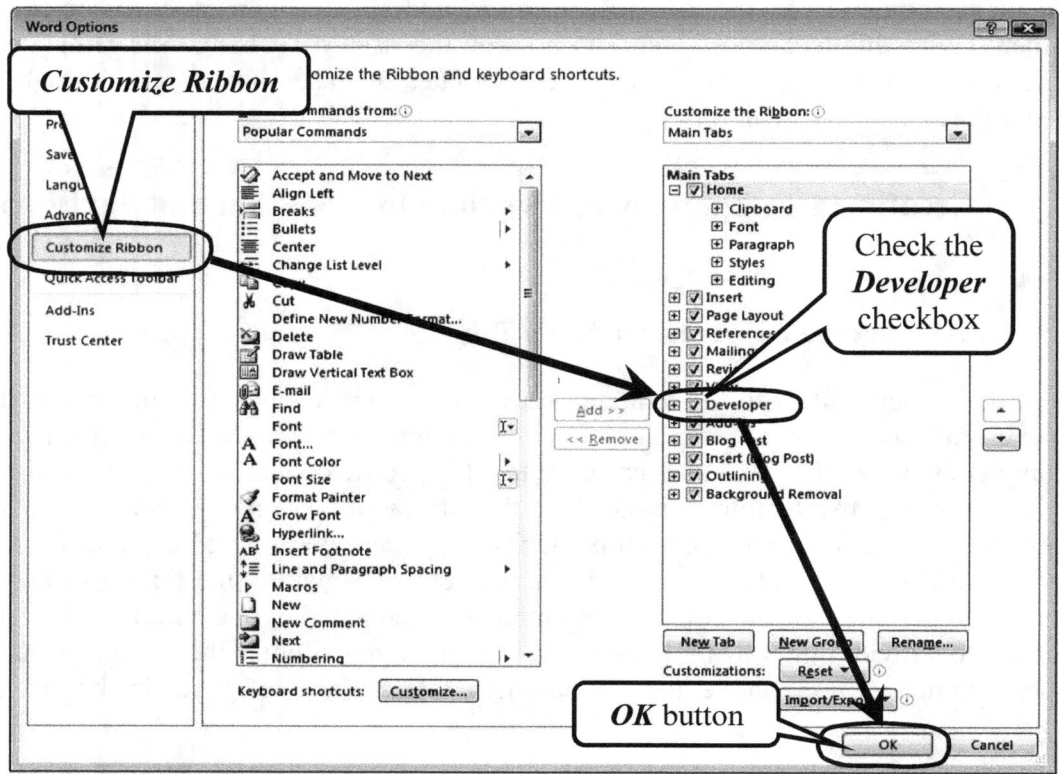

Figure 8-4: Adding *Developer* tab to the main menu

8.3.3   Showing Text Prompts in a Template

Some fields in a document may have quite unique content specific for each document, such as the fax cover page, which has the addressee name, company name, address, phone and fax numbers, total number of pages in the fax, and notes. This content is different for each fax transmission and for this reason cannot be hard coded in the template. However, it would be nice to provide prompts to the user about the type of content that needs to be entered into the document. For example, if the user sees "Click here to enter the addressee name" at the correct location in the document, it reminds the user that content should be entered in that field and also helps the user identify what type of content to enter.

To insert such a prompt, navigate to the *Developer* tab in the main menu and click on *Design Mode* in the *Controls* group of the ribbon as shown in Figure 8-6. When in this mode, place the cursor in the position where you want to insert the prompt and click on *Plan Text Content Control* from the *Controls* group of the ribbon in the *Developer* tab

(Figure 8-6). This action results in the prompt "Click here to enter text" being displayed in the position of the cursor as shown in Figure 8-6. The user can change the text of the prompt by clicking on this text and modifying it. For example, in the location where the addressee name should be entered it would be more appropriate to change the prompt to "Click here to enter the addressee name".

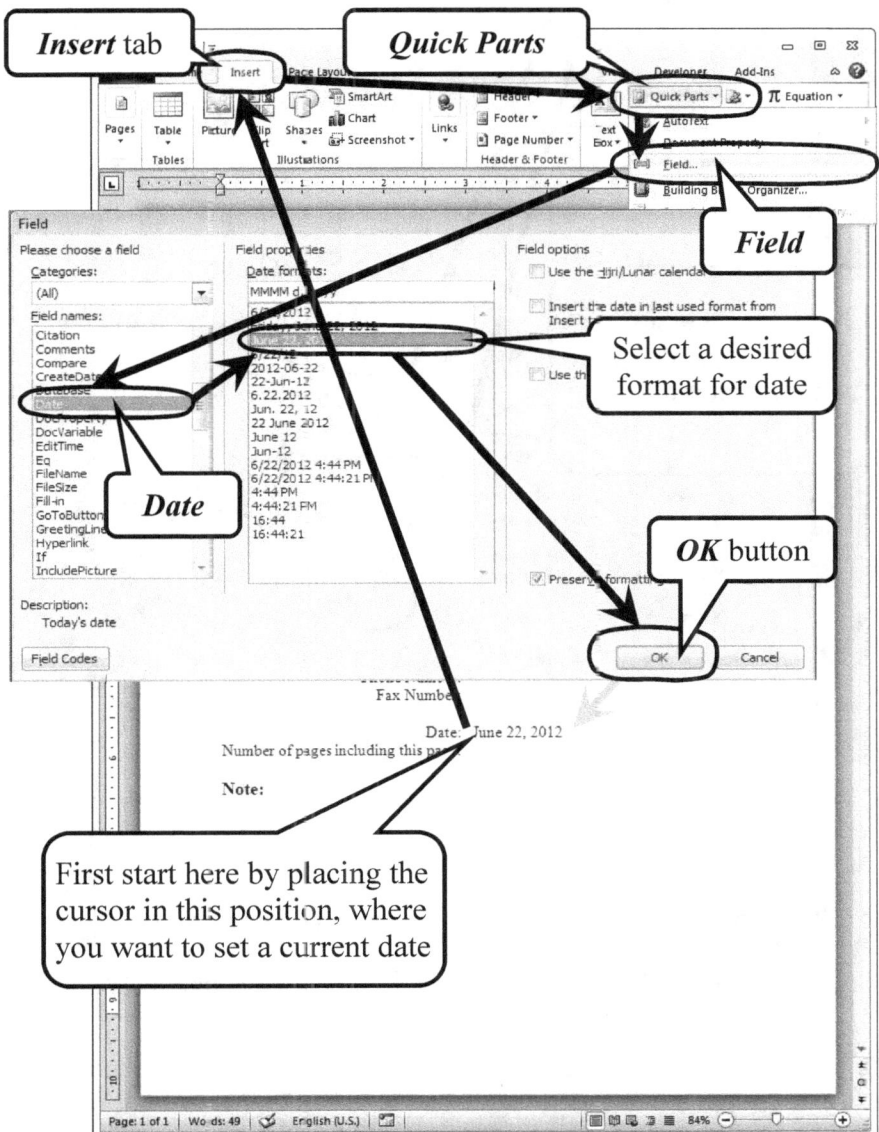

Figure 8-5: Adding a current date field to the fax cover page template

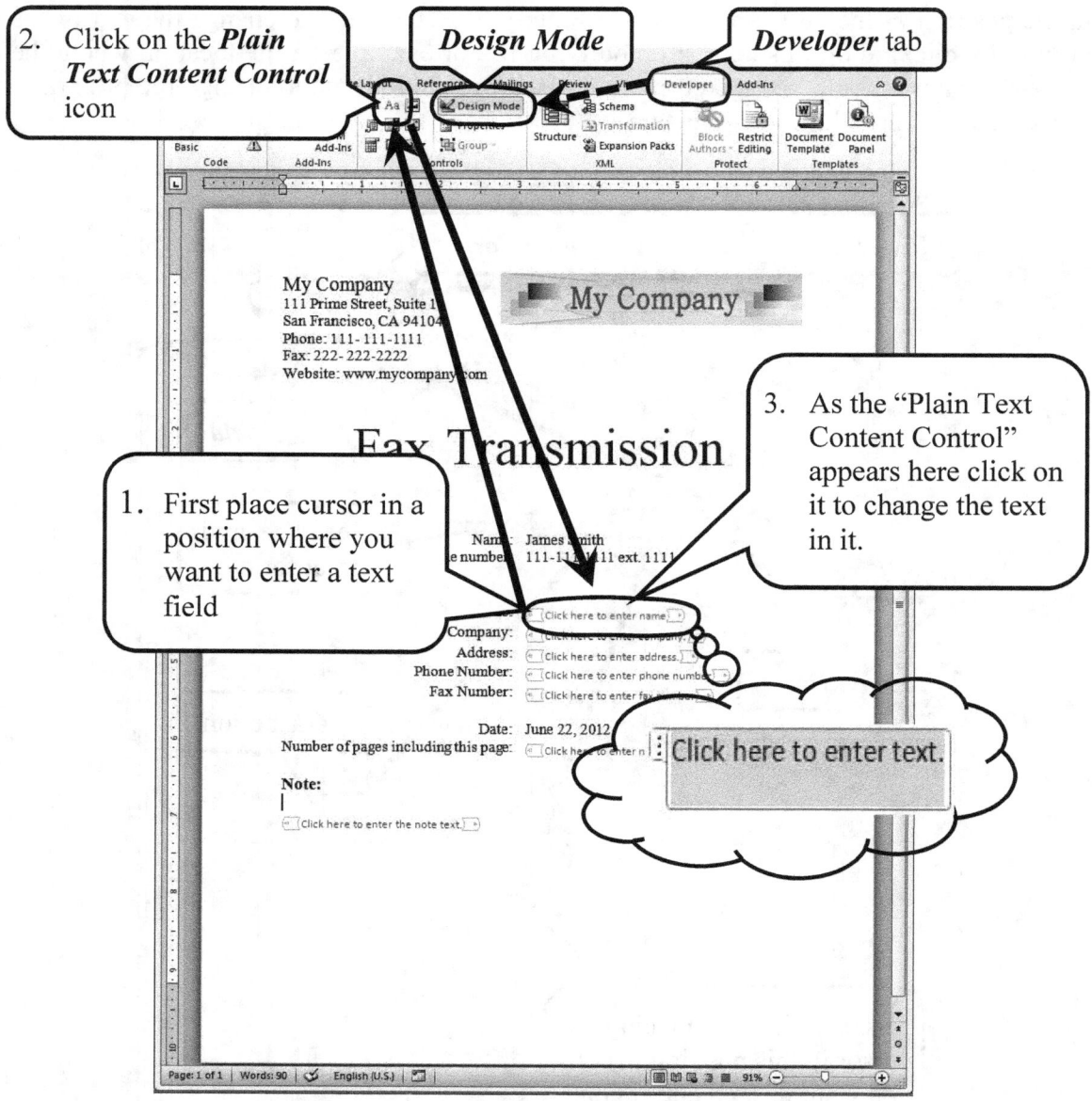

Figure 8-6: Adding text fields to the fax cover page template

As all prompts are inserted in the template and their content is modified as needed, the fax cover page template looks like Figure 8-7. Now go back to the ribbon and click again on the button **Design Mode**. This turns off the design mode.

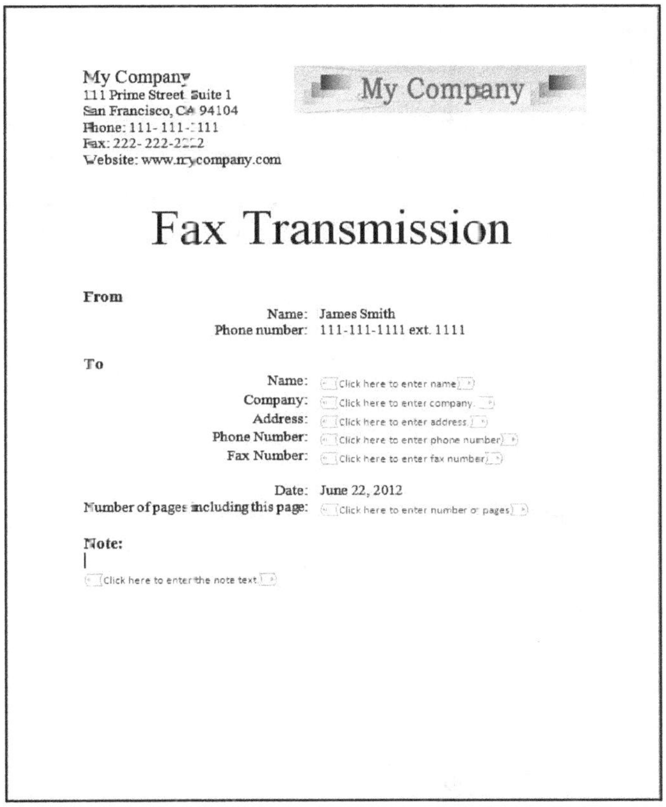
My Company
111 Prime Street Suite 1
San Francisco, CA 94104
Phone: 111-111-1111
Fax: 222-222-2222
Website: www.mycompany.com

My Company

Fax Transmission

From

Name: James Smith
Phone number: 111-111-1111 ext. 1111

To

Name: Click here to enter name.
Company: Click here to enter company.
Address: Click here to enter address.
Phone Number: Click here to enter phone number.
Fax Number: Click here to enter fax number.

Date: June 22, 2012
Number of pages including this page: Click here to enter number of pages.

Note:

Click here to enter the note text.

Figure 8-7: A fax cover page template with prompts and current date

As the template is ready, save it as a template in a convenient location on your computer as discussed in Section 8.2 and illustrated in Figure 8-3.

8.4 Using Templates

The user can open a Microsoft Word document from a template in a number of ways:

One way is to open a document from the exact location of the template that the user wants to use. To do so, the user should navigate to the folder where the template is stored and click on the template file name (*.dotx). This brings up a document that looks exactly like the template and uses the layout, formats, and styles used in the template. For example, if the user clicks on the fax cover template file, a document as shown in Figure 8-7 will open.

Another way is to open a document from a template chosen from the collection of templates associated with Microsoft Word. To do so, the user can navigate to the ***File*** tab in the main menu, then click on the *New* item in the submenu, and choose a desired template from the collection of templates.

Templates, their structure, and the development methods described in this chapter reveal only a small portion of template functionality. However, after working through this chapter hopefully the reader will be able to develop and use a variety of templates and accumulate enough knowledge to self-learn more sophisticated template technologies.

Questions and Exercises

Questions

1. What is a Microsoft Word template?
2. What advantage do templates offer?
3. How do you create a template from a document?
4. How do you save a template?
5. How do you show the Developer tab in the ribbon?
6. How do you set the current date in a template?
7. How do you set a prompt in a template?
8. How do you change prompt content?
9. How do you open a document from a template?

Exercises

1. Develop a template for a corporate letterhead.
2. Develop a template for a "Happy New Year" greeting letter.

9 Spreadsheets and Calculations

9.1 Introduction to Microsoft Excel

Microsoft Excel is the spreadsheet and calculation application of the Microsoft Office suite. Spreadsheet files created with Microsoft Excel have extension ".xlsx" for versions 2007 and 2010, and ".xls" 2003 and preceding versions. These two extensions imply differences in the internal structure of the documents, however files can be converted from one format into another if needed with some possible loss of formatting functionality.

This book addresses Microsoft Excel 2010 functionality. The structure of the user interface for Microsoft Excel is similar to that for Microsoft Word and is based on the concept of the **Ribbon** which was described in Chapter 4.

The main menu addresses major divisions of functionality and is accompanied by a group of related functions. Main menu items are referred to as *tabs*. For example, *Home* tab, *Insert* tab and so on as shown in Figure 9-1. Each tab (main menu item) corresponds to a submenu group of functions associated with it. Each group of such submenu functions is displayed on a panel below the main menu. This panel is referred to as a **Ribbon** and the group of functions displayed in the ribbon is specific to a tab. This means that switching a tab results in changes in the ribbon.

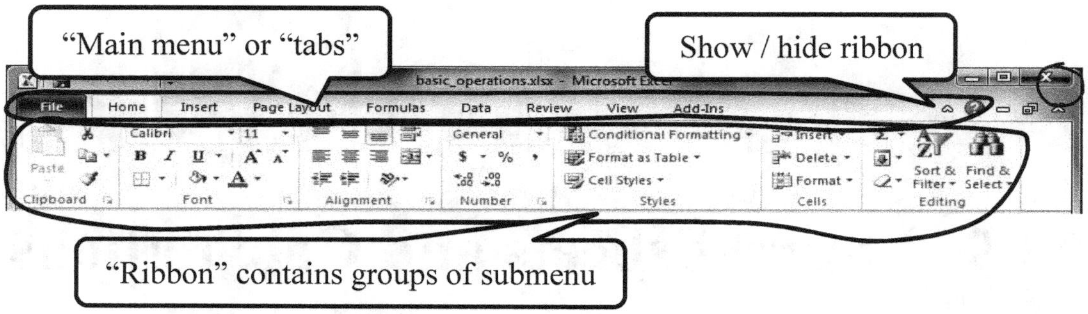

Figure 9-1: Tabs and ribbons

Users can show or hide the ribbon by pressing an icon indicated in Figure 9-1. Placing the cursor along a ribbon and scrolling causes sequential switching of the main menu tabs along with their ribbons.

In this book we presume that the reader is familiar with the elementary foundations of Microsoft Excel and that the reader knows how to perform calculations, use algebraic operations such as +, -, *, /, and ^, is familiar with some basic functions like sum, sqrt, exp, average, and others, and knows some other basic operations. Assuming this we will concentrate on the next level of proficiency in Microsoft Excel. In case the user is a very beginner, we recommend first learning the basic functions mentioned above before reading this chapter.

9.2   Cells and Basic Operations

9.2.1   Cell Address, Value and Operations

Every cell in Microsoft Excel has a formal address. For example, the selected cell in Figure 9-2 has address B5, which means column B and row 5 on the spreadsheet.

Every cell in Microsoft Excel has a value and an "Empty" cell is also a value. Please be aware that Microsoft Excel may treat values "Empty", " " (space), or "0" (zero) as the same value. A value could be entered in a cell explicitly as a constant, or in a form of expression that calculates the value from the values of some other cells. For example, textual values in cells A1, A3, A4, A5, B2, C2, D2 and E2 and numerical values in cells B3, C3, D3, B4, C4, and D4 (in the example shown in Figure 9-2 they were entered directly as they are). The values in cells E3, E4, B5, C5, D5, and E5 were entered in the form of expressions which calculate the appropriate values from the values of other cells as shown in Figure 9-2. For example, the formula (expression) in cell B5 is "=B3-B4" which means that the value of cell B6 is equal to the difference of values of cell B3 and B4.

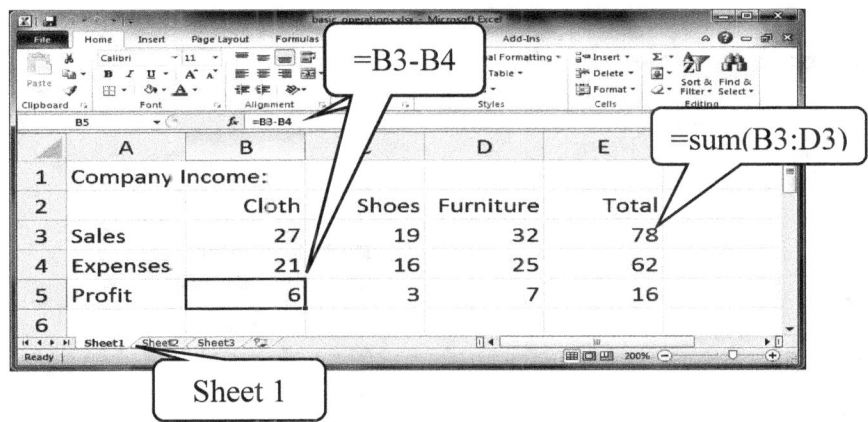

Figure 9-2: Microsoft Excel basic operations

9.2.2   Functions

The value in cell E3 (Figure 9-2) is equal to the sum of values of cells B3+C3+D3. Function sum(B3:D3) returns the sum of value of all cells in between B3 and D3. All expressions are supposed to start with symbol "=". You may start an expression with symbols "+" or "-" but it's better to start with "=" for consistency. Microsoft Excel has a broad variety of built-in functions covering many kinds of calculations. Among the most useful functions are average(), if(), sum(), sumif(), sumproduct(), count(), sqrt(), year(0), month(), day(), today(), and many others. You can use Microsoft Excel built-in help to find built-in functions that you need and learn how to use them.

9.2.3   Lists and Arrays

The user often needs to identify or set a list of cells on which an expression or a function acts. A list of cells can be set by a semicolon-separated list. For example, (A3; B1; B2; C1) means a list of cells which includes cells A3, B1, B2, and C1.

The term "array" in Microsoft Excel means a contiguous list of cells. For example, an array can be identified as (A1:A5) where the colon sign means A1 and A5 as well as all the cells in between, i.e. A1, A2, A3, A4, and A5. The list (A1:B5), as another example, includes A1, A2, A3, A4, A5, B1, B2, B3, B4, and B5.

9.2.4 Different Sheets of the Same File

The same Microsoft Excel file may contain multiple sheets as shown in Figure 9-3.

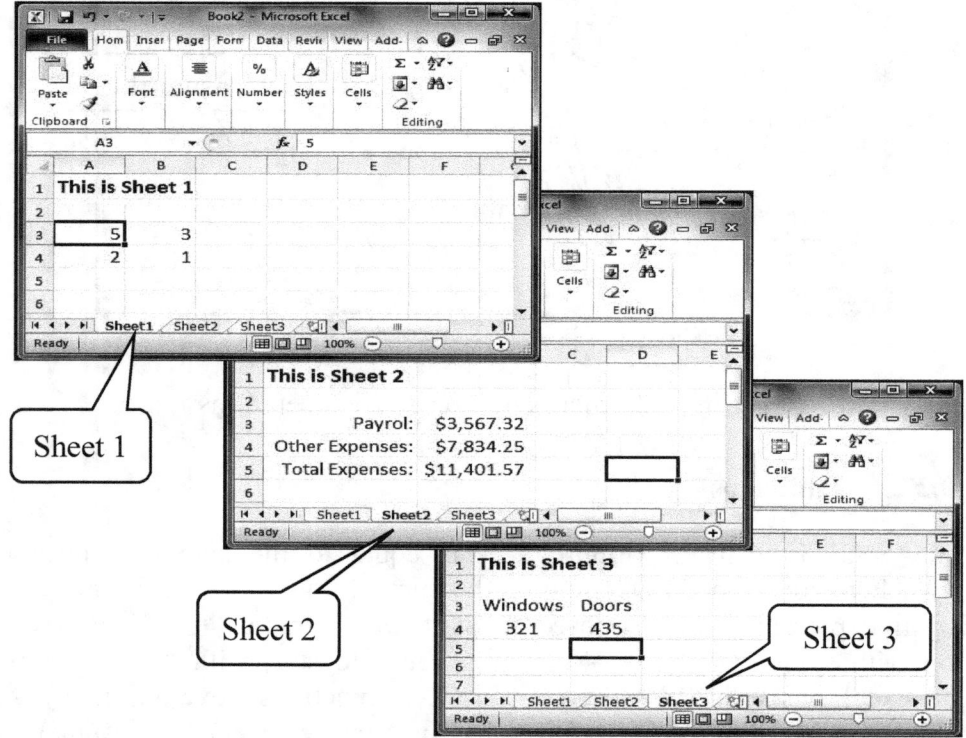

Figure 9-3: Different sheets in the same file

Each sheet has its own name and contains different information. By default sheets have names "Sheet1", "Sheet2", "Sheet3" (Figure 9-3) and so on. The user can rename sheets by right clicking on the sheet name, selecting **Rename** from the drop-down box, and typing a new name as shown in Figure 9-4.

Thus if the user wants to rename "Sheet2" to "Expenses", the user has to choose command **Rename** from the drop-down box and type "Expenses" on top of "Sheet2". The sheet name will then change to "Expenses" as shown in Figure 9-5.

The user can insert a new sheet or delete an existing sheet by using command **Insert** or **Delete** from the drop-down menu shown in Figure 9-5. The user also can click on the icon Insert to **Insert** (Figure 9-5) a new sheet.

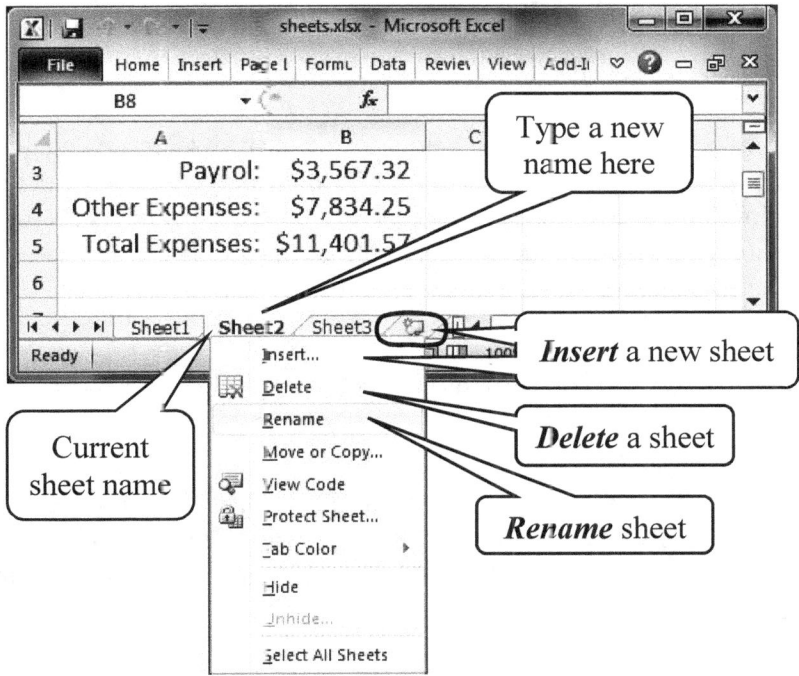

Figure 9-4: Renaming sheets

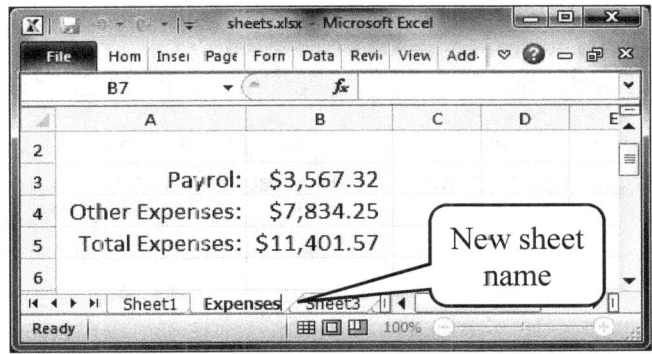

Figure 9-5: Renamed sheet

9.2.5   Global Cell Address

Microsoft Excel allows the user to operate with multiple sheets of the same file and also with sheets of different files. Every cell in such an environment has its own unique address. This unique address has the following structure:

'filepath\[filename]sheet_name'!local_cell_address

For example, suppose the user wants to place in a selected cell the value of cell B5 from sheet "Expenses" of file "sheets.xlsx" which is located in directory "company" on disk "D:". In this case "D:\company" is the path, "sheets.xlsx" is the file name, "Expenses" is the sheet name, and the local cell address is B5. Then the value should be referenced by the global address of the cell as

'D:\company\[sheets.xlsx]'!B5

If the cells referenced are within the same file, then the path and file name can be omitted in the address. If the cells referenced are within the same sheet then the path, file name, and sheet name can be omitted too. All this makes a good sense, so this rule should not be difficult to remember.

9.3   Copying and Moving Cell Content

9.3.1   Copying Content within one Sheet

The Copy-and-Paste procedure is commonly known. You can also use this technique to copy and paste the content of one cell to another cell or multiple cells.

Suppose you want to copy the content of cell C4 into cell E5. Right click on cell C4 and select *Copy* from the drop-down menu to copy it. An alternative way (or shortcut) to copy the content of cell C4 is to select cell C4 and press *Ctrl-C* on the keyboard. Once you've copied the content, move the cursor to cell E5 and right click on it and select *Paste* from the drop-down menu. This will paste the copied content of cell C4 to cell E5. The user will be offered different paste options, such as "paste the value", "paste the formula", and others. If the user chooses the "paste the value" option, then the exact value of cell C4 will be pasted into cell E5. If the user chooses to "paste the formula", then the formula in cell C4 will be copied into cell E5 and the value may change. Pressing *Ctrl-V* (the paste shortcut) on the keyboard will result in pasting the formula. The formula will be automatically modified by the offset between cells C4 and E5, i.e. the formula in E5 reflects the same relationship that C4 has with the cell addresses in its formula. Let's clarify the offset with the example shown in Figure 9-6.

Cell C4 contains formula =A1+B2 that results in a value of 3+5=8. The formula copied into cell E5 will be =C2+D3 to reflect the shift by two columns and one row between cells C4 and E5. Thus A1 and B2 in formula =A1+B2 in cell C4 turns into C2 and D3 in cell E5 (Figure 9-6).

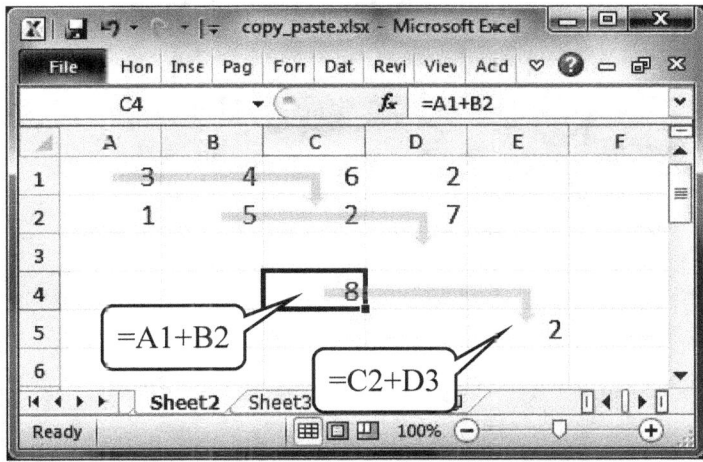

Figure 9-6: Copy-and-Paste

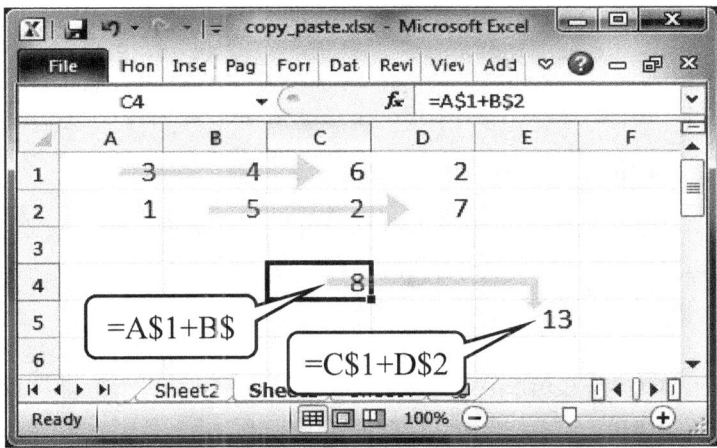

Figure 9-7: Copy-and-Paste without offset by rows

If the user does not want cell offsetting when copying, the appropriate part of the cell address in the formula should be marked with symbol $. For example, if cell C4 contains formula =A$1+B$2 and the cell content is copied to cell E5, the formula in cell E5 will be =C$1+D$2 because symbol $ is placed before the row numbers preventing offsetting the row. Likewise, since there is no symbol $ placed before the column letter, the offset by columns does take place as shown in Figure 9-7. For this reason the value calculated in cell E5 equals to 6+7=13.

To prevent all offsetting when copying, all address components have to be marked with symbol $ as shown in Figure 9-8. In this case both formulas in cells C4 and E5 are identical, i.e. =$A$1+$B$2.

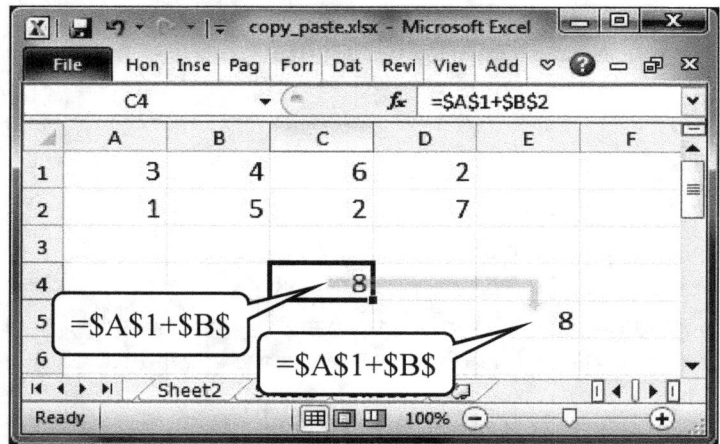

Figure 9-8: Copy-and-Paste without column and row offset

Controlling cell offset when copying cells is quite practical. Let's demonstrate it in examples.

9.3.2   Example 1: Profit Calculation

Suppose the user wants to calculate profit by year (Figure 9-9):
- The user enters year 2005 in cell A3 and enters formula =A3+1 into cell A4, making the value in cell A4 equal to 2006.
- Then the user copies the formula in cell A4 and pastes it into cell A5:A10. As is evident from Figure 9-9, the formulas are pasted with the appropriate offset by row resulting in a list of years in column A.
- The user enters values for the revenue and expenses by year in the appropriate cells (B3:C10)[5].
- The user enters formula =B3-C3 into cell D3 that leads cell D3 to show the difference between values of cells B3 and C3, i.e. profit.
- The user copies cells D3 and pastes it as a formula into cells D4:D10. In result, cell D4 contains formula = B4-C4, D5 contains formula = B5-C5, and

---

[5] Notation B3:C10 means an array of cells between cell B3 and C10 as defined in section 9.2.3 above.

so on (Figure 9-9), i.e. all copy-paste formulas are copied with an appropriate offset by row which was exactly the goal.

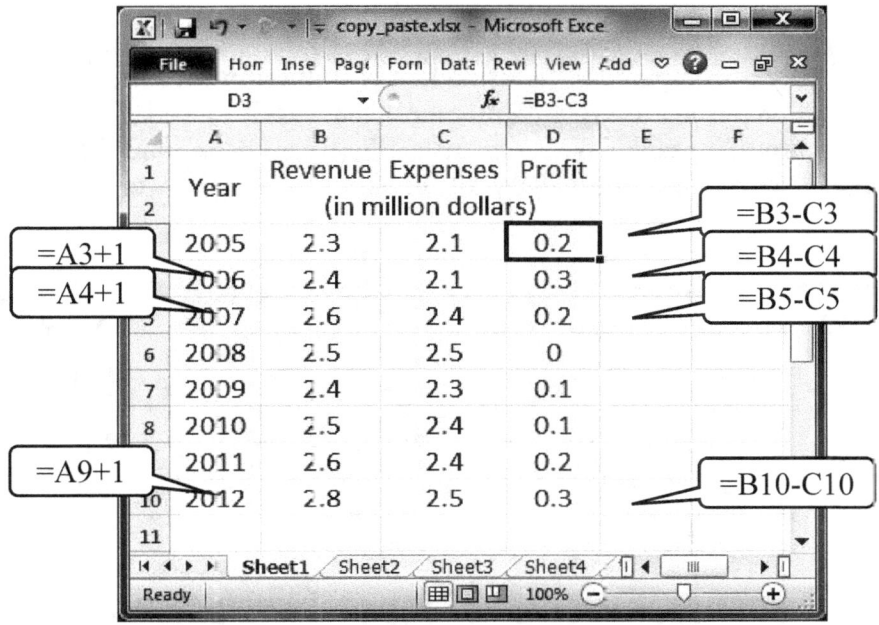

Figure 9-9: Copy and Paste

9.3.3   Example 2: Mortgage Calculation

Suppose the user wants to calculate a mortgage payment. We know that periodic mortgage payment is set in the form of annuity[6], which can be calculated as

$$A = PV / \sum_{m=1}^{nk} \left[1 / \left(1 + \frac{i}{k} \right)^m \right]$$ (9.1)

where A is the fixed periodic payment amount, PV is the present value or the borrowed amount, i is the annual interest rate, k is the number of payments and the number of compounding periods per year[7], and n is the total number of years to pay off the mortgage.

---

[6] Term annuity refers to periodic fixed payments on borrowed amount.
[7] We set this condition for the sake of simplicity. In the real world conditions compounding periods may be much shorter than payment periods

Consider a mortgage for three years with semiannual payments, i.e. six total payments, one made every six months. The borrowed amount is $10,000 and the annual interest rate is 7% compounding monthly. Thus in this case $PV = 10,000$, $i = 7\%$, $k = 12$, and $n = 3$.

First of all, let's prepare the fields and enter initial information into a spreadsheet as shown in Figure 9-10. We type "Mortgage Calculator" in cell A1 and make other entries in the appropriate cells. We align cells B2, B3, B4, F3, and F4 to the right by using the ***Align Right*** icon in the ***Ribbon*** of the ***Home*** tab. This is only done so that the document has a nicer look and feel.

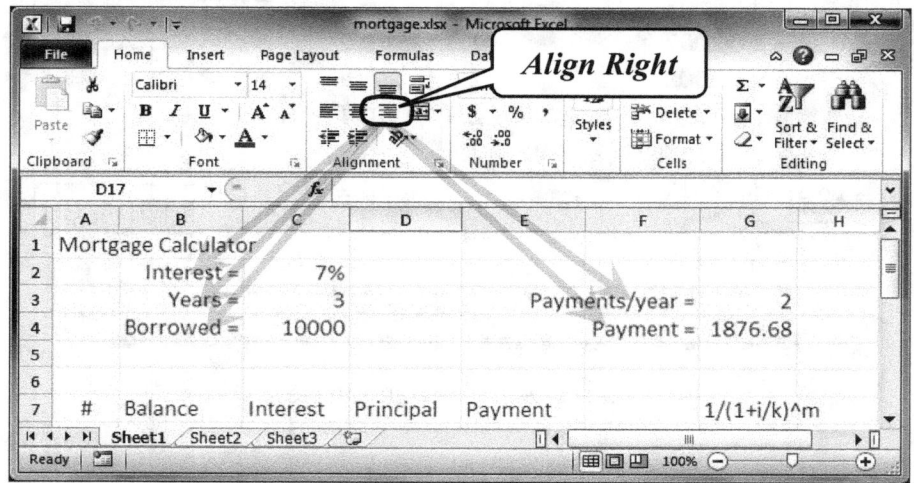

Figure 9-10: Mortgage calculator – Step 1: initial preparation of the spreadsheet

As the initial layout is done and initial information is entered, we make the following entries (Table 9-1 and Figure 9-11):

Table 9-1: Entries in the spreadsheet

Cell	Entry
A8	1
A9	=A8+1
G8	=1/(1+C$2/G$3)^A8
G4	=C4/SUM(G8:G13)

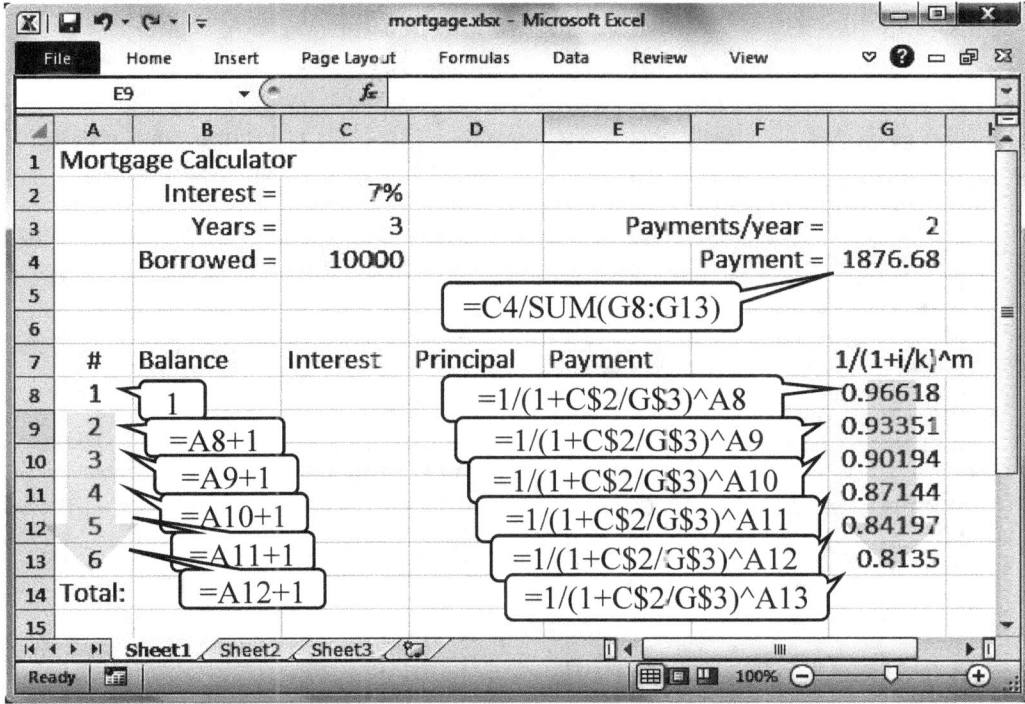

Figure 9-11: Mortgage calculator – Step 2

Calculating the mortgage (annuity) payment

We will use Equation (9.1) to calculate the mortgage (annuity) payment. The equation contains the sum by the number of payments. We set a pivot array G8:G13 for the appropriate components of the sum. To calculate the first component we enter =1/(1+C$2/G$3)^A8 into cell G8. Then we copy this formula to cells G9:G13 (Figure 9-11). Note that the copied formulas do not show offset for the parts which have "$" as explained previously.

As the components of the sum for Equation (9.1) are calculated in cells G8 G13, the annuity payment can be calculated using Equation (9.1) by entering formula =C4/SUM(G8:G13) in cell G4 as shown in Figure 9-11.

Calculating interest, principal payments, balances, and totals

As the annuity payment amount is calculated, we can calculate the portions of the payment that go toward paying interest (cells C8:C13 in Figure 9-12) and principal (cells D8:D13 in Figure 9-12). By knowing the principal payment we can calculate the appropriate balance changes (cells B8:B13 in Figure 9-12). The appropriate formulas and the copying paths are shown in Figure 9-12. First we enter appropriate formulas in cells

B8, C8, D8, E8 and B9 as shown in Figure 9-12. Then we copy cell B9 into array B10:B14, cell C8 into array C9:C13, cell D8 into array D9:D13, and cell E8 into array E9:E13. After that we calculate the total interest payment by entering =SUM(C8:C13) into cell C14 as show in Figure 9-12. To calculate the total principal payment and total payments we copy cell C14 into array D14:E14, which will be copied with the appropriate offset shown in Figure 9-12.

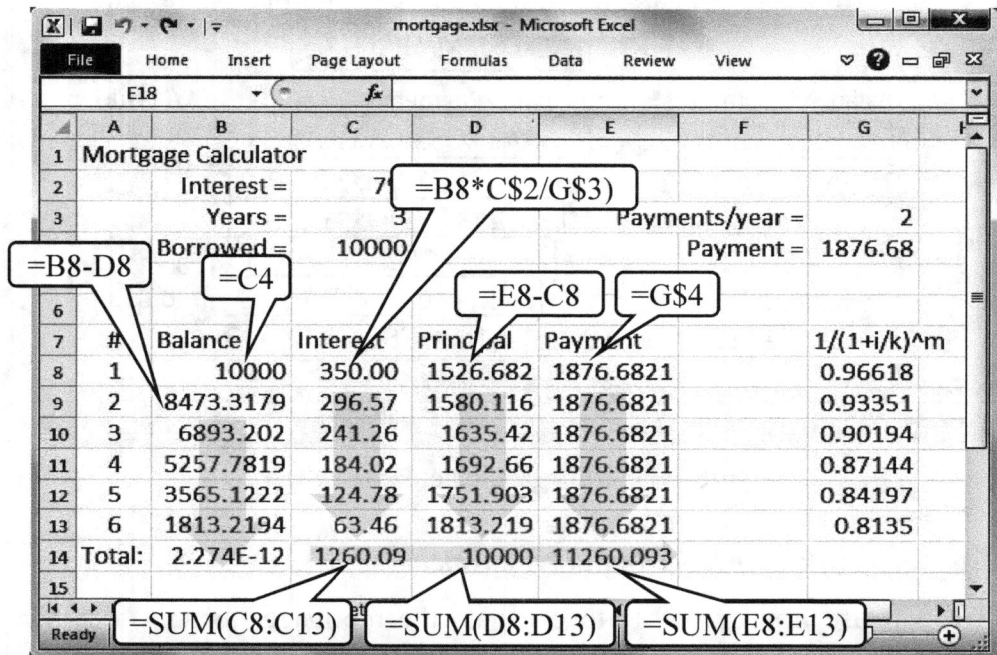

Figure 9-12: Mortgage calculator

Thus we have calculated all details of the mortgage set forth in the beginning of this example. If some numbers in Figure 9-12 looks strangely formatted to you—for example, the amount in cell B9 is calculated up to the hundredth fraction of a cent—we address this issue in section 9.4 .

9.3.4   Moving Content within one Sheet

As we discussed in the previous section, copying formulas from one cell to another (or to an array of cells) leads to the appropriate shift offset of the formulas unless the mark "$" is entered to prevent the offset.

If we move the content of a cell (or cells) using *Cut-and-Paste* or by just selecting a cell (or cells) and dragging it (them) to another location in the sheet, no offset will result from this operation. The hot key for **Cut** is ***Ctrl-X***.

9.4   Document Formatting

Documents developed with Microsoft Excel can be formatted to look nice and logical.

9.4.1   Data Types and Formats

As we can see from our exercise on mortgage calculation in Figure 9-12, the document may use some formatting to look nicer and be more logical. For example, the amounts in cells B8:E14 look strange when they have different numbers of digits after the decimal point. It looks even stranger when we see the amount calculated up to the fraction of a cent (Figure 9-12). This occurs because all the numbers were calculated in the general format and shown with as much accuracy as fits in the physical length of the appropriate cell.

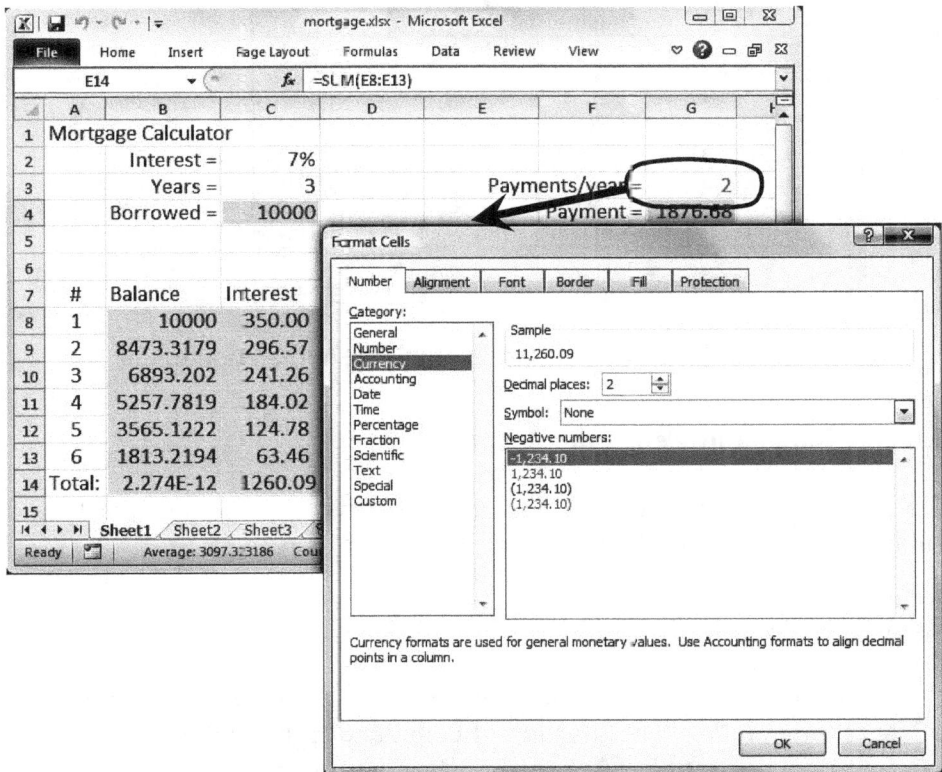

Figure 9-13: Setting up data types and formats

To address this issue, the user can control and change data types and formats. To change data format, the user right clicks on the selected cell or group of cells to bring up a "Format Cells" popup control, then chooses the **Number** tab in the control with the desired data type and format as shown in Figure 9-13.

The basic procedure of setting data types and formats is quite intuitive, so you will easily figure it out after a couple of minutes of "playing" with this feature.

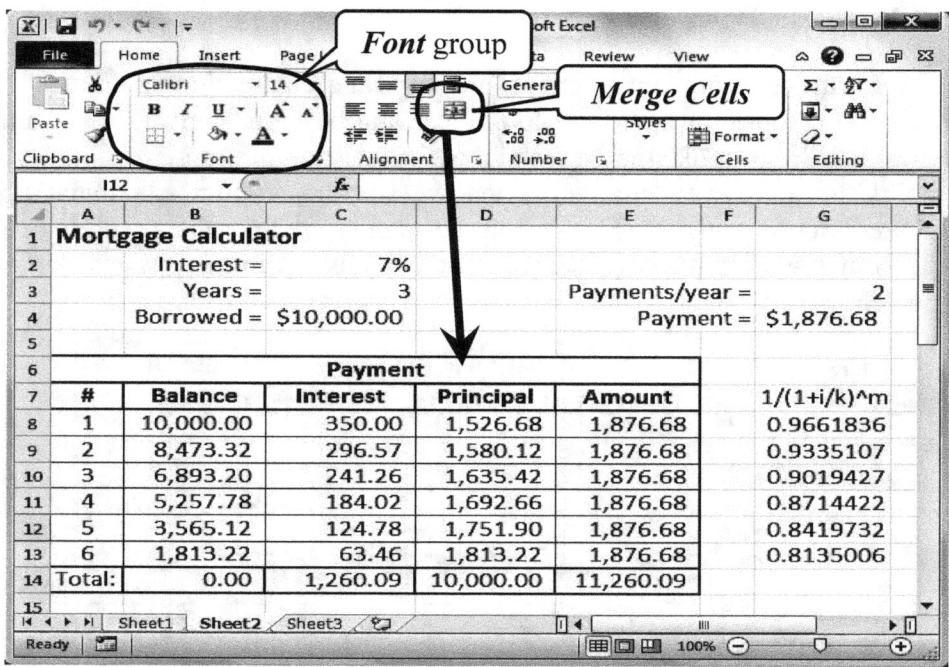

Figure 9-14: Mortgage calculator – formatted document

9.4.2   Fonts and Cells Fill

The user can set up font face, size, and color with the help of the features in the Font group in the ribbon of the **Home** tab as shown in Figure 9-14.

9.4.3   Borders

The table in Figure 9-12 would look better if it had distinct borders. To set up borders select the area on a sheet (a group of cells) and right click on it. This brings up a "Format Cells" popup control. Choose the **Border** tab in the control and set up the borders as shown in Figure 9-15. This procedure is very intuitive, so you will learn it virtually in no time.

9.4.4   Cells Merging

In the process of formatting, we want to place the common category "Payment" above all categories defined in A7:E7 of the table in Figure 9-14. To do this we can merge cells A6:E6. To merge cells, the user has to select the cells and click on the icon *Merge Cells* as shown in Figure 9-14. To unmerge cells the user has to select the merged cell and click on the icon *Merge Cells* again.

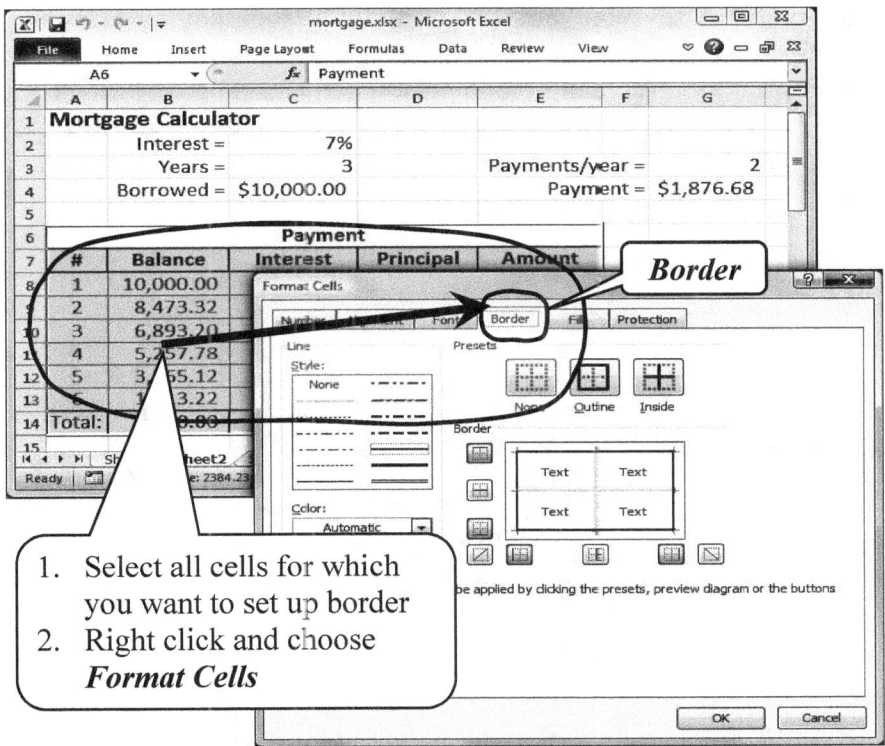

Figure 9-15: Setting up cell borders

9.5   Copying and Linking Content between Different Sheets and Files

The user can copy a cell within a sheet, between sheets of the same file, and also between different Microsoft Excel files. This functionality allows users to develop interacting and linked documents. For example, you have one Excel file which tracks your stock market operations and balances and another file which tracks your personal finances including balances from the stock market. If you link the stock market balance in your personal finance file with the balance in your stock market file, the stock market balance in the personal finance file will automatically updated whenever you make changes to the balance in your stock market file.

To copy the content of a cell to another location, select the location where you want to copy it and press the equal sign on the keyboard. The equal sign always indicates the beginning of a formula. Then go to the file and sheet from where you want to copy, place the cursor on the appropriate cell and *Left Click* (or *Enter*). This operation places an equal sign in the destination cell followed by the absolute address of the original cell.

For example, let's say you want to link the mortgage payment amount from cell G4 in file "mortgage.xlsx" in Figure 9-12 with cell B4 from the Microsoft Excel file "personal_finance.xlsx" that contains your personal finances as shown in Figure 9-16. First, you enter the equal sign into cell B5 in file "personal_finance.xlsx" as shown in Figure 9-16, then you *Left Click* (or *Enter*) on cell G4 in file "mortgage.xlsx" to which you want to link.

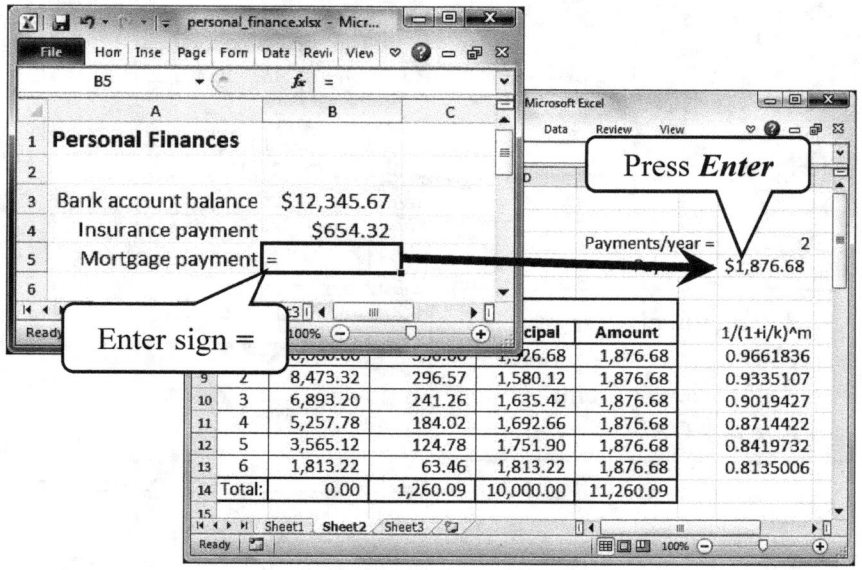

Figure 9-16: Linking cells in different sheet and files

In result of this operation, cell B4 in file "personal_finance.xlsx" contains formula equal sign and the full address of cell G4 from file "mortgage.xlsx" and looks like

$$=[mortgage.xlsx]Sheet2!\$G\$4$$

as shown in Figure 9-17. This formula copies the value written in cell G4 of Sheet 2 of file "mortgage.xlsx" to the cell B4 of Sheet 1 of file "personal.finance.xlsx". Thus, both values in both linked cells are $1,879.85.

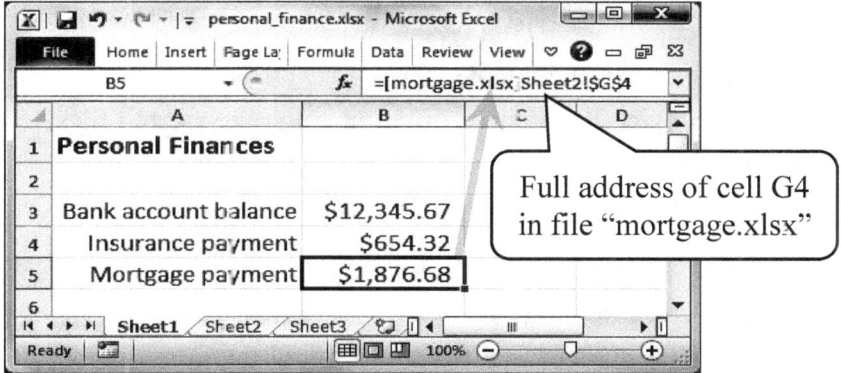

Figure 9-17: Linked cell

If the value in cell G4 of Sheet 2 of file "mortgage.xlsx" changes, then the value in cell B4 of Sheet 1 of file "personal.finance.xlsx" will be updated too.

Questions and Exercises

Questions

1. What is the format of the full address of a cell in Microsoft Excel?
2. What is the cell address from the same sheet?
3. What is the cell address from a different sheet of the same file?
4. What is the cell address from a different Microsoft Excel file?
5. What is the value of a cell?
6. How do you insert an operation into a cell?
7. What is an array in Microsoft Excel and how do you define it?
8. What is a function in Microsoft Excel?
9. How do you use functions in Microsoft Excel?
10. How do you find the function you need?
11. How do you copy cell content?
12. What kind of address offset occurs when copying cell content?
13. What is the practical purpose of the cell address offset in copying?
14. How do you use the cell address offset?
15. How do you prevent the cell address offset?

16. What is the data type in Microsoft Excel?

17. How many data types in Microsoft Excel do you know?

18. How do you set or change data type?

19. How do you format cell content?

20. How do you copy cell content to different cells, sheets, and files?

21. How do you link cell content in different sheets and files?

Exercises

1   Develop an invoice document.

2   Make a couple of invoices in different sheets of the same file.

3   Develop another Microsoft Excel document that summarizes the invoices and link the invoice amounts to that document.

10 Charts

10.1   Inserting a Chart

Microsoft Excel offers advanced functionality for creating graphs and charts. Suppose the user developed a Microsoft Excel sheet with sales data and wants to create a chart illustrating this data as shown in Figure 10-1.

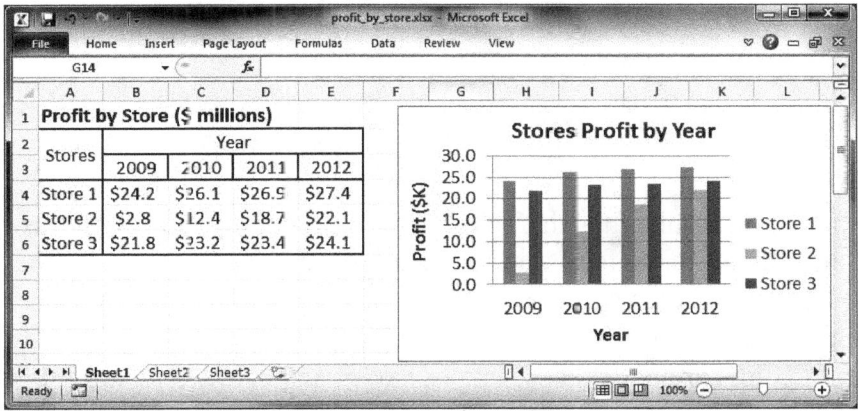

Figure 10-1: Store profit by year

There are several ways of inserting a chart. Let's build a chart from data. First of all let's select the arrays of data which we want to show in the chart. In the case of the table in Figure 10-1 this array is B4:E6. Navigate to the *Insert* tab in the main menu, then click on the chart icon in the *Charts* group of the ribbon, and select the type of chart you wish to use (Figure 10-2).

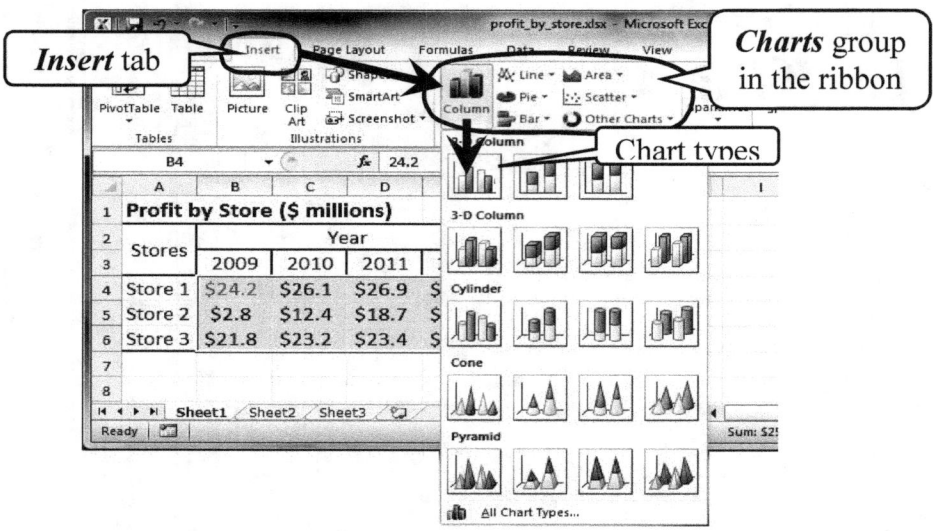

Figure 10-2: Inserting a chart

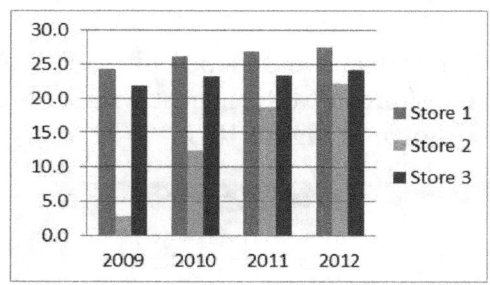

Figure 10-3: Initially generated chart

This operation results in a chart as shown in Figure 10-3. Though this chart shows the data, it is not yet complete for a number of reasons:

- the horizontal axis shows numbers 1, 2, 3, and 4 instead of years
- some strange legends such as "series" are shown in the right part of the chart
- chart colors are not exactly what we want and could be confused in gray scale printing
- the chart contains neither title, nor axis legends

- many other things we may want to change to make the chart exactly as we want.

We can fix all these problems and make the chart exactly as we wish by adjusting its layout and format.

You may also insert an empty chart without first selecting the data. In this case you have to build the chart from scratch in exactly the same way as you adjust its layout and format.

10.2   The Layout and Format of a Chart

A chart has different elements. The major elements of a chart are shown in Figure 10-4.

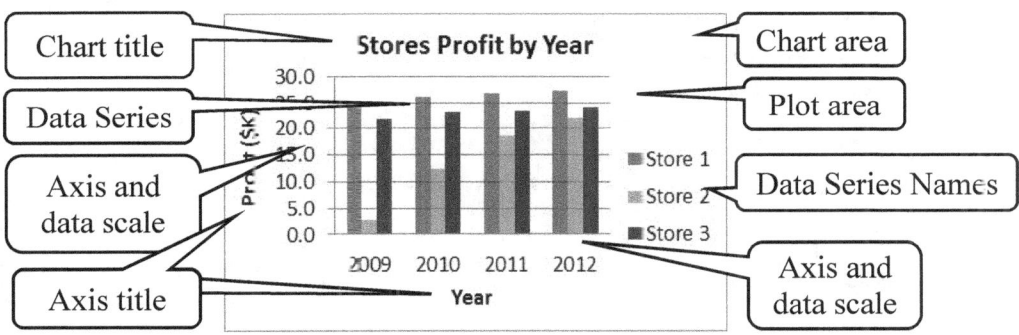

Figure 10-4: Chart components

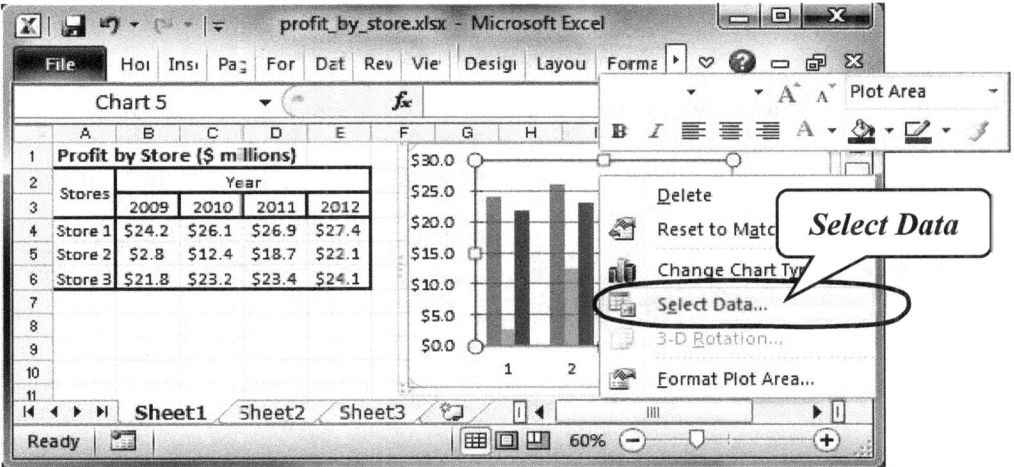

Figure 10-5: Navigating to data source

10.2.1   Data Series

The term "data series" refers to the named arrays shown in the chart. In our chart we have three data series, which are arrays B4:E4, B5:E5, and B6:E6. Also we have an array B3:E3 that represents the data on the horizontal axis (years in our case). To add, edit, or delete data series, right click on the data series part of the chart which is the area where the data is presented. This brings up a popup menu where you choose **Select Data** as shown in Figure 10-5.

The **Select Data** choice brings up a data editing control window as shown in Figure 10-6. Left clicking on the **Edit** button in the right pane of the control window brings up the popup **Axis Labels** data selection box where you can select data for the horizontal axis (Figure 10-7).

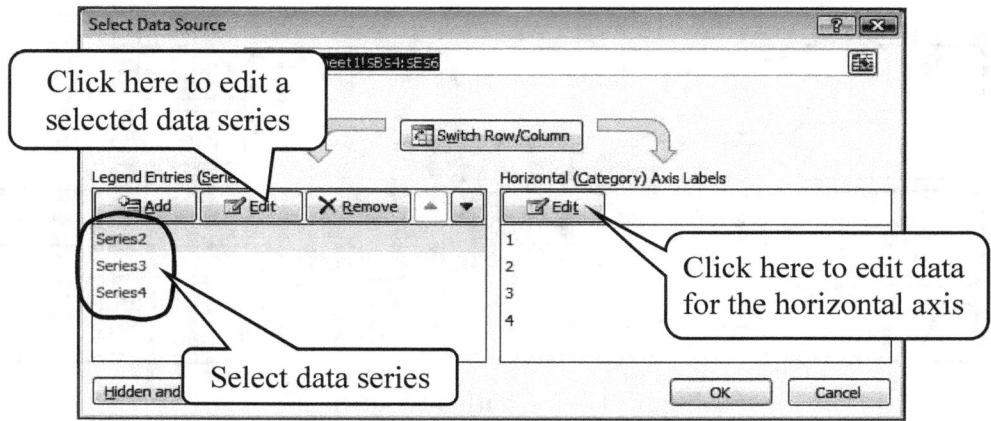

Figure 10-6: Editing data series

Simply place the mouse over the first cell of the data array, press and hold down the left mouse button, move the mouse to the last data cell of the array, and click on **OK** in the control window or press **Enter** key on the keyboard (Figure 10-7). You immediately see how initial values on the horizontal axis changed to the values in B3:E3.

You can also edit, add, or remove data series in the chart. Suppose you want to edit data series in the chart. To do so select a data series and click on the **Edit** button in the left pane of the control window in Figure 10-6. This brings up a popup **Edit Series** selection box similar to the selection box for the horizontal axis data described above. The only difference is that this box contains a **Series Name** field (Figure 10-8), where you enter the name you want to give to the series. For example, in our case the series name is "Store 1". Then select the data array for that series, which is B4:E4, and click **OK**. The data for the series is set and the series name on the chart is changed to "Store 1" (Figure 10-8).

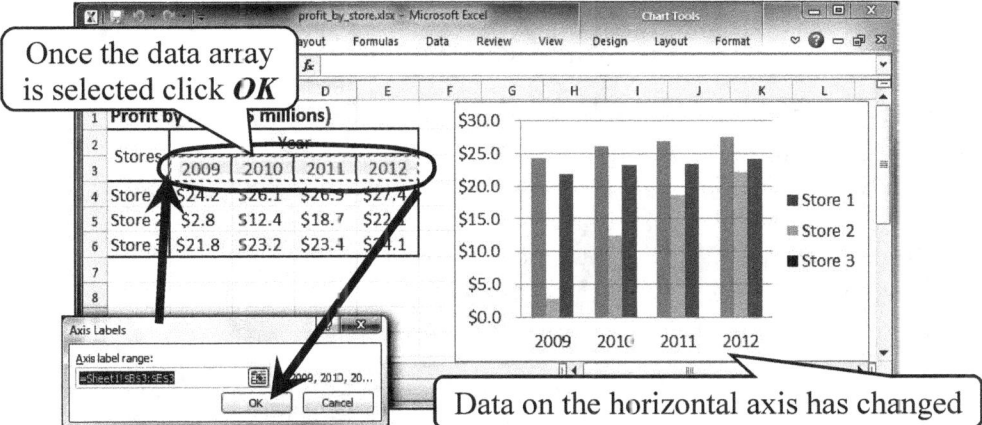

Figure 10-7: Editing data series

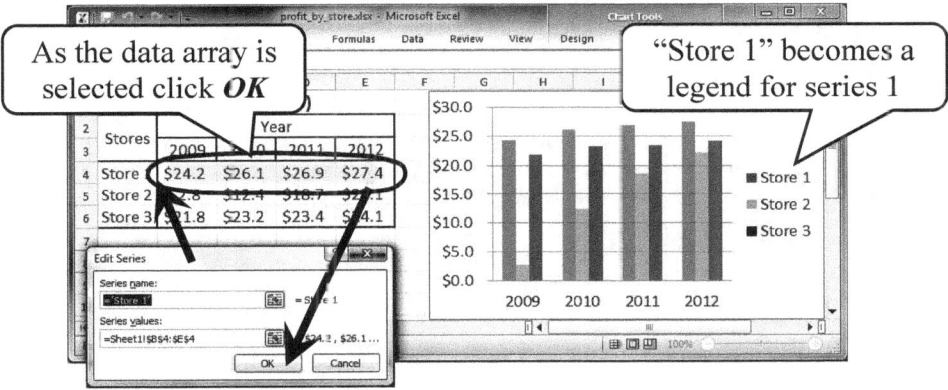

Figure 10-8: Editing data series

By using this functionality you can modify the data series and change the chart. This is also the way to populate the chart with data if you start doing it from scratch without selecting initial data.

10.2.2   Formatting Axes and Data Scales

To format an axis, first select the axis by left clicking in the axis area, including the axis data area, then right click on the selected axis to bring up the popup menu, and choose *Format Axis* as shown in Figure 10-9.

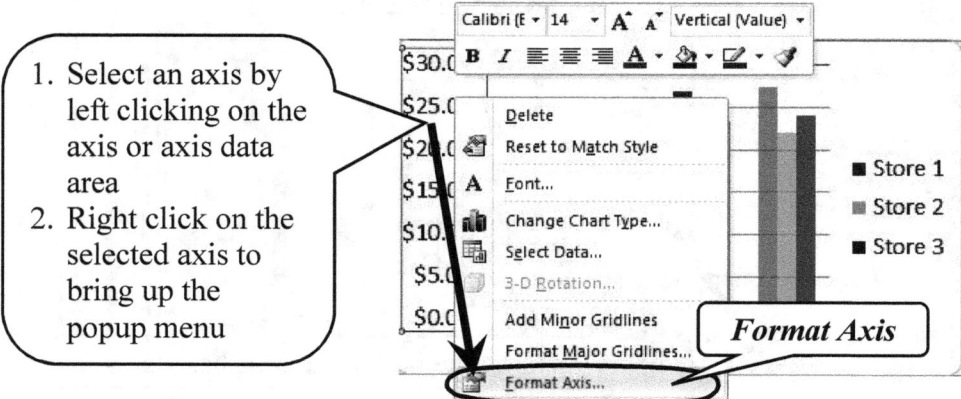

Figure 10-9: Formatting a chart axis

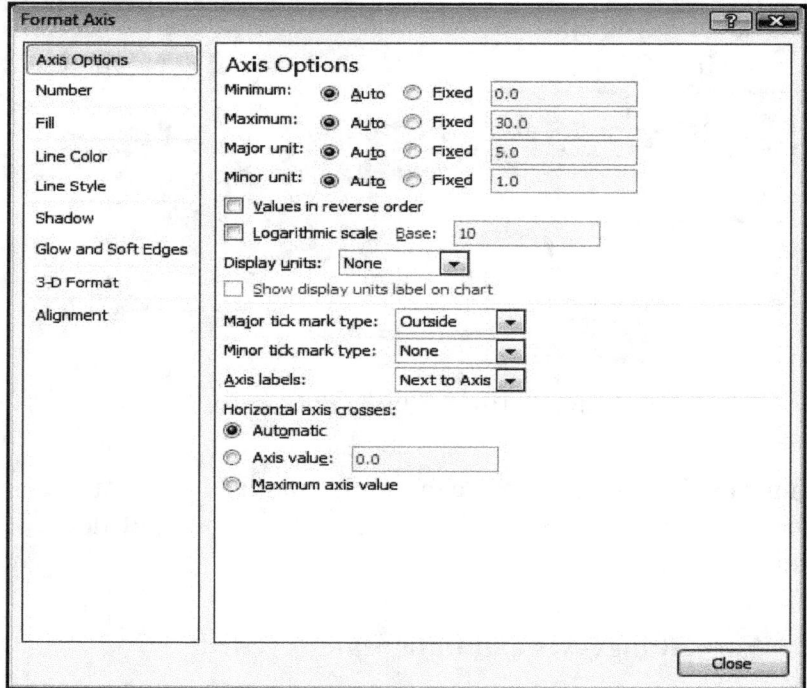

Figure 10-10: Format axis control

This brings up a ***Format Axis*** control window (Figure 10-10) where you can set up or change a desired format for the selected axis. This formatting consists of many features and parameters that are quite intuitive and can be easily learned by trying them out.

10.2.3   Chart and Axis Titles

The chart we have now contains neither a chart nor axis titles and looks as shown in Figure 10-11.

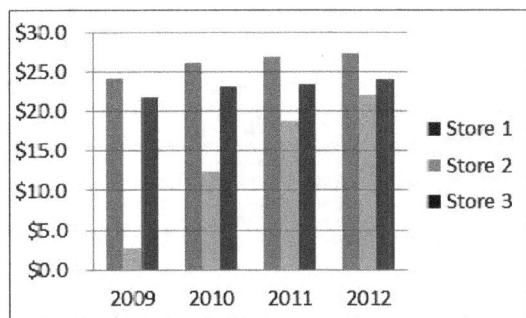

Figure 10-11: The chart after editing series and axis data

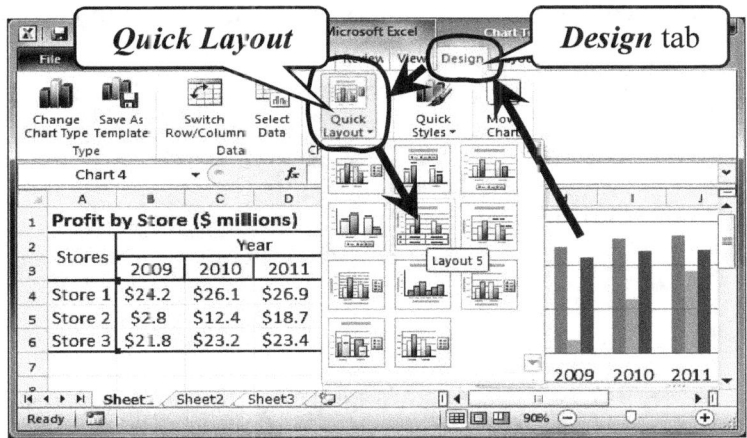

Figure 10-12: Changing a chart layout via *Design* tab

The user can insert a chart or axis titles, or change the chart layout in some other way, by selecting the chart and then either

- navigating to the ***Design*** tab in the ***Chart Tool*** section of the main menu and then choosing one of the layouts from the ***Quick Layout*** in the ***Ribbon*** as shown in Figure 10-12 or
- navigating to the ***Layout*** tab in the ***Chart Tool*** section of the main menu and then choosing the appropriate layout from ***Chart Title*** or ***Axis Title*** in the ***Labels*** group of the ***Ribbon*** as shown in Figure 10-13.

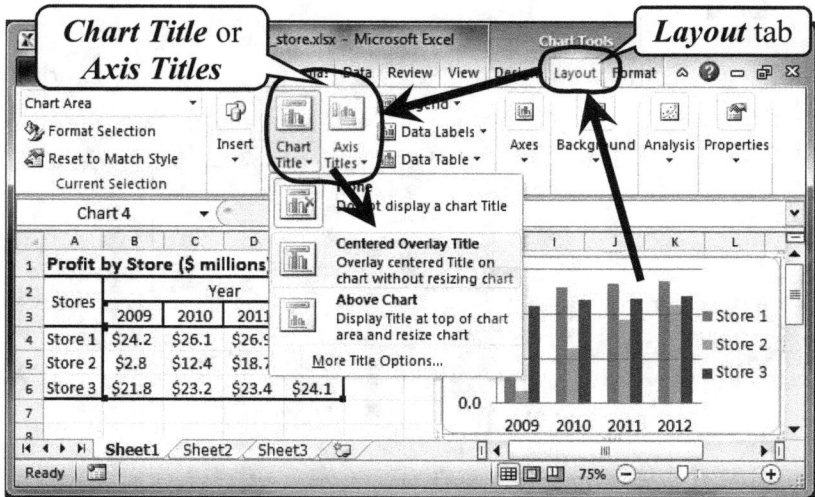

Figure 10-13: Changing a chart layout via *Layout* tab

Our chart after inserting the chart and axis titles as shown in Figure 10-14.

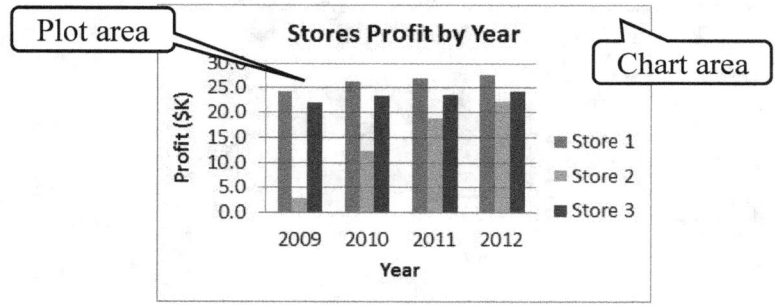

Figure 10-14: The chart after adding the chart and axis titles

10.2.4   Formatting Plot and Chart Areas

The "plot area" is the area where the actual chart is placed while the "chart area" is the entire area of the chart (Figure 10-14). To edit a plot area, right click on it and choose **Format Plot Area** from the popup menu. This brings up a plot area formatting control (Figure 10-15-a) that the user can use to edit the plot area.

Similarly, right click on the chart area outside the plot area and choose **Format Chart Area** from the popup menu to bring up the chart area formatting control (Figure 10-15-b) that the user can use to edit the chart area.

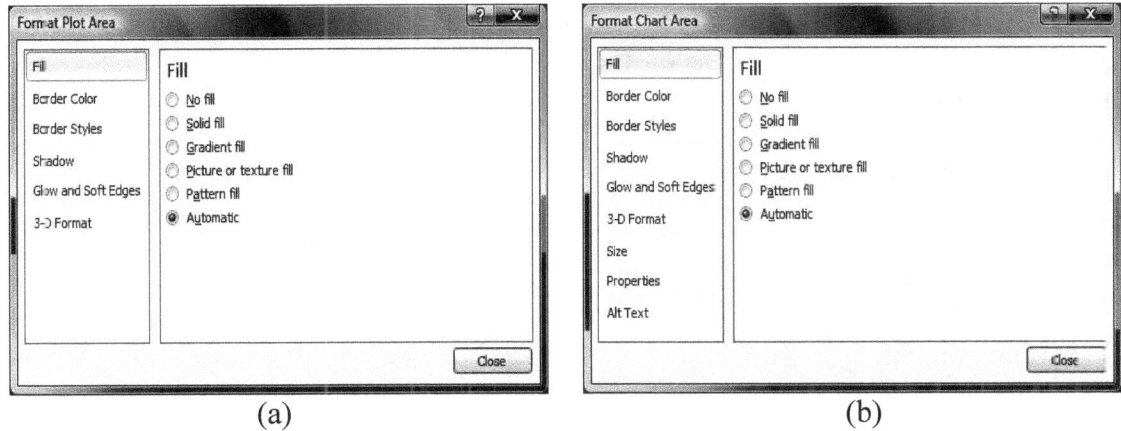

(a)   (b)

Figure 10-15: The plot and chart area formatting controls

Both, the plot and chart area formatting controls allow the user to change the background (fill) color, borders, size, and other properties. Just a few minutes of "playing" with their functionality (Figure 10-15) is sufficient to make you comfortable with plot and chart area formatting.

10.2.5   Changing the Chart Type

Sometimes the user wants to change the entire type of chart. For example, we developed a "bar" chart but the user wants to change it to a graph with lines. This can easily be changed. To change the chart type, right click on the chart and choose Change Chart Type from the popup menu. This brings up the *Change Chart Type* control dialog where you can select the chart type you want (Figure 10-16).

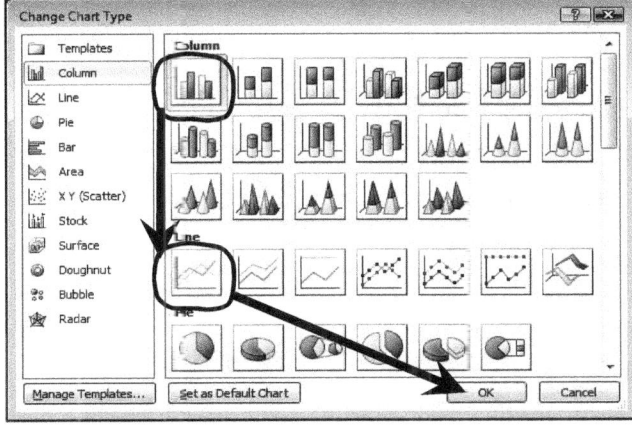

Figure 10-16: The change chart type control dialog

Suppose the user changed the chart type from "column" to "line" as shown in Figure 10-16. When the user clicks on the **OK** button in the ***Change Chart Type*** control dialog, the chart changes its look as shown in Figure 10-17.

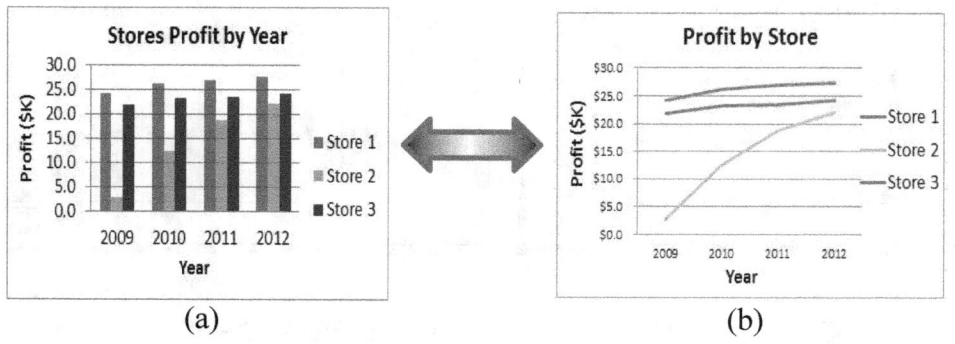

        (a)   (b)

Figure 10-17: Changing the chart type

10.3   Copying Charts to Other Documents

The user can copy-and-paste charts developed in Microsoft Excel to other Microsoft documents. This operation is very intuitive and does not require any special knowledge or skills.

Questions and Exercises

Questions

1.   How do you create a chart in an Excel document?
2.   What is the layout of a chart?
3.   What is data series?
4.   How do you set data series in a chart?
5.   How do you format axes in a chart?
6.   What is the plot area of a chart?
7.   What is the chart area of a chart?
8.   How do you format the plot area?
9.   How do you format the chart area?
10. How do you change a chart type?
11. How do you copy a chart to other documents?

Exercises

1   Develop a spreadsheet document that contains some numbers by year. For example, this could be revenue, expenses, profit, or return of an investment portfolio. Create a chart based on this data.

2   Format the chart developed in the previous exercise and make it look nice.

3   Copy the chart developed in the previous exercise to a Word document.

11   PowerPoint Presentations

11.1   Introduction to PowerPoint

PowerPoint is one of the major Microsoft Office applications. This application helps users develop and make presentations. A PowerPoint presentation consists of a series of slides. Each slide can have similar or different layouts and structures. Slide content can be static or animated. In the presentation mode, slides may be switched manually or automatically. In addition, presentations may be accompanied with a linked soundtrack.

PowerPoint files from 2007 have extension *.pptx for editable versions. Older versions have extension *.ppt. An editable version means the presentation can be presented as a slide show or it can also be edited and altered. PowerPoint files with an extension *.ppsx (for PowerPoint 2007 or more recent versions) or *.pps (for older versions) can only be shown as a slide show—it cannot be edited.

Typing text and inserting images in PowerPoint is similar to other office applications. Hopefully the reader has already learned how to do basic operations with PowerPoint slides, like insert a new slide, type text, insert an image, and switch between normal and slide show modes.

In "normal mode" the user can edit the presentation, while in "slide show mode" the user makes the presentation. The user can switch between normal and slideshow modes by clicking on the appropriate icon as illustrated in Figure 11-1. The user also can use function key **F5** to switch to slideshow mode and the **Esc** key to switch back to normal mode.

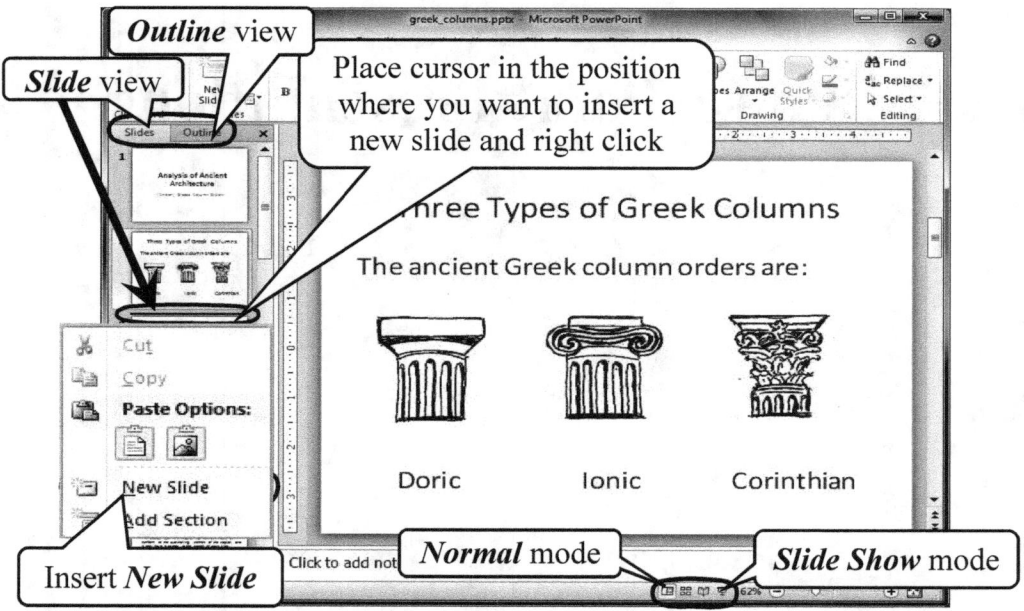

Figure 11-1: Inserting new slides, typing text and inserting images in the normal mode

The left pane in the normal mode may be in either the **Slide** or **Outline** view (left pane in Figure 11-1). The **Slide** view displays the sequence of slides in the presentation as they actually are. The **Outline** view displays the sequence of slides in the presentation with the text notes in the slides. To insert a new slide in the presentation, place the cursor between the slides where you want to insert a new slide, right click in that position, and select **New Slide** from the popup menu (Figure 11-1).

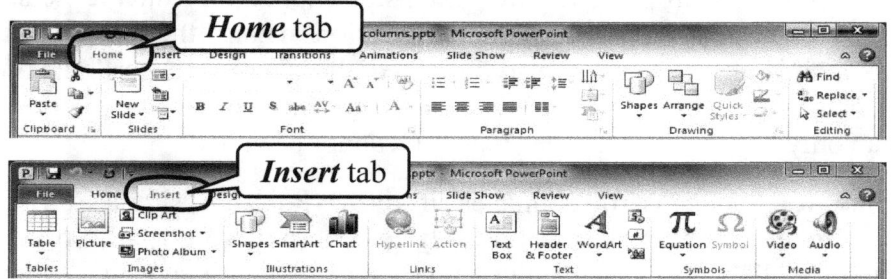

Figure 11-2: *Ribbons* for *Home* and *Insert* tabs in a PowerPoint presentation

Control over text and images in PowerPoint is quite similar to Word, so the reader can easily figure it out without special instructions. Figure 11-2 shows the **Home** and **Insert** tabs of the PowerPoint ***Ribbon***, most functions of which are quite intuitive and hopefully already somewhat familiar to the reader.

11.2   Slide Layout

Each slide in a presentation may use one of the preset layouts. Layouts for slides in PowerPoint play a similar role as styles play in a Word document. Layout defines a variety of content formats in a slide including text font face, type, size of text and image areas, title format and other design functions.

To change the layout of a slide, select the Slide view in the left pane of the screen in normal (editing) mode, right click on the slide you want to change the layout of, select the Layout item from the popup menu and choose a layout you wish from the collection as shown in Figure 11-3.

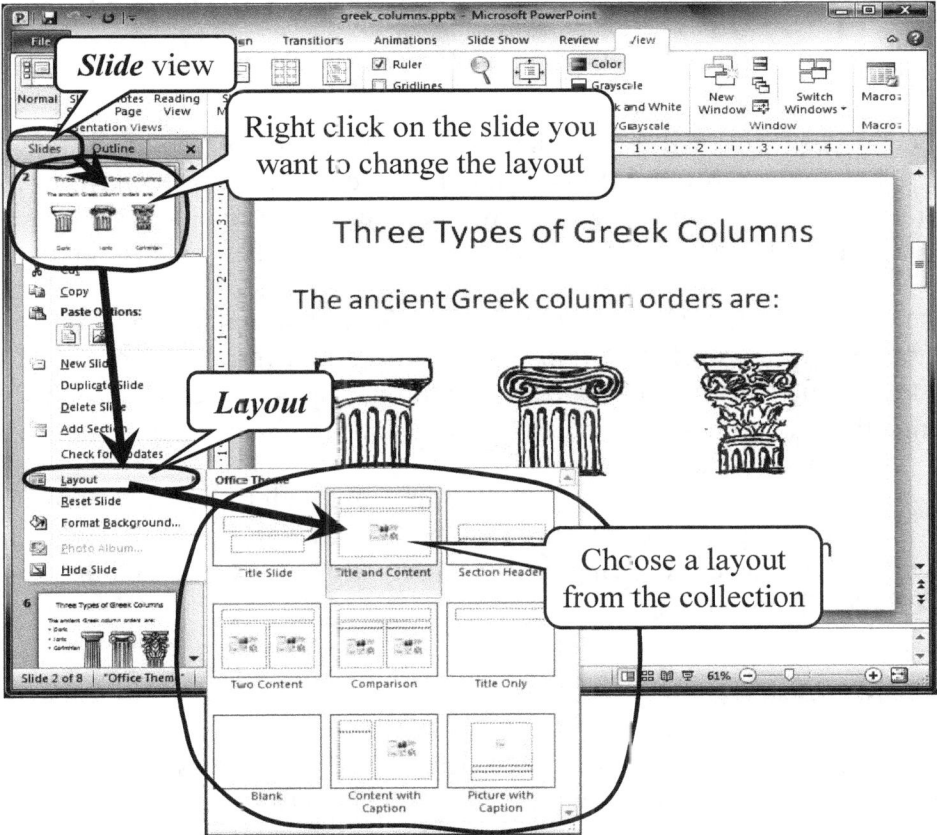

Figure 11-3: Changing the layout of a slide

11.3   Slides Design

The user can easily change a slide's design in PowerPoint. Actually, the user can design slides exactly as he/she wants them to be. Each slide in a presentation follows the generic design set forth for the entire presentation. The user can use one of the preset design themes as is, or has the option to modify it. Please note that "empty white background" is also a preset theme, so if the user decides to do a completely original design he/she starts with a preset empty white background theme.

To use a preset theme, navigate to the **_Design_** tab in the main menu and choose a theme from the choices in the **_Themes_** group as shown in Figure 11-4.

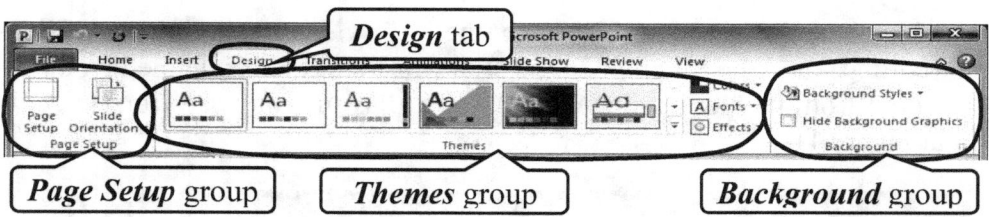

Figure 11-4: Typical functions of the **_Design_** tab

The chosen theme will be applied to all slides of the presentation, both existing ones and new slides that you insert later. Note that slides with different layouts may have a different look and feel when utilizing a different theme. This includes the title slide too. **_Colors_**, **_Fonts_**, and **_Effects_** in the **_Themes_** group help modify the selected themes.

The default **_Design_** tab also includes **_Page Setup_** and **_Background_** groups (Figure 11-4). With the **_Page Setup_** function the user can set up physical parameters of slides in the presentation, such as size and orientation. With the **_Background_** function the user can set or change the background of a slide by using colors, gradients, or even images.

To recap, we may change the design of the presentation shown in Figure 11-2 and Figure 11-3 by selecting a different preset theme as shown in Figure 11-5. We may also modify the design theme by changing the colors, fonts, effects, and background as described above (Figure 11-4).

11.4   Slide Master

All slides in a presentation follow certain slide templates that include design, layout, and formatting and may vary for different layouts (for example, see the left slide pane in Figure 11-5). These slide templates inherit design features from the main template, or "slide master". A slide master is at the top in aof the hierarchy of slide templates; it contains the primary information about the theme and formatting of slides in a presentation.

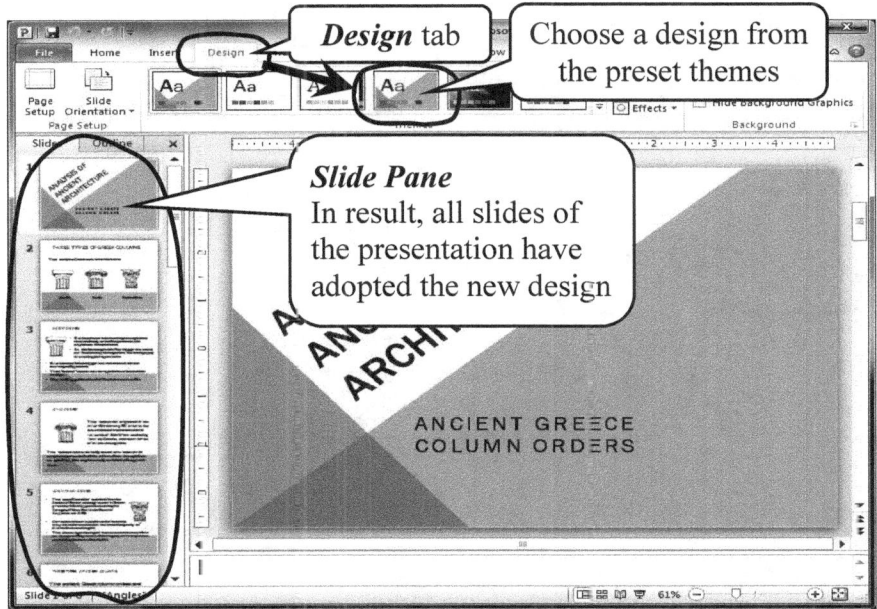

Figure 11-5: Modified design of the presentation

To access the slide master, navigate to the *View* tab in the main menu and click on the *Slide Master* icon in the *Master View* group in the *Ribbon* (Figure 11-6). You'll notice that the main menu has changed and the *Slide Master* tab appears. Navigate to the *Slide Master* tab. You will see the slide master on the top of the left pane in the PowerPoint window (Figure 11-6). Below the slide master are slide templates associated with this slide master.

Any theme or formatting change of the slide master will impact all associated templates. On the other hand, theme or formatting changes of an associated template will only affect that specific template. The user can design, change, or edit slide themes for all or specific slide templates in the *Slide Master* mode (Figure 11-6) similar to how it's done in the *Design* mode (Figure 11-5).

Setting up footers, slide numbering, or the current date will be discussed in the next section. Though these features can be activated via *Insert* → *Header & Footer*, placeholders for this information should be designed or edited in the *Slide Master* mode.

To exit the Master View and return to editing your presentation, click on the *Close Master View* icon in the ribbon of the *Slide Master* tab as shown in Figure 11-6.

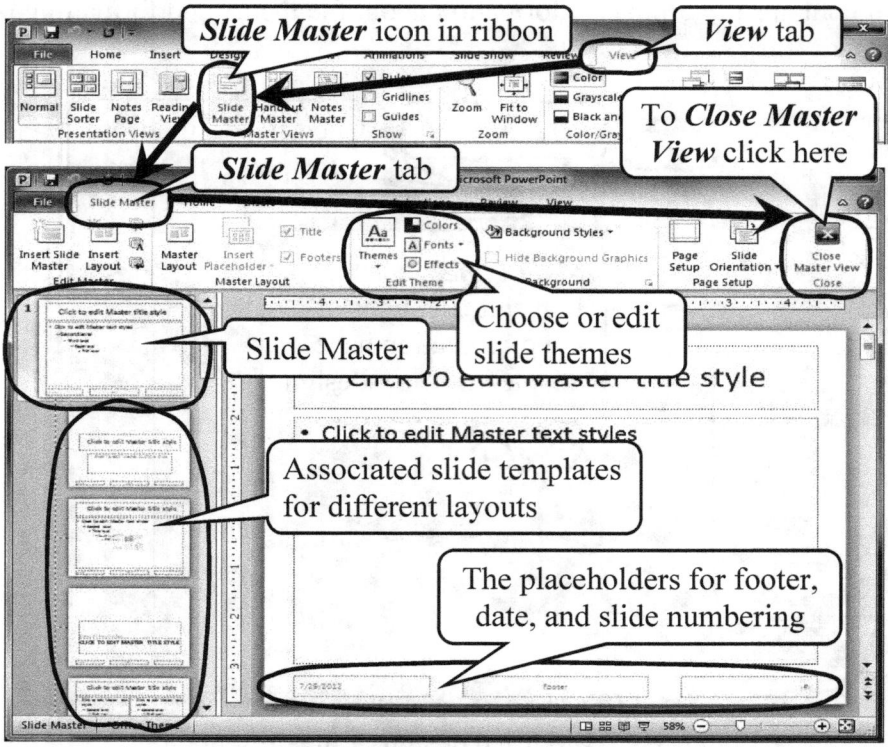

Figure 11-6: Slide master view

11.5 Footers, Page Numbering, and Current Date

As part of the design and layout, the user can set up a footer, page numbering, and a current date on each slide. This information can be set identically for all slides or differently for specific slide templates. To set up a footer, slide numbering, and a date, navigate to the Insert tab in the main menu and click on the *Header & Footer* icon in the *Text* group of the *Ribbon*. This opens a *Header & Footer* popup control window (Figure 11-7). The footer, slide number, and current date setup process with this control is quite intuitive. The placeholders for these features shown in Figure 11-7 should be setup or edited in the Slide Master mode as described in the previous section (Figure 11-6).

It is important to note that the footer, slide numbering, and current date features can be set for selected slide templates by choosing the appropriate templates before opening the **Header & Footer** control window. Even within the specific template type, these features could be applied to all slides or to a given slide by pressing on *Apply* or *Apply to All* buttons in the Header & Footer control window. The user can also control whether to show these features on the title slide by checking/unchecking the appropriate checkbox at the bottom of the *Header & Footer* control window

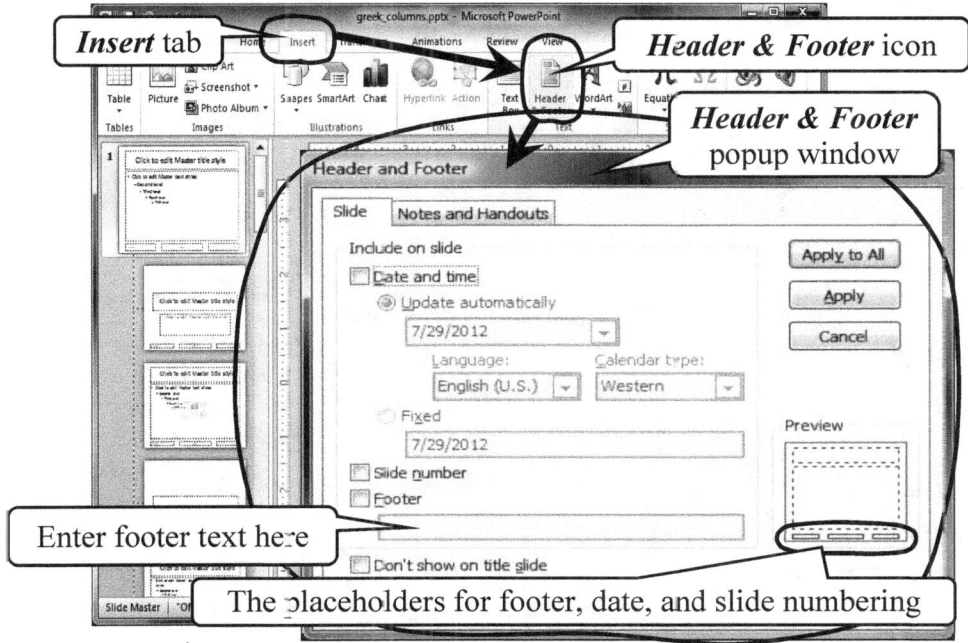

Figure 11-7: Setting up footer, slide numbering, and current date

11.6   Assigning a Layout to a Slide

You can easily assign a layout available (or developed) in Slide Master to any slide in your presentation. To do so right click on a slide in the Slide Pane, chose Layout from the popup menu and select a desired layout as shown in Figure 11-8.

11.7   Animation

Sometimes a presentation looks more compelling if some of its images or texts are animated. Animation may include a variety of actions, such as appearing later on a slide, disappearing from the slide, or moving within the slide. Animation actions can also be programmed to occur at a button click or on a timer.

Suppose we want to animate the slide shown in Figure 11-3, so that the Doric, Ionic, and Corinthian columns appear on the slide one-by-one and only after the column order names "fly-in" to the slide as shown in Figure 11-9.

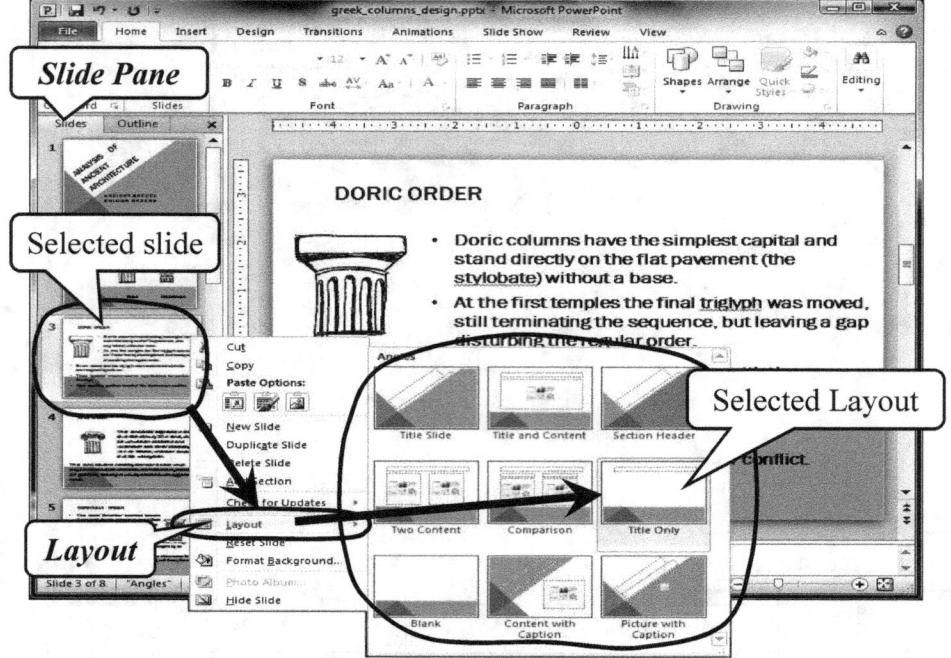

Figure 11-8: Assigning layout to a slide

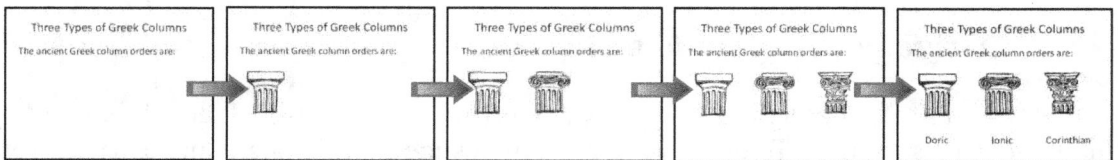

Figure 11-9: Slide animation sequence

To setup animation, first navigate to the *Animation* tab and click on the *Animation Pane* icon in the *Advanced Animation* group in the *Ribbon* as shown in Figure 11-10. This opens the *Animation Pane* where the animation sequence will be displayed. So far the animation pane is empty because no animation is set up for this slide.

When the animation pane is open, select the first object for animation by clicking on the image of the Doric column and then clicking on the *Add Animation* icon in the *Advanced Animation* group in the *Ribbon* (Figure 11-10). This action opens a drop-down box of animation options (Figure 11-11).

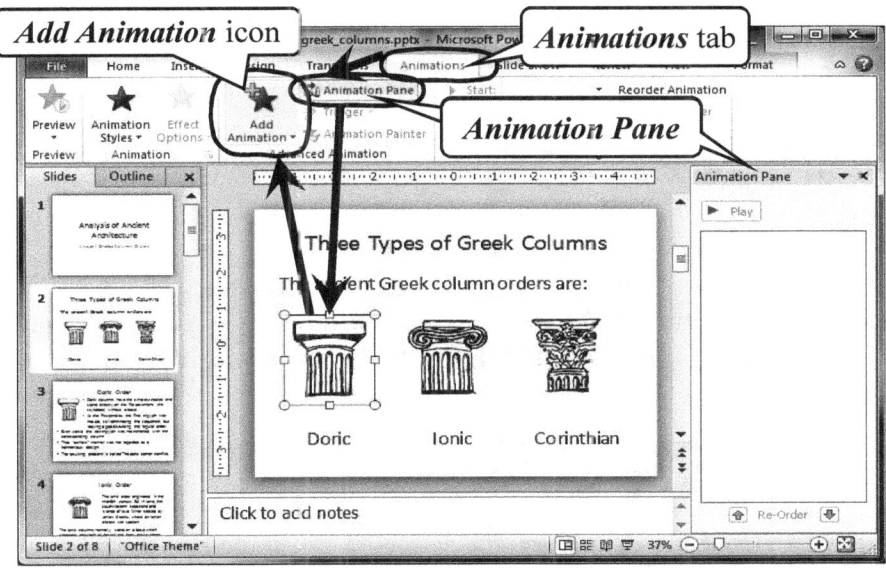

Figure 11-10: Animation setup beginning

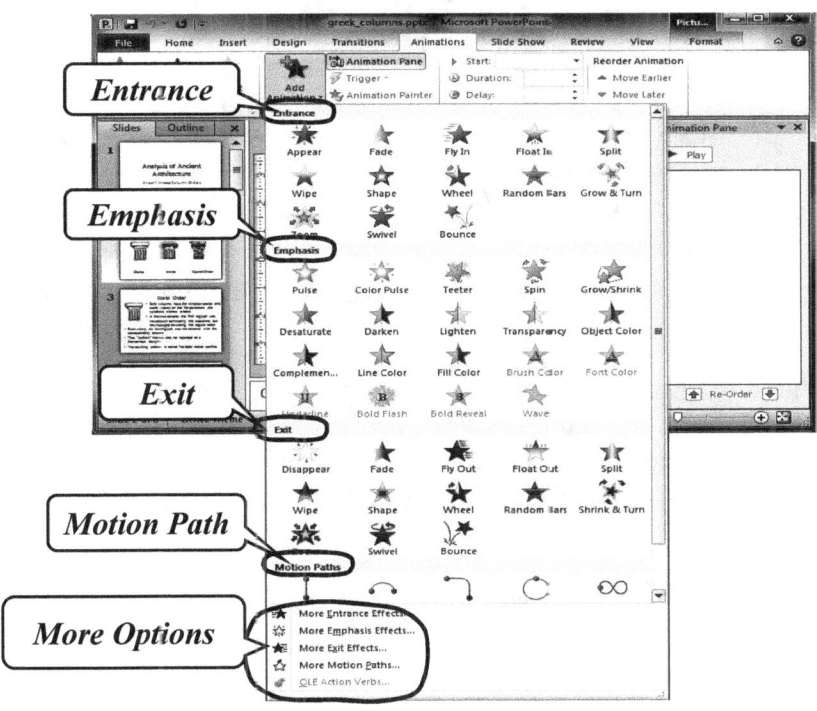

Figure 11-11: Animation action setup

The animation options include six sections:
- Entrance
- Emphasis
- Exit
- Motion Path
- More Options

In this particular case, we are interested in the ***Entrance*** options. Let's choose the ***Appear*** option for the picture of a Doric column. As soon as we click on that option, the first animation sequence is set. This animation sequence is shown in the Animation Pane and the sequence number is displayed next to the animated object (Figure 11-12).

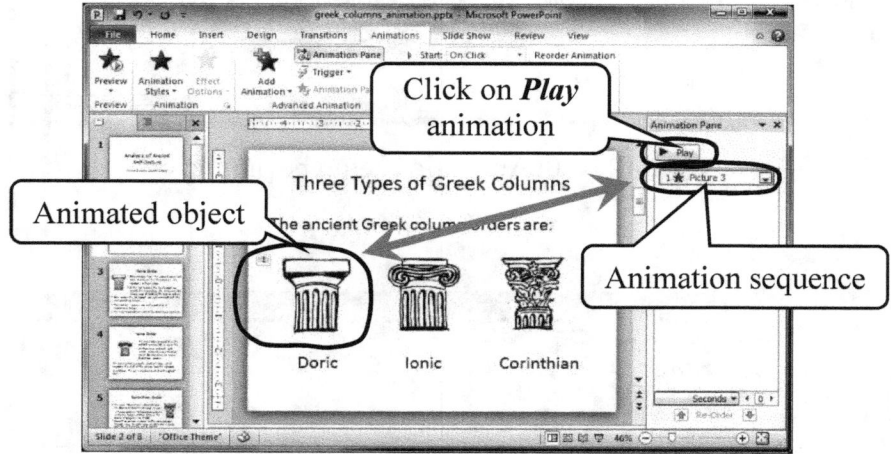

Figure 11-12: First animated object and animation sequence, and preview

Setting up all planned animation sequences one-by-one, we finally complete the animation sequence for this slide as shown in Figure 11-13.

The animation sequence consists of separate animation actions applied to each object. You can set each animation action to trigger either by a mouse click or by the status of the previous animation event, or by time elapsed from the previous event. Right clicking on an animation sequence opens the list of options for action triggers as shown in Figure 11-14.

The user can preview the completed animation by clicking on the ***Play*** button as described above and illustrated in Figure 11-12.

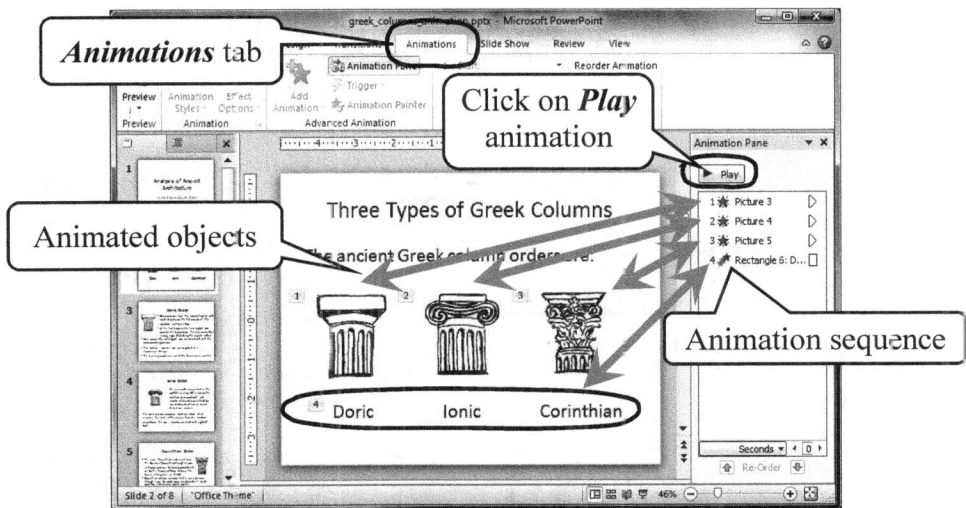

Figure 11-13: Animated objects, animation sequences, and preview

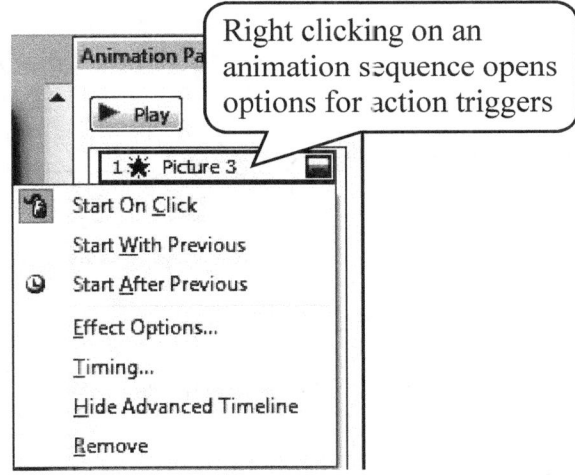

Figure 11-14: Animation action triggers

11.8   Soundtrack

Some presentations are better with music, narration, or other sounds. PowerPoint offers such functionality. To insert sound, navigate to the *Insert* tab, click on the *Media* icon in the ribbon, choose *Audio*, and select one of the sources from the list of *Audio Sources* as shown in Figure 11-15. When the soundtrack is added to the slide, an audio icon appears on that slide (Figure 11-15).

To preview the inserted audio clip, place the cursor over the audio clip icon on the slide. This action brings up the soundtrack control as shown in Figure 11-16. Press the "Play" button on the soundtrack control (Figure 11-16) to preview the audio clip.

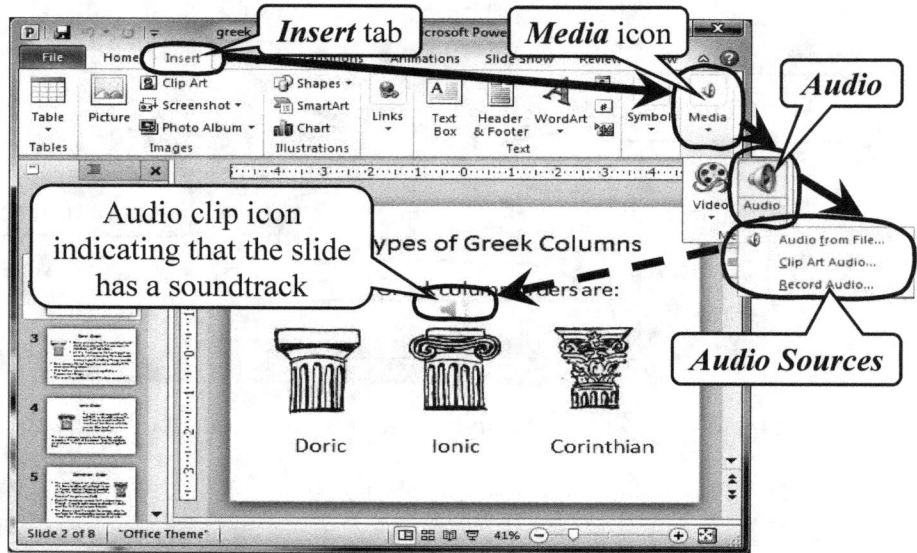

Figure 11-15: Adding sound to a PowerPoint presentation

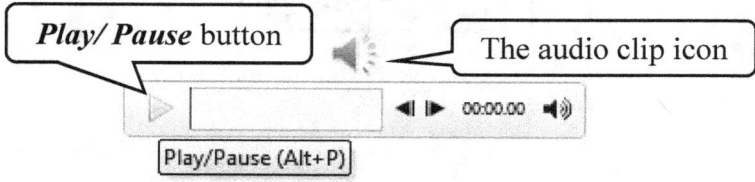

Figure 11-16: Soundtrack control

The user can display or hide the audio clip icon on the slide in the presentation mode. The user can also choose whether to play the sound automatically when the slide is shown or by clicking on the audio clip icon. To control the playback option, open the audio tool by navigating to the *Playback* tab as shown in Figure 11-17.

To hide the audio clip icon in the presentation mode, check the *Hide During Show* checkbox in the *Audio Options* group in the *Ribbon*. To control the sound volume, click on the Volume icon and choose from four volume options: low, medium, high, and mute as shown in Figure 11-17.

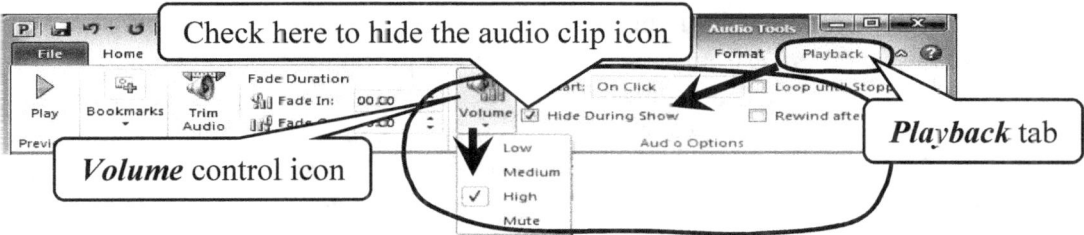

Figure 11-17: Playback audio tool

The user has three options to play the audio clip:
- automatically when slide is shown
- manually upon a click on the slide
- throughout all slides in the presentation

To choose one of the start options, click on the **Start** drop-down box in the ribbon and select an option of choice as shown in Figure 11-18.

Figure 11-18: Playback audio tool

The sound clip may not be long enough to play throughout the slide or the entire presentation time. To loop the sound clip, check the **Loop until Stopped** checkbox in the **Audio Options** group in the **Ribbon** of the **Playback** tab as shown in Figure 11-18. In this case, the sound clip will be played continuously.

11.9   Practical Hints in Developing PowerPoint Presentations

Developing a good PowerPoint presentation takes more than technical tools. There are several general practical rules which could be very helpful in presentation design and development. We will focus on presentations for public speeches that we presume will be shown via projector:
- The colors on your slides, though may look very good, vibrant, and distinct on the computer monitor, most likely will look worse on the projector screen.
- Be aware that some people have color vision problems, so try to choose colors that are visually well separated not only in Colors but also in Grayscale.
- Use a high-contrast slide background and text. Dark text on a light background is

normally seen more easily than light text on a dark background.

- Do not use very small font sizes. If people have problems reading your slides, the presentation is not well designed. Remember that some people do not have perfect vision. Unless you have a very good reason, try not to use a font size smaller than Calibri 24 or comparable sizes of other font faces. For example, Helvetica 20 and Times New Roman 24 look similar by size as Calibri 24.

- Do not put too much text on a slide. People are not comfortable and feel bored reading too much text or long stories on a slide during public presentations. Keep your slides concise and information bullet-wise.

- Try not to read your slides during your presentation. Use the slides as a detailed outline of your presentation but tell your own story. Remember that people can read faster than you can speak.

- Insert slide numbering. This is very important for referencing slides during a discussion after the presentation. It is also helpful to show the slide number out of the total number of slides in the presentation so that people will know what to expect about the length of the presentation.

- Do not include too much animation, video, or sound effects into your presentation. If your presentation is too busy with such effects, it may look annoying and defocus the audience from the main information stream of the presentation.

Questions and Exercises

Questions

1   What file extensions do PowerPoint files have?
2   In what modes can PowerPoint presentation be displayed?
3   How do you insert a new slide into a presentation?
4   How do you control and set a slide layout?
5   How do you design a slide's look and feel?
6   What is a slide theme?
7   How do you set a slide theme?
8   How do you edit a slide theme?
9   How do you change a slide background?
10   How do you change a theme for a group of slides?
11   What is a slide master?
12   How do you edit a slide master?
13   How do you switch to a master view?

14   What is a slide template?

15   How do you set placeholders for the current date, footer, or slide number?

16   How do you insert the current date, footer, or slide number on slides?

17   How do you set animation on a slide?

18   How do you control animation events, sequence, and effects?

19   How do you preview animation on slides?

20   How do you include a soundtrack in a presentation?

21   What audio sources can be used for the soundtrack?

22   How do you preview the soundtrack on a slide?

23   How do you setup automatic and manual play back options for a presentation?

24   How do you control the volume of sound in a presentation?

25   How do you loop an audio clip in a presentation?

26   What practical hints do you recall about developing a presentation?

Exercises

1   Select an interesting topic and develop a PowerPoint presentation with static slides.

2   Add some animation to the slides but keep it from being too busy.

3   Add soundtrack to the presentation but keep it within a reason.